War and Change in World Politics

War and Change in World Politics

ROBERT GILPIN
Princeton University

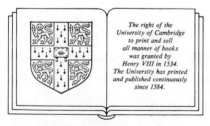

The right of the
University of Cambridge
to print and sell
all manner of books
was granted by
Henry VIII in 1534.
The University has printed
and published continuously
since 1584.

CAMBRIDGE UNIVERSITY PRESS

Cambridge

London   New York   New Rochelle

Melbourne   Sydney

Published by the Press Syndicate of the University of Cambridge
The Pitt Building, Trumpington Street, Cambridge CB2 1RP
32 East 57th Street, New York, NY 10022, USA
10 Stamford Road, Oakleigh, Melbourne 3166, Australia

First published 1981
First paperback edition 1983
Reprinted 1984, 1985 (twice), 1986

Printed in the United States of America

Library of Congress Cataloging in Publication Data

Gilpin, Robert

War and change in world politics.

Bibliography: p.
Includes index.
1. International relations-Research. I. Title.
JX1291.G53   327'.072   81-2885
ISBN 0 521 24018 2 hard cover   AACR2
ISBN 0 521 27376 5 paperback

IN MEMORY OF HAROLD SPROUT
1901–1980

The great events of history are often due to secular changes in the growth of population and other fundamental economic causes, which, escaping by their gradual character the notice of contemporary observers, are attributed to the follies of statesmen or the fanaticism of atheists.

John Maynard Keynes, *The Economic Consequences of the Peace*

Contents

Preface

In his excellent book *Sociologists, Economists and Democracy* (1970), Brian Barry identified and analyzed two of the foremost approaches to theorizing in contemporary social science: the sociological and economic modes of theory construction. This study will draw on the insights provided by these two types of social theories in an attempt to understand international political change. Each type of social theory makes its own contribution. However, in this study we shall regard both as suggestive, rather than as methodologies to be applied rigorously. Thus their strengths and weaknesses will be discussed here briefly to familiarize the reader with the intellectual background and underlying methodology of this book.

The fundamental feature of sociological theory is its emphasis on whole societies or whole social systems. Although definitions of social systems vary, they have in common the notion of a set of identifiable elements characterized by explicit or implicit interrelationships. Whether these elements are individuals, groups, social roles, or other factors, sociological theory assumes that individual behavior is explained by the nature of the system and one's place in it. The social system is the primary determinant of behavior, either by socializing the actor with respect to a particular set of norms and values or by exercising constraints on the actor. In brief, the whole is greater than the sum of its parts, and the social system itself must be the focus of theorizing.

In contrast to the holistic approach of sociological theory, economic theory, or what some call rational-choice theory, focuses on the individual (Becker, 1976, p. 5; Rogowski, 1978). It assumes that individual behavior is determined wholly by rationality; that is, individuals seek to maximize, or at least to satisfy, certain values or interests at the lowest possible cost to themselves. In this context, rationality applies only to endeavor, not to outcome; failure to achieve an objective because of ignorance or some other factor does not invalidate the rationalist premise that individuals act on the basis of a cost/benefit or means/ends calculation. Finally, it holds that individuals will seek to acquire their objectives until a market equilibrium is reached; that is, individuals will pursue an objective until the associated costs are equal to the realized benefits. Following these individualistic and rationalistic assumptions, economists attempt to explain human behavior.

The strength of the sociological approach is its focus on the structural and institutional determinants of individual behavior. Individuals make choices and act in a world of rules and norms not entirely of their own making. Moreover, these constraining rules and social structures cannot be reduced wholly to self-interest; in many cases individuals can even be viewed as behaving in ways opposed to their self-interest. Although individuals (acting alone or through groups or states) seek to change rules and structures in accordance with their interests, they can never escape completely the constraints of social structure. Moreover, as Percey S. Cohen has stressed (1968, p. 126), although individuals and groups attempt to promote their interests, their actions invariably lead to unanticipated consequences. Both self-interest and social structure are determinants of human behavior.

The strength of economic theory is that it embodies a general conception of social and political change that can be useful in understanding international political change. As John Harsanyi has argued, the problem of social change "must be ultimately explained in terms of personal incentives for some people to change their behavior" (1969, p. 532). That is, a theory of change seeks to explain why "some people have decided that their interests would be better served by a new type of institutional arrangement" (Harsanyi, 1969, p. 532). It focuses on how technological, economic, and other changes affect the power and interests of individuals (organized in coalitions and states) and thereby influence them to modify their behavior and institutions.

Underlying this economic view of social or political change is the assumption that the purposes and natures of social institutions are determined principally by the self-interest and relative power of individual members. In the words of James Buchanan, "political structure is conceived as something that *emerges* from the choice processes of individual participants" (1966, p. 26). Individuals, groups, and other actors use their powers to create social and political institutions that they believe will advance their interests. Thus the objectives of a social or political institution primarily reflect the interests of its more powerful members. When these interests or the relative powers of individuals (or of groups and states) change, there will be attempts to change the nature of the institution and its objectives in order to reflect significant changes in interest and power.

A second advantage of the theory of rational choice is that it can draw on a large and well-tested body of economic theory. In fact, economics provides a highly developed theory of social behavior, and for this reason economic theory has been applied to an ever-increasing range of social and political phenomena. In some cases the application of economic theory to conventionally conceived noneconomic behavior such as suicide or the choice of a marriage partner has bordered on the ridiculous. Yet, if used with discretion, the so-called laws of microeconomics (demand, marginal utility, and diminishing returns), as well as those from public finance and other subcategories of economics, can help explain political behavior.

Thus economic theory suggests that the study of international political change must consider how political, economic, and technological developments affect the relative incomes (powers) of political actors and the costs of obtaining the objectives sought by groups and states. Among these objectives, the most important ones are sociopolitical arrangements favorable to the interests of a group or state. Thus, this study will argue that a group or a state will attempt to change the political system in response to developments that increase its relative power or decrease the costs of modifying political arrangements and will continue its efforts until an equilibrium is reached between the costs and benefits of further change.[1]

Although it is helpful to assume that social systems and political institutions emerge from the decisions of powerful actors in pursuit of perceived interests, the resulting social arrangements are not completely willed or controlled by these actors. Furthermore, social and political institutions, once in place, operate according to a logic of their own. For example, the actions of individual consumers or sellers give rise to an economic market, but these individuals in a freely competitive market cannot control the price at which they buy or sell goods. Similarly, as Kenneth Waltz (1979) pointed out, individual states compose an international system, but they have only limited control over its operations and to varying degrees must conform to the logic of a competitive, anarchic system of interacting states. Waltz's insight is indicative of the value of the sociological approach (or systems approach) to the theory of international relations.

Because this book will analyze political change in the past, as well as in the modern world, a relevant question is whether or not economic theory is universally applicable. Is its utility restricted to market economies composed of acquisitive individuals pursuing rational self-interest?[2] In this book we shall assume that rationality is not historically or culturally bound but that individuals in all societies past and present attempt to achieve their interests and goals by the most efficient means possible. However, the specific interests or objectives that individuals pursue and the appropriateness of the means they employ are dependent on prevailing social norms and the material environment. For this reason, although here we employ the economic mode of analysis in an effort to understand political change, we appreciate that the sociological perspective is also necessary to an

---

[1] A noteworthy example of this approach to political change is that of Haskel (1976), who applied rational-choice theory to foreign-policy decision making. Haskel's book was a pioneering effort that deserves much more attention than it has thus far received.

[2] This so-called formal-substantive issue was the subject of a famous exchange between the anthropologist Melville Herskovits and the economist Frank Knight. Herskovits eventually conceded the argument and wrote a precedent-setting book applying formal economic theory to nonmarket and primitive societies (1952).

understanding of the context of rational behavior. In short, the economic and sociological approaches must be integrated to explain international political change.

Thus this study will draw on both the sociological approach and the economic approach to social theory in an attempt to develop a theory or conception of international political change. At the same time, we are mindful of the severe limitations of both types of social theories and of the fact that even though each approach partially compensates for the weaknesses of the other, a combination of the two approaches does not provide a comprehensive explanation of political change nor resolve the basic dilemma of social science: whether to explain trivial matters with exactitude or to treat significant matters with imprecision. In this study we have chosen to follow the latter course in the belief that possible errors and certain oversimplification are the price one must pay if one is to deal with the important issues of our age. This sacrifice of precision is justifiable only if this study clarifies the issues of war and change in world politics more than it obfuscates.

I have benefited enormously in the writing of this book from the assistance of others. The Lehrman Institute of New York City provided the initial funding and intellectual encouragement. Additional financial support was received from the Rockefeller Foundation and its program on conflict studies. Princeton University granted me leave from my teaching and academic responsibilities; its Woodrow Wilson School and the Center of International Studies helped me in financial and other ways. I thank all these institutions for making it possible for me to complete the book.

Further, I would like to thank those individuals who criticized the manuscript or helped me in other ways. I would like particularly to express my deep appreciation to several colleagues, students, and others for their comments on the manuscript: David Caploe, Michael Doyle, Robert Heilbroner, Miles Kahler, Peter Katzenstein, Marion J. Levey, Jr., Jim Keagle, Robert Keohane, Michael Loriaux, Michael Mastanduno, Ralph Pettman, Mark A. Sinz, David Spiro, and Kenneth N. Waltz. A special debt is owed to my colleague William Branson for his suggestion of the appropriateness of economic theory in seeking to explain political change and for his tutoring in economics over the years. Participants in my graduate seminar on international relations and colloquia at Boston College and Stanford University were very helpful. They raised more issues than I could possibly answer. My secretary, Dorothy Gronet, and the professional typing service of Winifred Donahue have my thanks for preparing the typescript. Behind the scenes, my wife Jean orchestrated it all as editor, prodder, and critic par excellence.

Finally, I would like to express my appreciation of the late Harold Sprout, to whom I have dedicated this volume. He never read the text, nor even knew of its existence, and probably would have disagreed with much of it. Yet he contributed to its conception and influenced it, and its author, in more ways than he ever appreciated. He was an outstanding leader in the American study of international relations, forever at the frontier of the field. Those of us who had the privilege of knowing him and being his colleagues will always treasure our memories of him.

Introduction

During the 1970s and early 1980s a series of dramatic events signaled that international relations were undergoing a significant upheaval. Long-established and seemingly stable sets of relationships and understandings were summarily cast aside. Political leaders, academic observers, and the celebrated "man in the street" were suddenly conscious of the fact that the energy crisis, dramatic events in the Middle East, and tensions in the Communist world were novel developments of a qualitatively different order from those of the preceding decade. These developments and many others in the political, economic, and military realms signaled far-reaching shifts in the international distribution of power, an unleashing of new sociopolitical forces, and the global realignment of diplomatic relations. Above all, these events and developments revealed that the relatively stable international system that the world had known since the end of World War II was entering a period of uncertain political changes.

Ours is not the first age in which a sudden concatenation of dramatic events has revealed underlying shifts in military power, economic interest, and political alignments. In the twentieth century, developments of comparable magnitude had already taken place in the decades preceding World War I and World War II. This awareness of the dangers inherent in periods of political instability and rapid change causes profound unease and apprehension. The fear grows that events may get out of hand and the

1

the world may once again plunge itself into a global conflagration. Scholars, journalists, and others turn to history for guidance, asking if the current pattern of events resembles the pattern of 1914 or 1939 (Kahler, 1979–80).

These contemporary developments and their dangerous implications raise a number of questions regarding war and change in international relations: How and under what circumstances does change take place at the level of international relations? What are the roles of political, economic, and technological developments in producing change in international systems? Wherein lies the danger of intense military conflict during periods of rapid economic and political upheaval? And, most important of all, are answers that are derived from examination of the past valid for the contemporary world? In other words, to what extent have social, economic, and technological developments such as increasing economic interdependence of nations and the advent of nuclear weapons changed the role of war in the process of international political change? Is there any reason to hope that political change may be more benign in the future than it has been in the past?

The purpose of this book is to explore these issues. In this endeavor we shall seek to develop an understanding of international political change more systematic than the understanding that currently exists. We do not pretend to develop a general theory of international relations that will provide an overarching explanatory statement. Instead, we attempt to provide a framework for thinking about the problem of war and change in world politics. This intellectual framework is intended to be an analytical device that will help to order and explain human experience. It does not constitute a rigorous scientific explanation of political change. The ideas on international political change presented are generalizations based on observations of historical experience rather than a set of hypotheses that have been tested scientifically by historical evidence; they are proposed as a plausible account of how international political change occurs.[1]

---

[1] However, in principle these ideas are translatable into specific testable hypotheses. At least we would argue that this is possible for a substantial fraction of them. The carrying out of this task, or part of it, would require another volume.

To this end we isolate and analyze the more obvious regularities and patterns associated with changes in international systems. However, we make no claim to have discovered the "laws of change" that determine when political change will occur or what course it will take.[2] On the contrary, the position taken here is that major political changes are the consequences of the conjuncture of unique and unpredictable sets of developments. However, the claim is made that it is possible to identify recurrent patterns, common elements, and general tendencies in the major turning points in international history. As the distinguished economist W. Arthur Lewis put it, "The process of social change is much the same today as it was 2,000 years ago. . . . We can tell how change will occur if it occurs; what we cannot foresee is what change is going to occur" (Lewis, 1970, pp. 17–18).

The conception of political change presented in this book, like almost all social science, is not predictive. Even economics is predictive only within a narrow range of issues (Northrop, 1947, pp. 243–5). Most of the alleged theories in the field of political science and in the sub-field of international relations are in fact analytical, descriptive constructs; they provide at best a conceptual framework and a set of questions that help us to analyze and explain a type of phenomenon (Hoffmann, 1960, p. 40). Thus, Kenneth Waltz, in his stimulating book, *Man, the State and War*, provided an explanation of war in general terms, but not the means for predicting any particular war (1959, p. 232). In similar fashion, this study seeks to explain in general terms the nature of international political change.

The need for a better understanding of political change, especially international political change, was well set forth by Wilbert Moore in the latest edition of the *International Encyclopedia of the Social Sciences:* "Paradoxically, as the rate of social change has accelerated in the real world of experience, the scientific disciplines dealing with man's actions and products have tended to emphasize orderly interdependence and static continuity" (Moore, 1968, p. 365).

[2] The term "law" is used several times in this book. In each case, law is to be interpreted as a general tendency that may be counteracted by other developments. This conception of law is taken from Baechler (1975, p. 52).

Moore's judgment concerning the inadequate treatment of political change by social scientists is borne out by analyses of
international-relations textbooks and theoretical works. Although
there are some recent outstanding exceptions (Choucri and
North, 1975; Keohane and Nye, 1977; Waltz, 1979), few of
these books have addressed the problem of political change in
systematic fashion. As David Easton rightly commented, "students of political life have . . . been prone to forget that the
really crucial problems of social research are concerned with the
patterns of change" (Easton, 1953, p. 42).[3]

It is worth noting, as Joseph Schumpeter pointed out, that the
natural development of any science is from static analysis to dynamic analysis (1954b, p. 964). Static theory is simpler, and its
propositions are easier to prove. Unfortunately, until the statics of
a field of inquiry are sufficiently well developed and one has a
good grasp of repetitive processes and recurrent phenomena, it is
difficult if not impossible to proceed to the study of dynamics.
From this perspective, systematic study of international relations
is a young field, and much of what passes for dynamics is in reality
an effort to understand the statics of interactions of particular
international systems: diplomatic bargaining, alliance behavior,
crisis management, etc. The question whether or not our current
understanding of these static aspects is sufficiently well advanced
to aid in the development of a dynamic theory poses a serious
challenge to the present enterprise.

A second factor that helps to explain the apparent neglect,
until recent years, of the problem of political change is what K.
J. Holsti called the decline of "grand theory" (1971, pp. 165–77).
The political realism of Hans Morgenthau, the systems theory of
Morton Kaplan, and the neofunctionalism of Ernst Haas, as well
as numerous other "grand theories," have one element in common: the search for a general theory of international politics.
Each in its own way, with varying success, has sought, in the
words of Morgenthau, "to reduce the facts of experience to mere

---

[3] It is symptomatic of this continued general neglect that the *Handbook of Political
Science* does not contain a section devoted specifically to the problem of political
change (Greenstein and Polsby, 1975), nor does the entry "political change" appear in
its cumulative index.

specific instances of general propositions" (quoted by Holsti, 1971, p. 167). Yet none of these ambitious efforts to understand the issues (war, imperialism, and political change) has gained general acceptance. Instead, "the major preoccupations of theorists during the past decade have been to explore specific problems, to form hypotheses or generalizations explaining limited ranges of phenomena, and particularly, to obtain data to test those hypotheses"(Holsti, 1971, p. 171). In brief, the more recent emphasis on so-called middle-range theory, though valuable in itself, has had the unfortunate consequence of diverting attention away from more general theoretical problems.[4]

A third reason for neglect of the study of political change is the Western bias in the study of international relations. For a profession whose intellectual commitment is the understanding of the interactions of societies, international relations as a discipline is remarkably parochial and ethnocentric. It is essentially a study of the Western state system, and a sizable fraction of the existing literature is devoted to developments since the end of World War II. Thus the profession has emphasized recent developments within that particular state system. Although there are exceptions, the practitioners of this discipline have not been forced to come to terms with the dynamics of this, or any other, state system.[5] As Martin Wight suggested (1966), international relations lacks a tradition of political theorizing. In large measure, of course, this is because of the paucity of reliable secondary studies of non-Western systems. This situation in itself is a formidable obstacle to the development of a theory of international political change.

A fourth reason for neglect of the theoretical problem of political change is the widespread conviction of the futility of the task. Prevalent among historians, this view is also held by many social scientists (Hirschman, 1970b). The search for "laws of change" is held to be useless because of the uniqueness and complexity of

---

[4] Several important books have recently indicated revival of interest in general theory (Choucri and North, 1975; Bull, 1977; Keohane and Nye, 1977; Hoffmann, 1978; Pettman, 1979; Waltz, 1979). Marxist scholars, of course, never lost interest in "grand theory."

[5] Three recent exceptions are Luard (1976), Wesson (1978), and Wight (1977).

historical events. Thus the search for generalizations or patterns in human affairs is regarded as a hopeless enterprise. Such a position, if taken at face value, denies the very possibility of a science or history of society; yet one should note its admonitions that there are no immutable laws of change and that although repetitive patterns may exist, social change is ultimately contingent on unique sets of historical events.

Finally, the development of a theory of political change has been inhibited by ideology and emotion. In part this is due to a conservative bias in Western social science. Most academic social scientists have a preference for stability or at least a preference for orderly change. The idea of radical changes that threaten accepted values and interests is not an appealing one. This issue is especially acute for the theorist of international political change, who must confront directly the fundamental problem of international relations: war. The inhibiting effect of this dreadful issue has been well put by John Burton in a sweeping indictment of contemporary international-relations scholarship:

The chief failure of orthodoxy has been in relation to change. The outstanding feature of reality is the dynamic nature of International Relations. No general theory is appropriate which cannot take into consideration the rapidly changing technological, social and political environment in which nations are required to live in peace one with the other. But the only device of fundamental change which is possible in the context of power politics is that of war, for which reason war is recognized as a legitimate instrument of national policy. It is not surprising that International Relations has tended to be discussed in static terms, and that stability has tended to be interpreted in terms of the maintenance of the *status quo*. A dynamic approach to International Relations would immediately confront the analyst with no alternative but to acknowledge war as the only available mechanism for change (Burton, 1965, pp. 71–2).

Burton's challenge to orthodox theory of international relations goes to the heart of the present study. In recent years theorists of international relations have tended to stress the moderating and stabilizing influences of contemporary developments on the behavior of states, especially the increasing economic interdependence among nations and the destructiveness of modern weapons. These important developments have encouraged many individuals to believe that peaceful evolution has replaced military conflict as the principal means of adjusting relations among nation-states in the contemporary world. This assumption has been accompanied by a belief that economic and welfare goals have triumphed over the traditional power and security objectives of states. Thus, many believe that the opportunity for peaceful economic intercourse and the constraints imposed by modern destructive warfare have served to decrease the probability of a major war.

In the present study we take a very different stance, a stance based on the assumption that the fundamental nature of international relations has not changed over the millennia. International relations continue to be a recurring struggle for wealth and power among independent actors in a state of anarchy. The classic history of Thucydides is as meaningful a guide to the behavior of states today as when it was written in the fifth century B.C. Yet important changes have taken place. One of the subthemes of this book, in fact, is that modern statecraft and premodern statecraft differ in significant respects, a situation first appreciated by Montesquieu, Edward Gibbon, and other earlier writers on the subject. Nevertheless, we contend that the fundamentals have not been altered.[6] For this reason, the insights of earlier writers and historical experience are considered relevant to an understanding of the ways in which international systems function and change in the contemporary era.

Thus, although there is obviously an important element of truth in the belief that contemporary economic and technological developments have altered relations among states, events in Asia, Africa, and the Middle East in the 1970s and early 1980s force us once again to acknowledge the continuing unsolved problem of war and the role of war in the process of international political change. Even more than in the past, in the last decades of the twentieth century we need to understand the relationship of war and change in the international system. Only in this way can we hope to fashion a more peaceful alternative. As E. H.

---

[6] The reasons for this belief are set forth in Chapter 6.

Carr (1951) reminded us, this is the basic task of the study of international relations: "To establish methods of peaceful change is . . . the fundamental problem of international morality and of international politics." But if peace were the ultimate goal of statecraft, then the solution to the problem of peaceful change would be easy. Peace may always be had by surrender to the aggressor state. The real task for the peaceful state is to seek a peace that protects and guarantees its vital interests and its concept of international morality.

1

The nature of international political change

The argument of this book is that an international system is established for the same reason that any social or political system is created; actors enter social relations and create social structures in order to advance particular sets of political, economic, or other types of interests. Because the interests of some of the actors may conflict with those of other actors, the particular interests that are most favored by these social arrangements tend to reflect the relative powers of the actors involved. That is, although social systems impose restraints on the behavior of all actors, the behaviors rewarded and punished by the system will coincide, at least initially, with the interests of the most powerful members of the social system. Over time, however, the interests of individual actors and the balance of power among the actors do change as a result of economic, technological, and other developments. As a consequence, those actors who benefit most from a change in the social system and who gain the power to effect such change will seek to alter the system in ways that favor their interests. The resulting changed system will reflect the new distribution of power and the interests of its new dominant members. Thus, a precondition for political change lies in a disjuncture between the existing social system and the redistribution of power toward those actors who would benefit most from a change in the system.

This conception of political change is based on the notion that the purpose or social function of any social system, including the international system, may be defined in terms of the benefits that various members derive from its operation (Harsanyi, 1969, p. 532). As is the case with domestic society, the nature of the international system determines whose interests are being served by the functioning of the system. Changes in the system imply changes in the distribution of benefits provided to and costs imposed on individual members by the system. Thus the study of international political change must focus on the international system and especially on the efforts of political actors to change the international system in order to advance their own interests. Whether these interests are security, economic gain, or ideological goals, the achievement of state objectives is dependent on the nature of the international system (i.e., the governance of the system, the rules of the system, the recognition of rights, etc.). As is the case in any social or political system, the process of international political change ultimately reflects the efforts of individuals or groups to transform institutions and systems in order to advance their interests. Because these interests and the powers of groups (or states) change, in time the political system will be changed in ways that will reflect these underlying shifts in interest and power. The elaboration of this approach for the understanding of international political change is the purpose of the subsequent discussion in this book.

A FRAMEWORK FOR UNDERSTANDING INTERNATIONAL POLITICAL CHANGE

The conceptualization of international political change to be presented in this book rests on a set of assumptions regarding the behavior of states:

1   An international system is stable (i.e., in a state of equilibrium) if no state believes it profitable to attempt to change the system.

2   A state will attempt to change the international system if the expected benefits exceed the expected costs (i.e., if there is an expected net gain).

3   A state will seek to change the international system through territorial, political, and economic expansion until the marginal costs of further change are equal to or greater than the marginal benefits.

4 Once an equilibrium between the costs and benefits of further change and expansion is reached, the tendency is for the economic costs of maintaining the status quo to rise faster than the economic capacity to support the status quo.

5 If the disequilibrium in the international system is not resolved, then the system will be changed, and a new equilibrium reflecting the redistribution of power will be established.

Obviously these assumptions are abstractions from a highly complex political reality. They do not describe the actual decision processes of statesmen, but as in the case of economic theory, actors are assumed to behave as if they were guided by such a set of cost/benefit calculations. Moreover, these assumptions are not mutually exclusive; they do overlap. Assumptions 2 and 4 are mirror images of one another, assumption 2 referring to a revisionist state and assumption 4 referring to a status quo state. For analytical purposes, however, each assumption will be discussed separately in subsequent chapters.

On the basis of these assumptions, the conceptualization of international political change to be presented here seeks to comprehend a continuing historical process. Because history has no starts and stops, one must break into the flow of history at a particular point. The following analysis of political change begins with an international system in a state of equilibrium as shown in Figure 1. An international system is in a state of equilibrium if the more powerful states in the system are satisfied with the existing territorial, political, and economic arrangements. Although minor changes and adjustments may take place, an equilibrium condition is one in which no powerful state (or group) believes that a change in the system would yield additional benefits commensurate with the anticipated costs of bringing about a change in the system (Curry and Wade, 1968, p. 49; Davis and North, 1971, p. 40). Although every state and group in the system could benefit from particular types of change, the costs involved will discourage attempts to seek a change in system. As one writer has put it, "a power equilibrium represents a stable political configuration provided there are no changes in returns to conquest" (Rader, 1971, p. 50). Under these conditions,

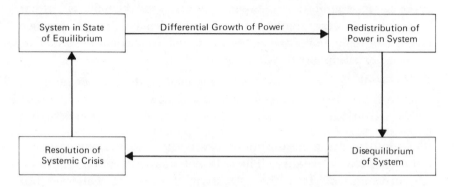

Figure 1. Diagram of international political change.

where no one has an incentive to change the system, the status quo may be said to be stable.

In the more traditional language of international relations, the international status quo is held to be a legitimate one, at least by the major states in the system. The meaning of legitimacy was defined by Henry Kissinger as follows:

[Legitimacy] implies the acceptance of the framework of the international order by all major powers, at least to the extent that no state is so dissatisfied that, like Germany after the Treaty of Versailles, it expresses its dissatisfaction in a revolutionary foreign policy. A legitimate order does not make conflicts impossible, but it limits their scope. Wars may occur, but they will be fought *in the name of* the existing structure and the peace which follows will be justified as a better expression of the "legitimate," general consensus. Diplomacy in the classic sense, the adjustment of differences through negotiations, is possible only in "legitimate" international orders (1957, pp. 1–2).

What this quotation suggests is that an international system or order exists in a condition of homeostatic or dynamic equilibrium. Like any other system, it is not completely at rest; changes at the level of interstate interactions are constantly taking place. In general, however, the conflicts, alliances, and diplomatic interactions among the actors in the system tend to preserve the defining characteristics of the system. Thus, as Kissinger demonstrated, the legitimate order or equilibrium created at the Congress of Vienna (1814) survived limited conflicts and diplomatic maneuvering until it finally collapsed in response to the profound economic, technological, and political upheavals of the latter part of the nineteenth century. This issue of legitimacy will be discussed later.

In every international system there are continual occurrences of political, economic, and technological changes that promise gains or threaten losses for one or another actor. In most cases these potential gains and losses are minor, and only incremental adjustments are necessary in order to take account of them. Such changes take place within the existing international system, producing a condition of homeostatic equilibrium. The relative stability of the system is, in fact, largely determined by its capacity to adjust to the demands of actors affected by changing political and environmental conditions. In every system, therefore, a process of disequilibrium and adjustment is constantly taking place. In the absence of large potential net benefits from change, the system continues to remain in a state of equilibrium.

If the interests and relative powers of the principal states in an international system remained constant over time, or if power relations changed in such a way as to maintain the same relative distribution of power, the system would continue indefinitely in a state of equilibrium. However, both domestic and international developments undermine the stability of the status quo. For example, shifts in domestic coalitions may necessitate redefinition of the "national interest." However, the most destabilizing factor is the tendency in an international system for the powers of member states to change at different rates because of political, economic, and technological developments. In time, the differential growth in power of the various states in the system causes a fundamental redistribution of power in the system.

The concept of power is one of the most troublesome in the field of international relations and, more generally, political science. Many weighty books have analyzed and elaborated the concept. In this book, power refers simply to the military, economic, and technological capabilities of states. This definition obviously leaves out important and intangible elements that affect the outcomes of political actions, such as public morale, qualities of leadership, and situational factors. It also excludes what E. H. Carr called "power over opinion" (1951, p. 132). These psychological and frequently incalculable aspects of power and international relations are more closely associated with the concept of prestige as it is used in this book. The relationship between power and prestige and its significance for international political change will be discussed herein.

As a consequence of the changing interests of individual states, and especially because of the differential growth in power among states, the international system moves from a condition of equilibrium to one of disequilibrium. Disequilibrium is a situation in which economic, political, and technological developments have increased considerably the potential benefits or decreased the potential costs to one or more states of seeking to change the international system. Forestalling one's losses or increasing one's gains becomes an incentive for one or more states to attempt to change the system. Thus there develops a disjuncture between the existing international system and the potential gains to particular states from a change in the international system.

The elements of this systemic disequilibrium are twofold. First, military, technological, or other changes have increased the benefits of territorial conquest or the benefits of changing the international system in other ways. Second, the differential growth in power among the states in the system has altered the cost of changing the system. This transformation of the benefits and/or the costs of changing the system produces an incongruity or disjuncture among the components of the system (Table 1). On the one hand, the hierarchy of prestige, the division of territory, the international division of labor, and the rules of the system remain basically unchanged; they continue to reflect primarily the interests of the existing dominant powers and the relative power distribution that prevailed at the time of the last systemic change. On the other hand, the international distribution of power has undergone a radical transformation that has weakened the foundations of the existing system. It is this disjuncture between the several components of the system and its implications for relative gains and losses among the various states in the system that cause international political change.

This disjuncture within the existing international system involving the potential benefits and losses to particular powerful actors from a change in the system leads to a crisis in the international system. Although resolution of a crisis through peaceful adjustment of the systemic disequilibrium is possible, the principal mechanism of change throughout history has been war, or what we shall call hegemonic war (i.e., a war that determines which state or states will be dominant and will govern the system). The peace settlement following such a hegemonic struggle reorders the political, territorial, and other bases of the system. Thus the cycle of change is completed in that hegemonic war and the peace settlement create a new status quo and equilibrium reflecting the redistribution of power in the system and the other components of the system.

DEFINITION OF BASIC TERMS

In the remainder of this chapter the basic terms and issues embodied in this conceptualization of political change will be defined and elaborated. In the first place, every theory of international relations requires a theory of the state. In addition, the conception of state interest and the objectives of foreign policy must be set forth. Third, the nature of the international system must be defined. The conceptualization or definition of these three factors determines who it is (the state) that seeks to change social arrangements (the international system) in order to secure what interests (the objectives of foreign policy). Although the definitions used in this book are arbitrary, they are derived from our overall conception of international political change as previously developed.

Definition of the state

The theory of the state that we shall use in this study is that the state is "an organization that provides protection and [welfare] . . . in return for revenue" (North and Thomas, 1973, p. 6). The state is the principal mechanism by which society can provide these "public goods" and overcome the free-rider problem.[1] Principally through its definition and enforcement of property rights the state protects the welfare of its citizens against the actions of other individuals and states and also provides a basis for the resolution of disputes.[2] These tasks are essential because of the ubiquitous nature of conflict in a world of scarce resources.

State and society are conceived in this book to be composed of individuals and groups that are distinguishable yet mutually influence one another. The state, i.e., those particular individuals who hold authority, has interests of its own. The absolute monarch or contemporary politician has personal objectives he seeks to achieve, the primary one being to maintain himself in office. Yet, even the most ruthless dictator must satisfy the interests of those individuals and groups who also wield power in a society. Powerful groups set constraints on and may even determine the actions of state authority. They constitute the society that is protected by the state; their particular concept of justice reigns. The definition and functioning of property rights tend to advance their interests and welfare. Thus, while the states in the Soviet Union, the United States, and South Africa perform the same set of general functions, the individuals and groups in society benefited by these states differ very greatly. Throughout this book, although the term "state" will be used as if it were an autonomous entity, the reader should appreciate that the meaning given here applies.

The key role of property rights in the functioning of society was expressed by one writer in the following terms:

Property rights are an instrument of society and derive their significance from the fact that they help a man form those expectations which

---

[1] A public good is one "which all enjoy in common in the sense that each individual's consumption of such a good leads to no subtraction from any other individual's consumption of that good" (Samuelson, 1954, p. 387). A free-rider is an individual who consumes the good at no personal expense or little expense. For an excellent discussion of the application of public-goods theory to international relations, see the work of Hart and Cowhey (1977).

[2] This responsibility of the state revolves particularly around the so-called problem of externalities (i.e., the rendering of services or disservices to an individual for which neither payment nor compensation is made) (Baumol, 1965, pp.24–36).

he can reasonably hold in his dealings with others. These expectations find expression in the laws, customs, and mores of a society. An owner of property rights possesses the consent of fellowmen to allow him to act in particular ways. An owner expects the community to prevent others from interfering with his actions, provided that these actions are not prohibited in the specifications of his rights (Demsetz, 1967, p. 347).

The delineation of property rights is necessary if any society is to operate effectively; property rights function by conveying "the right to benefit or harm oneself or others. Harming a competitor by producing superior products may be permitted, while shooting him may not. A man may be permitted to benefit himself by shooting an intruder but be prohibited from selling below a price floor" (Demsetz, 1967, p. 347). Thus the nature and distribution of property rights determine which individuals will be most benefited and which will pay the most costs with respect to the functioning of different types of social institutions. For this reason the basic domestic function of the state is to define and protect the property rights of individuals and groups.

The primary external function of the state is to protect the property rights and personal security of its members vis-à-vis the citizens and actions of other states. In the words of Ralf Dahrendorf, the state is thus a "conflict group." Whereas obviously there are other conflict groups (tribes, labor unions, feudal fiefdoms, guerrilla bands, etc.), the essence of the state is its territoriality (Dahrendorf, 1959, p. 290). Within the territory it encompasses the state exercises a monopoly of the legitimate use of force and embodies the idea that everyone in that territory is subject to the same law or set of rules. Thus the authority of the state is believed superior to that of all other groups in the territory controlled by the state.

These internal and external functions of the state and the ultimate nature of its authority mean that it is the principal actor in the international system. The state is sovereign in that it must answer to no higher authority in the international sphere. It alone defines and protects the rights of individuals and groups. Individuals possess no rights except those guaranteed by the state itself; they have no security save that afforded by the state.

If the state is to protect its citizens and their rights, and in the absence of any higher authority and in a competitive state system, the state must be "self-regarding" and must look on all other states as potential threats.[3]

The argument that the state (as herein conceived) is the principal actor in international relations does not deny the existence of other individual and collective actors. As Ernst Haas cogently put it, the actors in international relations are those entities capable of putting forth demands effectively; who or what these entities may be cannot be answered a priori (Haas, 1964, p. 84). However, the state is the principal actor in that the nature of the state and the pattern of relations among states are the most important determinants of the character of international relations at any given moment. This argument does not presume that states need always be the principal actors, nor does it presume that the nature of the state need always be the same and that the contemporary nation-state is the ultimate form of political organization. Throughout history, in fact, states and political organizations have varied greatly: tribes, empires, fiefdoms, city-states, etc. The nation-state in historical terms is a rather recent arrival; its success has been due to a peculiar set of historical circumstances, and there is no guarantee that these conditions will continue into the future. Yet it would be premature to suggest (much less declare, as many contemporary writers do) that the nation-state is dead or dying.

Interests and objectives of states

Strictly speaking, states, as such, have no interests, or what economists call "utility functions," nor do bureaucracies, interest groups, or so-called transnational actors, for that matter. Only individuals and individuals joined together into various types of coalitions can be said to have interests.[4] From this perspective

---

[3] "Self-regarding" is the apt expression of Kenneth Waltz (1979, p. 91). The idea that the state is the principal actor in international relations is strongly supported by Waltz's discussion (1979, pp. 93–7).

[4] A coalition is defined as "a group of persons working together who have some but not all goals in common" (Downs, 1967, p. 76).

the state may be conceived as a coalition of coalitions whose objectives and interests result from the powers and bargaining among the several coalitions composing the larger society and political elite. In the language of Brian Barry (1976, p. 159), collective choice and determination of political objectives are coalition processes (Cyert and March, 1963, p. 28).

The objectives and foreign policies of states are determined primarily by the interests of their dominant members or ruling coalitions. When one inquires what these interests or objectives are, one confronts a long-standing debate between what Stanley Hoffmann (1973) called the *classiques* and the *modernes*. The former, mainly political realists, argue that national security and power have been in the past and continue to be in the present the primary objectives of states. The latter counter that, however true this may have been in the past, attaining domestic economic stability and ensuring the welfare of the populace have become the foremost objectives of states in the contemporary world.

We believe that both the *classiques* and the *modernes* have confused the issue. Both positions assume that one can speak of a hierarchy of the objectives of states and that states seek to maximize one or another set of interests. These assumptions misrepresent the behavior and decision-making processes of states (or, for that matter, any actor). Every action or decision involves a trade-off, and the effort to achieve one objective inevitably involves costs with respect to some other desired goal. Thus, whereas political realists are correct in stating that security is a primary objective in the sense that if it is not satisfied, all other objectives are placed in jeopardy, the pursuit of security involves the sacrifice of other desired social goals and a real cost to the society. Similarly, the maximization of efforts to attain economic and welfare goals entails the diversion of resources from national security. In a world of scarce resources, where every benefit entails a cost, societies seldom, if ever, choose guns or butter, at least over the long run.

Modern economic analysis substitutes the concept of the indifference curve for the notion that individuals (or states) possess a hierarchy of goals, demands, or utilities. Indifference analysis seeks to explain how income, price, and taste (as well as changes in these variables) affect the demand for goods and the supply of goods (Waldman, 1972, p. 241). In particular, in accordance with the law of demand, it accounts for the way in which changes in market conditions (e.g., income and price) affect the quantity of goods desired.[5] It is difficult, if not impossible, to draw an indifference curve for an individual and still more difficult for a whole society, and substitution of indifference analysis for the notion of a hierarchy of objectives does help clarify the issue posed by the *classique—moderne* controversy (Figure 2).

Indifference analysis assumes that individuals have numerous objectives and are willing to accept varying bundles of these objectives. In contrast to the idea of a hierarchy of goals, with its associated emphasis on maximization, indifference analysis assumes individuals make trade-offs among these objectives and pursue "satisficing" strategies rather than maximizing strategies (Simon, 1957, p. 250). That is to say, an individual will be satisfied by any one of a large number of different combinations of the desired goals. The individual (or state) will not seek to achieve one objective at the sacrifice of all others but will seek to find some optimum position on the set of indifference curves. Thus the state will not seek to maximize power (*classique*) or welfare (*moderne*) but will endeavor to find some optimum combination of both objectives (as well as others, for that matter), and the amount sought will depend on income and cost.

Several important implications for the study of international relations, and especially for our understanding of political change, flow from this emphasis on the concept of the indifference curve. In the first place, the slope of the indifference curve (i.e., the satisficing mix of objectives) differs from one society to another, depending on the specific interests of ruling domestic elites and

---

[5] The so-called law of demand is one of the most important assumptions underlying economic analysis. It holds, in effect, that "if the price of a good or service falls, *ceteris paribus,* people will buy more of it" (McKenzie and Tullock, 1975, p. 15). Also, if relative income rises, ceteris paribus, it is assumed that people will demand more of a good. This increased demand is limited, of course, by the law of diminishing utility. Unfortunately for economic predictions of human behavior, other things do not always remain the same, and economists lack an adequate theory for predicting changes in demand itself (Northrop, 1947, p. 245).

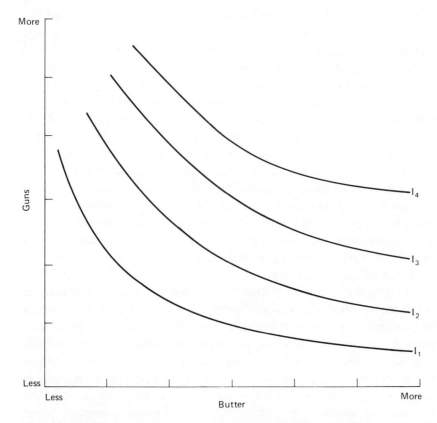

Figure 2. Indifference curves, each representing equally valued allocations of the two valued objects. [Adapted from Steinbruner (1974, p. 30).]

the international environment. For example, a continental European state with powerful neighbors will undoubtedly place greater emphasis on security than will an insular state with global economic interests, such as Great Britain in the nineteenth century or the United States in the twentieth.[6] Thus it is impossible in general terms to determine what bundles of security, economic, or other objectives will satisfy states.

---

[6] It is perhaps worth noting that nearly all theorists who argue that economic welfare has displaced security in the hierarchy of state objectives are American. The *moderne* position is really not so new, but rather a resurgence of what Arnold Wolfers and Laurence Martin (1956) called the Anglo-Saxon tradition in international relations.

Throughout history, states and ruling elites have sought a wide range of political, economic, and ideological objectives. During different eras the mix of objectives has varied in terms of the proportions of various sets of objectives. The ratio of security objectives to economic objectives, for example, may vary depending on internal and external factors. Objectives important in one age may be relatively unimportant in another. Thus, in the early modern era, religious objectives weighed heavily in the foreign policy of western European states.[7] Following the French Revolution, the political ideologies of liberalism and conservatism became important determinants of foreign policy. In the late twentieth-century world, economic ideologies and interests (as the *modernes* contend) are increasingly important objectives of states; yet it is the mix and trade-offs of objectives rather than their ordering that is critical to an understanding of foreign policy.

Second, the slope of a state's indifference curve may shift in response to both internal and external changes. The distribution of power among domestic coalitions may change over time, and with it the mix of interests or objectives of the foreign policy of the state will be altered. For example, the ruling elite may desire a revised mix weighted in favor of security goals. It is equally possible that the slope of the indifference curve may shift because of economic, technological, or other environmental changes that alter the costs of one or more objectives sought by states. For example, a military or technological innovation may dramatically reduce the cost and increase the benefits of territorial conquest and thereby encourage military expansion.

Third, the indifference curve selected by a state is to some degree a function of the wealth and power of the society. As the wealth and power of a society increase, the choice of indifference curve shifts outwardly. That is, an increase in a state's resources and power will cause a shift from I_1 to I_2. A more wealthy

[7] Actually, religious interests have been among the foremost objectives of states and other collectivities in all ages. This has resulted from the fact that the actors have been whole civilizations with differing and conflicting religious conceptions. The modern era has, in fact, been unique in this regard. Modern man has tended to substitute political and economic ideological passions for religious passion. Recent events in Iran may point toward a return to religious conflict.

and more powerful state (up to a point of diminishing utility) will select a larger bundle of security and welfare goals than a less wealthy and less powerful state (the production-possibility frontier is said to have shifted outwardly). As a consequence, the redistribution of wealth and power toward a particular state in an international system tends to stimulate the state to demand a larger bundle of welfare and security objectives.

Thus, a change in the relative cost of the objectives sought by a state or a change in the capacity of the state to achieve these objectives tend to induce a change in state behavior. A change in the relative costs of security objectives and welfare objectives or a change in a state's power and wealth usually causes a corresponding change in the foreign policy of the state. The explanation of international political change is in large measure a matter of accounting for shifts in the slopes and positions of the indifference curves of states and in the specific objectives of foreign policy. In general, these state objectives have been of three types.

Throughout history a principal objective of states has been the conquest of territory in order to advance economic, security, and other interests. Whether by means of imperialist subjugation of one people by another or by annexation of contiguous territory, states in all ages have sought to enlarge their control over territory and, by implication, their control over the international system. For this reason, a theory of international political change must of necessity also be a theory of imperialism and political integration.

Prior to the modern age, and particularly prior to the Industrial Revolution, conquest of territory was the primary means by which a group or state could increase its security or wealth. In an era of relatively stable technology and low productivity gains in both agriculture and manufacturing, a group or state could best increase its wealth and power by increasing its control over territory and conquering other peoples. In fact, until the technological revolution of the late eighteenth century, the international distribution of territory and the distribution of power and wealth were largely synonymous. Although this close relationship has changed because of modern industrial and military technology, it is obvious that control over territory is still an important objective of groups and states.

The second objective of states is to increase their influence over the behavior of other states. Through the use of threats and coercion, the formation of alliances, and the creation of exclusive spheres of influence, states attempt to create an international political environment and rules of the system that will be conducive to the fulfillment of their political, economic, and ideological interests. Thus, another aspect of the process of international political change involves the efforts of states (or, again, groups) to gain control over the behavior of other actors in the international system.

The third objective of states, and in the modern world an increasingly important objective, is to control or at least exercise influence over the world economy, or what may more properly be called the international division of labor. This objective, of course, cannot easily be isolated from the first two. Both the control of territory and the political domination of one state over another have profound consequences for international economic relations. However, since the emergence of an international market economy in the seventeenth century and its extension throughout the globe in the nineteenth century, market power or economic power has itself become a principal means by which states seek to organize and manipulate the international division of labor to their own advantage.

In the modern world the international division of labor has become a significant determinant of the relative wealth, security, and prestige of states; the organization and management of the world economy have become important objectives of states. The terms of trade, the flow of resources (capital, technology, commodities), and the nature of the international monetary system are today primary concerns of state policy. Therefore, the distribution of economic power and the rules governing international economic regimes have become critical aspects of the process of international political change (Keohane and Nye, 1977).

In particular, creation and operation of the interdependent world economy have required recognition and enforcement of individual property rights on a global scale. The progressive extension of these rights of individuals (or corporations) geographically and from the relatively simple area of commercial intercourse to the complex arena of foreign investment has become a central feature of international relations in the modern world. The idea that a citizen of one country can exercise property rights across national boundaries is a revolutionary feature of the modern world, especially on the scale it is now practiced in the 1980s. Determination of the rules governing these rights has been an important aspect of international political change.

Among these objectives of states, the most important are those that a state considers its vital interests and for which it is prepared to go to war. Although the concept of vital interest is imprecise, and the definition of a vital interest may change because of economic, technological, or political change, every state regards the safeguarding of certain interests to be of overriding importance to its security. Thus, Great Britain fought several wars over a period of three centuries to secure the independence of the Low Countries from hostile powers. Since World War II, eastern Europe and western Europe have been accepted by all concerned as vital interests of the Soviet Union and the United States, respectively. Therefore, despite its vagueness, the idea of vital interest (Wight, 1979, pp. 95–9) remains an important idea for understanding the foreign policies of states:

So long as international relations are based on force, power will be a leading object of national ambition. There results a vicious circle. When a political leader says that war is necessary in his country's vital interests, what he usually means is that war is necessary to acquire or to avoid losing some factor of national strength. The interest is only vital in the sense that it is vital to success in war. The only end vital enough to justify war is something arising out of the prospect of war itself (Hawtrey, 1952, p. 19).

The nature of the international system

States create international social, political, and economic arrangements in order to advance particular sets of interests. However, obviously they do not have complete control over this process. Once in place, the international system itself has a

reciprocal influence on state behavior; it affects the ways in
which individuals, groups, and states seek to achieve their
goals. The international system thus provides a set of constraints and opportunities within which individual groups and
states seek to advance their interests.

The term "international system" is itself ambiguous. It can
cover a range of phenomena from sporadic contacts among states
to the tightly interlocked relationships of late-nineteenth-century
Europe. Until the modern era there was no single international
system, but rather several international systems, with little or no
contact one with another. Thus, except for the modern world,
one cannot really speak of the international system. In this study
the term "international system" will be used to refer to the com-
partmentalized systems of the past, as well as the worldwide
system of the present era.

The definition of international system to be used here is
adapted from the definition used by Robert Mundell and Alexander Swoboda: "A system is an aggregation of diverse entities
united by regular interaction according to a form of control"
(Mundell and Swoboda, 1969, p. 343).[8] According to this formulation, an international system has three primary aspects. In the
first place, there are the "diverse entities," which may be processes, structures, actors, or even attributes of actors. Second, the
system is characterized by "regular interaction," which can vary
on a continuum from infrequent contacts to intense interdependence of states. Third, there is some "form of control" that regu-
lates behavior and may range from informal rules of the system to
formal institutions. Furthermore, by implication, the system must
have some boundaries that set it apart from other systems and its
larger environment. Let us consider each aspect in more detail.

Diverse entities.   As noted earlier, the principal entities or actors
are states, although other actors of a transnational or international
nature may also play important roles under certain sets of circumstances. The nature of the state itself also changes over time, and
the character of the international system is largely determined by
the type of state-actor: city-states, empires, nation-states, etc. A

[8] The writer in endebted to Edward Morse for bringing this definition to his attention.

Waltz – Like units?

fundamental task of a theory of international political change is
to inquire into the factors that influence the type of state characteristic of a particular era and international system.

Regular interactions.   Every international system is characterized by various types of interactions among its elements. The
nature, regularity, and intensity of these interactions vary
greatly for different international systems. The interactions
among the actors in the system may range from intermittent
armed conflict to the high levels of economic and cultural interdependence of the modern world. Together, diplomatic, military,
economic, and other relationships among states constitute the
functioning of the international system.

In the modern world, these interactions among states have
become increasingly intense and organized, principally because
of revolutionary advances in transportation and communications.
Diplomatic, alliance, and cultural relationships among states
have been institutionalized and governed by formally agreed
rules. In particular, economic interdependence, or what may be
called the international division of labor, has evolved to the point
that trade, money relations, and foreign investment are among
the most important features of the international system in the
contemporary world. The evolution and functioning of the international division of labor have become critical aspects of the
process of international political change.

Form of control.   Undoubtedly the most controversial aspect of
the definition of the term "international system" as used here is
the notion of control over the system. A view prevalent among
many scholars of political science is that the essence of international relations is precisely the absence of control. International politics, in contrast to domestic politics, are said to take
place in a condition of anarchy; there is no authority or control
over the behavior of the actors, and many writers believe that it
is a contradiction in terms to speak of control over the international system. Because of the centrality of this issue to the argument of this study, it requires a more extended treatment than
the other aspects of the international system.

Table 1. *Mechanisms of control (components of system)*

Domestic	International
Government[a]	Dominance of great powers[b]
Authority	Hierarchy of prestige
Property rights	Division of territory
Law	Rules of the system
Domestic economy	International economy

[a]Based on distribution of power among domestic groups, coalitions, classes, etc.
[b]Based on distribution of power among states in the system.

The argument of this study is that the relationships among states have a high degree of order and that although the international system is one of anarchy (i.e., absence of formal governmental authority), the system does exercise an element of control over the behavior of states (Bull, 1977; Young, 1978). However, the nature and extent of this control differ from the nature and extent of the control that domestic society exercises over the behavior of individuals. Yet it is possible to identify similarities in the control mechanisms of domestic systems and international systems (Table 1).

When we speak of control over the international system, this term must be understood as "relative control" and "seeking to control." No state has ever completely controlled an international system; for that matter, no domestic government, not even the most totalitarian, has completely controlled a domestic society. The degree of control obviously differs also in various aspects of international relations and over time (Keohane and Nye, 1977, p. 31). If a group or state were completely in control of a society, change could not take place. Indeed, it is precisely because economic, political, and technological forces escape the control of dominant groups and states that change does take place.

Control over or governance of the international system is a function of three factors. In the first place, governance of the system rests on the distribution of power among political coalitions. In domestic society these coalitions are primarily classes, strata, or interest groups, and the distribution of power among these entities is a principal aspect of the governance of domestic society. In international society the distribution of power among coalitions of coalitions (or states) determines who governs the international system and whose interests are principally promoted by the functioning of the system.

In the words of E. H. Carr, "international government is, in effect, government by that state [or states] which supplies [supply] the power necessary for the purpose of governing" (1951, p. 107). In every international system the dominant powers in the international hierarchy of power and prestige organize and control the processes of interactions among the elements of the system. Or, as Raymond Aron put it, "the structure of international systems is always *oligopolistic*. In each period the principal actors have determined the system more than they have been determined by it" (1966, p. 95). These dominant states have sought to exert control over the system in order to advance their self-interests.

Throughout history, three forms of control or types of structure have characterized international systems. The first structure is imperial or hegemonic: A single powerful state controls or dominates the lesser states in the system. This type of system has, in fact, been most prevalent, at least until modern times, and scholars of international relations have detected a propensity for every international system to evolve in the direction of a universal empire. The second structure is a bipolar structure in which two powerful states control and regulate interactions within and between their respective spheres of influence; despite important exceptions, the tendency has always been for such systems to be unstable and relatively short-lived. The third type of structure is a balance of power in which three or more states control one another's actions through diplomatic maneuver, shifting alliances, and open conflict. The classic example of this system is, of course, the European balance of power that may be said to have existed from the Treaty of Westphalia (1648) to the eve of World War I (1914).

The distribution of power among states constitutes the principal form of control in every international system. The dominant states and empires in every international system organize and maintain the network of political, economic, and other relationships within the system and especially in their respective spheres of influence. Both individually and in interaction with one another, those states that historically have been called the great powers and are known today as the superpowers establish and enforce the basic rules and rights that influence their own behavior and that of the lesser states in the system.

The second component in the governance of an international system is the hierarchy of prestige among states. In international relations, prestige is the functional equivalent of the role of authority in domestic politics. Like the concept of authority, prestige is closely linked to but is distinct from the concept of power. As defined by Max Weber, power is the "probability that one actor within a social relationship will be in a position to carry out his own will despite resistance, regardless of the basis on which this probability rests." Authority (or prestige) is the "probability that a command with a given specific content will be obeyed by a given group of persons" (Dahrendorf, 1959, p. 166). Thus, both power and prestige function to ensure that the lesser states in the system will obey the commands of the dominant state or states.

Prestige, like authority, has a moral and functional basis (Carr, 1951, p. 236). To some extent the lesser states in an international system follow the leadership of more powerful states, in part because they accept the legitimacy and utility of the existing order. In general, they prefer the certainty of the status quo to the uncertainties of change. Also, the ruling elites and coalitions of subordinate states frequently form alliances with the dominant powers and identify their values and interests with those of the dominant powers. Empires and dominant states supply public goods (security, economic order, etc.) that give other states an interest in following their lead. Finally, every dominant state, and particularly an empire, promotes a religion or ideology that justifies its domination over other states in the system (Moore, 1958, pp. 10, 16). In short, numerous factors, including respect and common interest, underlie the prestige of a state and the legitimacy of its rule. Ultimately, however, the hierarchy of prestige in an international system rests on economic and military power.

Prestige is the reputation for power, and military power in particular. Whereas power refers to the economic, military, and related capabilities of a state, prestige refers primarily to the perceptions of other states with respect to a state's capacities and its ability and willingness to exercise its power. In the language of contemporary strategic theory, prestige involves the credibility of a state's power and its willingness to deter or compel other states in order to achieve its objectives. Thus, power and prestige are different, and, as will be argued later, the fact that the existing distribution of power and the hierarchy of prestige can sometimes be in conflict with one another is an important factor in international political change.

Prestige, rather than power, is the everyday currency of international relations, much as authority is the central ordering feature of domestic society. As E. H. Carr put it, prestige is "enormously important," because "if your strength is recognized, you can generally achieve your aims without having to use it" (quoted in Wight, 1979, p. 98). It is for this reason that in the conduct of diplomacy and the resolution of conflicts among states there is actually relatively little use of overt force or, for that matter, explicit threats. Rather, the bargaining among states and the outcomes of negotiations are determined principally by the relative prestige of the parties involved. But behind such negotiations there is the implicit mutual recognition that deadlock at the bargaining table could lead to decision on the battlefield (Kissinger, 1961, p. 170). For this reason, the eras of relative peace and stability have been those historical epochs during which the prestige hierarchy has been clearly understood and has remained unchallenged. Conversely, a weakening of the hierarchy of prestige and increased ambiguity in interpreting it are frequently the prelude to eras of conflict and struggle.

The central role of prestige in the ordering and governance of the international system was well set forth in the following statement by Ralph Hawtrey:

If war is an interruption between two periods of peace, it is equally true that peace is an interval between two wars. That is not a mere verbal epigram. It is significant in a very real sense. War means the imposition of the will of the stronger on the weaker by force. But if their relative strength is already known, a trial of strength is unnecessary; the weaker will yield to the stronger without going through the torments of conflict to arrive at a conclusion foreknown from the beginning. The reputation for strength is what we call *prestige*. A country gains prestige from the possession of economic and military power. These are matters partly of fact and partly of opinion. Were they exactly ascertainable and measurable, conflicts of prestige could always take the place of conflicts of force. But it is not possible to measure exactly either the wealth of a country or the degree of its mobility, and even if the military force that could be maintained were precisely known, there are imponderables to take account of, the military qualities of the men, the proficiency of the leaders, the efficiency of the administration, and, last, but not least, pure luck. The result is that there is a wide margin of error. Prestige is not entirely a matter of calculation, but partly of indirect inference. In a diplomatic conflict the country which yields is likely to suffer in prestige because the fact of yielding is taken by the rest of the world to be evidence of conscious weakness. The visible components of power do not tell the whole story, and no one can judge better of the invisible components than the authorities governing the country itself. If they show want of confidence, people infer that there is some hidden source of weakness.

If the country's prestige is thus diminished, it is weakened in any future diplomatic conflict. And if a diplomatic conflict is about anything substantial, the failure is likely to mean a diminution of material strength.

A decline of prestige is therefore an injury to be dreaded. But in the last resort prestige means reputation for strength in war, and doubts on the subject can only be set at rest by war itself. A country will fight when it believes that its prestige in diplomacy is not equivalent to its real strength. Trial by battle is an exceptional incident, but the conflict of national force is continuous. That is inherent in the international anarchy (1952, pp. 64–5).

There are several aspects of this excellent statement that merit emphasis. In the first place, although prestige is largely a function of economic and military capabilities, it is achieved primarily through successful use of power, and especially through victory in war. The most prestigious members of the international system are those states that have most recently used military force or economic power successfully and have thereby imposed their will on others. Second, both power and prestige are ultimately imponderable and incalculable; they cannot be known absolutely by any a priori process of calculation. They are known only when they are tested, especially on the field of battle. Third, one of the principal functions of war, and particularly what we shall call hegemonic war, is to determine the international hierarchy of prestige and thereby determine which states will in effect govern the international system.

The critical role of prestige in the ordering and functioning of the international system is significant for our primary concern with the process of international political change. What Hawtrey's analysis suggests is that an inconsistency may, and in time does, arise between the established hierarchy of prestige and the existing distribution of power among states.[9] That is, perceptions of prestige lag behind changes in the actual capabilities of states. As a consequence, the governance of the system begins to break down as perceptions catch up with realities of power. The once-dominant state is decreasingly able to impose its will on others and/or to protect its interests. The rising state or states in the system increasingly demand changes in the system that will reflect their newly gained power and their unmet interests. Finally, the stalemate and issue of who will run the system are resolved through armed conflict.

It is frequently asserted that in the contemporary world economic success has largely displaced political and military success as the basis of international prestige. Japan and West Germany are cited as outstanding examples of defeated powers who have recouped their international positions by creating strong economies; in the areas of international trade, foreign investment, and world monetary affairs, these two nations now exert powerful influences throughout the world. This is correct; yet, several further points should be made. First, this emphasis on economic power is consistent with the book's definition of prestige as resting on the capabilities of the state (Hawtrey, 1952, p. 71). Second, Japan and West Germany have increased their prestige in part because they could translate their economic capabilities into

---

[9] The idea of status inconsistency is one that goes back to Max Weber and has been stressed by several recent writers such as Galtung (1964), Michael Haas (1974), and Wallace (1973).

military power. Third, as I have argued elsewhere, economic power can play the role that it does in today's world because of the nature of the economic and political order created and defended militarily primarily by the United States (Gilpin, 1975).

In summary, the legitimacy of the "right to rule" on the part of a great power may be said to rest on three factors. First, it is based on its victory in the last hegemonic war and its demonstrated ability to enforce its will on other states; the treaties that define the international status quo and provide the constitution of the established order have authority in that they reflect this reality. Second, the rule of the dominant power is frequently accepted because it provides certain public goods, such as a beneficial economic order or international security. Third, the position of the dominant power may be supported by ideological, religious, or other values common to a set of states. In contrast to the situation with domestic society, however, the last two factors are usually weak or nonexistent.[10]

In addition to the distribution of power and the hierarchy of prestige, the third component of the governance of an international system is a set of rights and rules that govern or at least influence the interactions among states (Hoffmann, 1965). As far back as our knowledge extends, states have recognized certain rules of the system, although in some instances these rules have been very primitive. These rules have ranged from simple understandings regarding spheres of influence, the exchange of ambassadors, and the conduct of commerce to the elaborate codification of international law in our own era.

Every system of human interaction requires a minimum set of rules and the mutual recognition of rights. The need for rules and rights arises from the basic human condition of scarcity of material resources and the need for order and predictability in human affairs. In order to minimize conflict over the distribution of scarce goods and to facilitate fruitful cooperation among indi-

---

[10]This concept of legitimacy has very little to do with the justice of the system. Although individual states seek justice for themselves, they very seldom rise above self-interest and promote a just system. For contrasting treatments of the role of justice in world politics, three contemporary books are noteworthy: Beitz (1979), Bull (1977, especially Chapter 4), and Falk (1971).

viduals, every social system creates rules and laws for governing behavior. This is as true for international systems as for domestic political systems (Bull, 1977, pp. 46–51).

In general, the rules affecting the interactions among states cover three broad areas. In the first place, they relate to the conduct of diplomacy and political intercourse among states. In some primitive systems such rules may be very rudimentary indeed. In the modern world, these matters have become highly institutionalized and governed by elaborate legal codes. Second, there may be certain rules of war. This is particularly true in the case of states sharing a religion or civilization. In the modern world, under the influence of Western civilization, the law of war, covering such topics as treatment of prisoners and rights of neutrals, has become highly developed, and frequently violated. Third, the rules of a system cover economic and other areas of intercourse among states. In all systems the mutual interest in trade has guaranteed some protection for the trader and merchant. In the modern world the rules or regimes governing international commerce, technical cooperation, and such matters are among the most important rules influencing interstate behavior.

The sources of rights and the rules embodying them range from custom to formally negotiated international treaties. In part, rights and rules rest on common values and interests and are generated by cooperative action among states. The European state system was noteworthy in the relatively high degree of consensus that existed regarding the nature of these rights and rules; this system constituted, in the view of Hedley Bull, not merely a system of states but a society of states sharing a common set of values and norms (Bull, 1977, pp. 15–16). One could say the same thing about the classical Greek city-state system. Whether or not the contemporary global system can also be characterized as a society of states that share common values and interests is a matter of intense scholarly controversy today.

Although the rights and rules governing interstate behavior are to varying degrees based on consensus and mutual interest, the primary foundation of rights and rules is in the power and interests of the dominant groups or states in a social system. As Harold Lasswell and Abraham Kaplan put it, political and other rules are "the pattern of ruler practices" (1950, p. 208). In every social system the dominant actors assert their rights and impose rules on lesser members in order to advance their particular interests. The Persian empire, which was perhaps the first lawgiver, imposed on other states the rules governing international economic relations and mediated disputes among its lesser neighbors (Bozeman, 1960, p. 53). Rome gave the Mediterranean world its own code of law and left as a legacy to Western civilization the first law of nations. In the modern era, what we call international law was imposed on the world by Western civilization, and it reflects the values and interests of Western civilization.

The most significant advance in rulemaking has been the innovation of the multilateral treaty and formalization of international law. This has been one of the major achievements of the European society of states. Prior to the Treaty of Westphalia (1648), international treaties were negotiated bilaterally and covered a limited range of subjects. The Congress of Westphalia brought together for the first time in history all the major powers of an international system. The rules agreed on covered the broad range of religious, political, and territorial matters at issue in the Thirty Years' War. The statesmen who gathered at Westphalia reordered the map of Europe and established a set of rules that brought relative peace to Europe for the rest of the century.

The treaties negotiated at the conclusions of the great wars of European civilization served as the constitution of the state system. The peace settlements of Westphalia (1648), Utrecht (1713), Vienna (1815), and Versailles (1919) attempted to fashion a stable status quo and establish a mutually recognized set of rules and rights. These treaties provided for the resolution of disputes, the imposition of penalties on the losers, the mutual recognition of security guarantees, etc. Most important of all, these peace treaties redistributed territory (and hence resources) among the states in the system and thereby changed the nature of the international system. In the words of one student of these treaties, "the territorial settlement . . . restratified the state system on a new basis" (Randle, 1973, p. 332).

In domestic society, as we have already seen, the principal mechanism for regulating the distribution of scarce goods is the concept of property. Property rights and the rules embodying them are the basic means for ordering domestic social, economic, and political affairs. The definition and distribution of such property rights reflect the powers and interests of the dominant members of society. For this reason, the process of domestic political change is fundamentally one of redefining and redistributing property rights.

In international affairs, territoriality is the functional equivalent of property rights. Like the definition of property, the control of territory confers a bundle of rights. The control and division of territory constitute the basic mechanism governing the distribution of scarce resources among the states in an international system. Whereas domestic political change involves redefinition and redistribution of property rights, international political change has been primarily a matter of redistributing territory among groups or states following the great wars of history. Although the importance of territorial control has lessened somewhat in the modern world, it continues to be the central ordering mechanism of international life. Contemporary nation-states, especially newly formed states in the Third World, are as fiercely jealous of their territorial sovereignty as their eighteenth-century European predecessors.

The foregoing definition of an international system, based as it is primarily on structural characteristics, obviously tells us very little about the political, economic, and moral content of specific international systems. Dominant powers have had very different sets of ideologies and interests that they have sought to achieve and incorporate into the rules and regimes of the system. Rome and Great Britain each created a world order, but the often oppressive rule of the Pax Romana was in most respects different from the generally liberal rule of the Pax Britannica. Napoleonic France and Hitlerite Germany gave very different governances to the Europe each united. The Pax Americana differs from what a Pax Sovietica would contain. A general and truly comprehensive theory of international relations would assess types of international systems (tyrannical–liberal, Christian–Islamic, communist–capitalist, etc.) for their characteristic features and dynamics. Where appropriate, this study will address these matters; however, they raise fundamental questions far beyond the limited purposes of this study.

Boundaries of the system. An international system, like every other system, has a set of boundaries that set it apart from its larger environment. In the case of an international system, determination of these boundaries is a difficult problem. With the exception of totally isolated systems, such as the pre-Columbian American empires, for example, there are no sharp geographic breaks between one system and another. What to one observer is a self-contained international system may be to another merely a subsystem of a larger and encompassing international system. For example, Thucydides treated the warring Greek city-states as a relatively autonomous system. Yet, on a larger canvas, these city-states were part of a much greater system dominated by imperial Persia, which was temporarily diverted from Greek affairs by troubles elsewhere in its empire. In short, what constitutes an international system (or subsystem) lies to some extent in the eye of the beholder.

Therefore, definition of the boundaries of an international system must of necessity be somewhat arbitrary and subjective. What constitutes an international system is determined partially by the perceptions of the actors themselves. The system encompasses those actors whose actions and reactions are taken into account by states in the formulation of foreign policy. The system is in effect an arena of calculation and interdependent decision making. The boundaries of the system are defined by the area over which great powers seek to exert control and influence. Thus, although imperial Rome and China were functionally interdependent and were profoundly affected by the disturbances caused by the massive migration of the steppe nomads of Central Asia, it would be absurd to regard ancient China and Rome as parts of the same international system (Teggart, 1939).

Nevertheless, geographic boundaries do matter, in that they affect which other actors and considerations a state must take into account in the formulation of its foreign policy. The topography of the land, the existence of water communications, and the climate obviously greatly facilitate or inhibit interactions among states. It is no accident, for example, that international systems tend to form around water communications: the ancient river basins of Asia and the Middle East, the Mediterranean Sea until modern times, and the Atlantic and Pacific oceans in the modern period. But it is equally true that geographic boundaries are elastic and are altered by changes in technology and other factors.

TYPES OF INTERNATIONAL CHANGES

It is obvious that international changes can be and are of varying degrees of magnitude and that individuals may place quite different weights on their significance. What to one person may be but a change within a particular international system may be for another a transformation of the system itself. For example, throughout the history of European diplomacy there was a continuous succession of differing distributions of power, a variety of actors, and changing memberships of political alliances. Because these changes were of different magnitudes, the theorist of international political change has the task of classifying them before formulating a theory to explain them. Thus, whereas Arthur Burns, in his *Of Powers and Their Politics,* regarded many of these changes, such as the emergence of revolutionary France and the Bismarckian unification of Germany in 1871, as merely modifications within the European state system (Burns, 1968, Chapter 5), Richard Rosecrance, in his *Action and Reaction in World Politics* (1963), classified them as changes of the international system itself. Underlying this difference in interpretation, of course, are contrasting theories of political change.

Although a typology of changes is largely an arbitrary matter, the classification used must be a function of one's theory of change and of one's definition of the entity that changes. Thus, in this study we draw on our earlier definition of an international system to distinguish three broad types of changes characteristic of international systems (Table 2). The first and most fundamental type of change is a change in the nature of the actors or diverse entities that compose an international system; this type

Table 2. *Types of international changes*[a]

Type	Factors that change
Systems change	Nature of actors (empires, nation-states, etc.)
Systemic change	Governance of system
Interaction change	Interstate processes

[a]All three types of changes may or may not involve a change in the boundaries of the system. Most likely, however, systems change involving a different set of principal actors also means a change in the boundaries of the system.

of change will be called *systems change*. The second type of change is a change in the form of control or governance of an international system; this type of change will be labeled *systemic change*. Third, a change may take place in the form of regular interactions or processes among the entities in an ongoing international system; this type of change will be labeled simply *interaction change*.

Unfortunately, it is not always easy to distinguish among these three types of change. Because of its all-encompassing nature, for example, systems change also involves both systemic and interaction changes. Furthermore, changes at the level of interstate interactions (viz., formation of diplomatic alliances or major shifts in the locations of economic activities) may be the prelude to systemic change and eventually systems change. The stuff of history is messy, and it is difficult, if not impossible, to sort it out into neat analytical categories.

The classification of a change is also a function of the level of analysis. What at one level of analysis may be classified as an interaction or systemic change may at another level be regarded as a systems change. For example, the unification of Germany in 1871 was an interaction change at the overall level of European politics, a systemic change at the level of central European politics, and a systems change at the level of intra-German politics. It all depends on the system of interstate interactions that one has in mind.

These three categories of change are what Max Weber called

ideal types. Although they may never take place in pure form, one type or another may best characterize the nature of change at a given moment in time. For this reason alone they are useful analytical devices, and they help to clarify the process of change. With this qualification in mind, each type will be discussed briefly.

Systems change

As implied by its label, systems change involves a major change in the character of the international system itself. In speaking of the character of the system, we refer primarily to the nature of the principal actors or diverse entities composing the system. The character of the international system is identified by its most prominent entities: empires, nation-states, or multinational corporations. The rise and decline of various types of entities and state systems must of necessity be a fundamental concern of a comprehensive theory of international change.

Although students of international relations have given little attention to this category of change and have left it (perhaps wisely) to the philosophers of history, it should be more central to their concerns. The rise and decline of the Greek city-state system, the decline of the medieval European state system, and the emergence of the modern European nation-state systems are examples of systems change. To study such changes properly and systematically would necessitate a truly comparative study of international relations and systems. In the absence of such studies, a theoretical analysis of systems change is obviously handicapped.

This issue is particularly relevant in the present era, in which new types of transnational and international actors are regarded as taking on roles that supplant the traditional dominant role of the nation-state, and the nation-state itself is held to be an increasingly anachronistic institution. There have, of course, been numerous valuable studies analyzing this subject, but the more general question of why one or another type of entity is best suited for a particular historical environment has been inadequately addressed by students of international relations.

In effect, what this question asks is why, at various times and in differing contexts, individuals and groups believe one political form rather than another is best suited to advance their interests. Although each political organization serves a general set of interests (protection, welfare, status), the particular type of organization that best serves a specific interest depends on the nature of the interest and the historical circumstances. As interests and circumstances change, the type of organization that is required to secure and defend the interests of individuals also changes. Any development that affects the costs and benefits of group or institutional membership for particular individuals will bring about organizational changes. For this reason, a systems change relates to the cost/benefit aspects of organizational membership and the ways in which economic, technological, and other developments affect the scale, efficiency, and viability of different types of political organizations. Although in this study we cannot hope to provide a definitive answer to this question, we can hope to shed some light on the issues involved.

Systemic change

Systemic change involves a change in the governance of an international system. That is to say, it is a change within the system rather than a change of the system itself. It entails changes in the international distribution of power, the hierarchy of prestige, and the rules and rights embodied in the system, although these changes seldom, if ever, occur simultaneously. Thus, whereas the focus of systems change is the rise and decline of state systems, the focus of systemic change is the rise and decline of the dominant states or empires that govern the particular international system.

The theory of international political change to be developed here rests on the assumption that the history of an international system is that of the rise and decline of the empires and dominant states that during their periods of reign over international affairs have given order and stability to the system. We shall argue that the evolution of any system has been characterized by successive rises of powerful states that have governed the system and have determined the patterns of international interactions and established the rules of the system. Thus the essence of systemic change involves the replacement of a declining dominant power by a rising dominant power.

Although scholars of international relations and diplomatic historians have devoted considerable attention to this type of change, most of these studies have been concerned primarily with the modern European nation-state system. There have been relatively few studies of earlier systems or non-Western systems by scholars in the field. Moreover, these studies have seldom addressed the problem of systemic change in a systematic, comparative, or theoretical vein; rather, most have tended to be historical or descriptive. There is a need for a comparative study of international systems that concentrates on systemic change in different types of international systems.

Such a comparative examination is obviously beyond the scope of this study, in which we do not presume to have presented a study of specific systemic changes even in the modern era. At best, this study may succeed in presenting a better understanding of the nature and process of systemic change as a historical process and point the way to empirical studies of change. If so, the purpose of this study will have been fulfilled.

Interaction change

By interaction change, we mean modifications in the political, economic, and other interactions or processes among the actors in an international system.Whereas this type of change does not involve a change in the overall hierarchy of power and prestige in the system, it usually does entail changes in the rights and rules embodied in an international system. However, it should be noted that interaction changes frequently do result from the efforts of states or other actors to accelerate or forestall more fundamental changes in an international system and may presage such changes.

In general, when scholars of international relations write of the dynamics of international relations, they are referring to modifications of the interactions among states within a particular state system (at least as defined in our study). This is the case, for example, in Richard Rosecrance's *Action and Reaction in World Politics* (1963), in which he analyzed the causes of changes in European diplomatic style from 1740 onward. The vast literature on alliance formation, regime change, and transnational relations is also on the level of intrasystemic interactions.[11] Whereas there has been little research on systems change and systemic change, there is a vast literature on changes in the interactions among states, though it is largely confined to the Western state system and more especially to international relations since 1945. Therefore, although interaction changes are the most frequent changes and constitute much of the stuff of international relations, we shall devote little attention to them. They have been well analyzed by others (e.g., Keohane and Nye, 1977). Instead, the focus of the study is mainly on systemic change and, to a lesser extent, systems change. We shall discuss interaction changes only insofar as they are relevant to a broader understanding of systemic change and systems change.

INCREMENTAL CHANGE VERSUS REVOLUTIONARY CHANGE

The explanation of political change raises a fundamental issue in social theory, namely whether the transformation of a social system can take place through incremental evolutionary changes or whether it must of necessity be the consequence of political upheavel and violence – revolution at the domestic level and major war at the international level. On one side of this controversy is the liberal, democratic tradition exemplified by the experience of the United States and Great Britain; both societies have witnessed peaceful changes in important social and political institutions in response to economic, technological, and other developments. Proponents of this position hold that a similar process of peaceful continuous change is possible at the international level. On the other side is the Hegelian-Marxist perspective, which ex-

[11] A position similar to ours is taken by Waltz (1979, especially Chapter 7).

plains major change in terms of a contradiction between the existing social system and underlying forces of change. Change is believed to be discontinuous and the consequence of a systemic
crisis that can be resolved only by the use of force, because no
dominant group gives up its privileges without a struggle. According to this view, peaceful change is merely the granting of mean-
ingless concessions designed to buy off revolutionary forces.

In contrast with the liberal conception of social change as being continuous incremental adjustments of social systems to the
forces of change, the Hegelian-Marxist perspective embodies
three quite different generalizations regarding the nature of social change. In the first place, the pattern of history is regarded
as a discontinuous series of "developing contradictions that lead
to intermittent abrupt changes" (Moore, 1965, p. 138). Second,
these contradictions or crises arise because of incompatibility
between existing social arrangements and underlying forces of
change (economic, technological, etc.). Third, the resolution of
the contradiction and the transformation of the social system are
the consequences of a power struggle among potential gainers
and losers.

The position we take in this study is that in an international
system both types of changes take place. The most frequently
observed types of changes are continuous incremental adjustments within the framework of the existing system. Territory
changes hands, shifts in alliances and influences take place, and
patterns of economic intercourse are altered. Such incremental
changes at the level of interstate interaction cause the international system to evolve as states seek to advance their interests
in response to economic, technological, and other environmental
developments. As a consequence, the process of international
political change is generally an evolutionary process in which
continual adjustments are made to accommodate the shifting interests and power relations of groups and states.

This gradual evolution of the international system is characterized by bargaining, coercive diplomacy, and warfare over specific and relatively narrowly defined interests (Young, 1978, p.
250). The system may be described as being in a state of homeostatic equilibrium. Territorial, political, and economic adjust-

ments among states in response to conflicting interests and shifting power relationships function to relieve pressure on the system, thereby preserving it intact. In brief, international political change takes place through the process of peaceful accommodation and limited conflicts at the level of interstate interactions.

Although changes at the level of interstate interactions constitute the bulk of international relations, obviously they are not the only types of changes one observes in the international sphere. Whereas most changes are continuous responses to slowly changing circumstances, adjustments do not always occur immediately. Major economic, technological, or military developments may occur at critical junctures, developments that promise significant gains or losses to one or another actor. If these gains cannot be realized in the framework of the existing system, states (or rather the domestic coalitions they represent) may believe that their interests can be served only by more sweeping and more profound changes in the international system. Conversely, other states will believe that the meeting of such demands will jeopardize what they regard as their own vital interests. At these critical moments, the issue is the nature and governance of the system itself and/or, more rarely, the character of the international actors themselves. The former type of change is labeled systemic change; the latter is systems change.

Both systemic change and systems change raise the basic issue of whose security, economic, and ideological interests will be most benefited by the functioning of the international system. The crisis may be said to be constitutional, because the pattern of political authority (hierarchy of prestige) is at stake in the crisis, as are the rights of individuals (or states) and the rules of the system. Furthermore, resolution of the crisis will most likely involve armed conflict (Table 3.). In domestic politics, constitutional crises are most frequently resolved by civil war and revolution; in international politics they usually are resolved by hegemonic war.

The Hegelian-Marxist conception of political change maintains that the critical junctures that lead to revolutionary change are produced by contradictions in the system. According to this viewpoint, contradictions are inevitable consequences of irreconcilable components in the social system. Furthermore, it is be-

Table 3. *Comparison of domestic change and international change*

	Domestic	International
Principal method of incremental change	Bargaining among groups, classes, etc.	Bargaining among states
Principal method of revolutionary change	Revolution and civil war	Hegemonic war
Principal objective of incremental change	Minor adjustments of domestic system	Minor adjustments of international system
Principal objective of revolutionary change	Constitution	Governance of system

lieved that it is possible a priori to determine when a crisis or conflict in a system is in fact irreconcilable and must inevitably cause a change in the system; it is also believed that the outcome of the contradiction can be predicted in advance. In brief, this influential school of thought has a deterministic view of the nature, causes, and consequences of political change.[12]

We reject this overly deterministic type of interpretation of political change.[13] Although it is certainly possible to identify crises, disequilibrium, and incompatible elements in a political system, especially a disjuncture between the governance of the system and the underlying distribution of power, it is most certainly not possible to predict the outcome. In the social sciences, we do not possess a predictive theory of social change in any sphere; we probably never shall.[14] Although we observe international crises and corresponding responses in the behavior of states, it cannot be known in advance if there will be an eventual return to equilibrium or a change in the nature of the system. The answer is dependent, at least in part, on what individuals choose to do.

[12] A number of Marzists, I am sure, would dispute this characterization of their doctrine.
[13] For an excellent critique of the Hegelian-Marxist conception of social change, see the work of Dupré (1977).
[14] A good critique of the problems of predictive theory in the social sciences is provided by Northrop (1947, pp. 235–64).

Despite this limitation, the Hegelian-Marxist approach to the problem of political change has heuristic value. What it suggests is that the locus of change must be found in the differential rates of change in the major components composing the social system. If all aspects of the social system were to change in unison, there would develop no contradiction requiring resolution by an abrupt change in the system. Instead, there would be incremental evolution of the system. In Marxist theory, the means of economic production evolve more rapidly than those elements in the superstructure of social and political relationships, such as law and class structure, thereby producing a contradiction between the forces of production and the relations of production. Thus the resulting revolutionary change in the system is caused by the fact that productive technology develops more rapidly than other aspects of the system; this systemic change, once it occurs, in turn further accelerates the development of productive forces. In other words, the development of the means of production is both the cause and the consequence of systemic change.

International political change is similarly caused by the differential rates of change for the major components composing the international political system. The international balance of power among the actors (like the forces of economic production) underlying the international system evolves more rapidly than the other components of the system, particularly the hierarchy of prestige and the rules of the system. Again, if all components were to change in unison, peaceful evolution of the system would take place. It is the differential rate of change between the international distribution of power and the other components of the system that produces a disjuncture or disequilibrium in the system that, if unresolved, causes a change in the system. This change in the system, once it occurs, in turn further accelerates (up to a point) the shift in the balance of power in the direction of the rising state or states in the system. Thus, in the language of social science, the differential growth of power in the system is both the cause and the consequence of international political change.

Contrary to the Hegelian-Marxist position, however, it is impossible to predict political outcomes or that revolutionary change will in fact take place and, if it does occur, what the consequences will be. Although one might devise a general theory of political change, ultimately the study of change cannot be divorced from specific historical contexts and those static elements that influence the triggering and the direction of political change. An explanation of change involves the bringing together of an explanatory theory and some set of initial conditions (Harsanyi, 1960, p. 141). The nature of these static elements determines the character of the outcome. No two hegemonic conflicts are alike; a hegemonic war may serve to strengthen the position of a dominant power, or it may produce far-reaching unanticipated changes in the system. Thus, although a theory of political change can help explain historical developments, such a theory can go only part way; it is no substitute for an examination of both the static and dynamic elements responsible for a particular international political change.

This nondeterministic approach to the problem of political change should help clarify a major issue currently being debated by scholars of international relations. The prevalent view that the contemporary international system is characterized by the erosion of American hegemony tells us little about the outcome of current developments and the future of the present international system or what would follow its abrupt ending, for example. In its place a new hegemonic power might arise, a global balance of power much like the European balance of power might take shape, or, as in the case of the decline of the Roman imperium, the world might once again be plunged into chaos and a new Dark Age. The ideas discussed in the subsequent chapters of this book embody this nondeterministic conception of political change.

2

Stability
and change

Assumption 1. An international system is stable (i.e., in a state of equilibrium) if no state believes it profitable to attempt to change the system.

Assumption 2. A state will attempt to change the international system if the expected benefits exceed the expected costs (i.e., if there is an expected net gain).

The argument of this chapter is that states make cost/benefit calculations in the determination of foreign policy and that a goal of a state's foreign policy is to change the international system in ways that will enhance the state's own interests. Whether these interests are power and security (as political realists argue), capitalistic profits (as Marxists allege), or welfare gains (as many contemporary theorists contend), every state desires to increase its control over those aspects of the international system that make its basic values and interests more secure.

However, although a group or state may desire to change the international system in order to advance its interests, the effort to do so necessarily involves costs; the group or state not only must have sufficient resources to meet these costs but also must be willing to pay such costs. Therefore, a group or state will attempt to change the system only if the expected benefits exceed the expected costs; that is, there must be an expected net gain. To put it another way, the group or state will seek to change the system only if it is believed that such change will be profitable (Davis and North, 1971, p. 40).

Unless it is judged to be profitable to one or another state to change the system, the system tends to remain relatively stable. This is a point that political realists tend to forget in arguing that states seek to maximize their power. Acquisition of power entails an opportunity cost to a society; some other desired good must be abandoned.[1] There have been many cases throughout history in which states have forgone apparent opportunities to increase their power because they judged the costs to be too high. This helps to account for the relative stability during certain long historical periods.

Whether or not it is profitable for a state to attempt to change the system is obviously dependent on a large number of factors, in particular on the way in which the state (more properly, its ruling elite) perceives the relative costs and benefits involved in changing the system. Thus, although one speaks of costs and benefits as if they were objective and quantifiable, both are highly subjective and psychological in nature; the benefits sought by a group and the price it is willing to pay depend ultimately on the perceived interests of the ruling elites and coalitions in a society (Buchanan, 1969).

Foremost among the determinants of these perceptions is the historical experience of the society. What, in particular, have been the consequences for the country from past attempts of its own and others to change the international system, and what lessons has the nation learned about war, aggression, appeasement, etc.? Has the society become a "mature" society, to use the term of Martin Wight (1979, p. 155), and come to believe that war does not pay? Or has it learned, to the contrary, that its security requires complete domination over its neighbors? The answers given to questions such as these influence the perceptions of political leaders when weighing the costs and benefits of seeking to change the international system. In the words of a former secretary of state, Henry Kissinger, referring to the stability of a balance of power and the legitimacy of the system,

---

[1] For applications of the concept of opportunity cost to noneconomic issues, see the work of Posner (1977, pp. 6–7) and Haskel (1976, pp. 34–5).

"while powers may appear to outsiders as factors in a security arrangement, they appear domestically as expressions of a historical existence. No power will submit to a settlement, however well balanced and however 'secure,' which seems totally to deny its vision of itself" (Kissinger, 1957, p. 146). And, a state will never cease in pressing what it regards as its just claims on the international system.

Moreover, it should be understood that when one speaks of expected net gains or benefits from changing the system, this can mean either of two things. In the first place, it can refer to an attempt to increase future benefits. In the second place, it can mean an attempt to decrease threatened losses (Buchanan and Tullock, 1962, p. 46). Both potential gainers and losers from ongoing developments in an international system may seek to change the system, the first because the long-term benefits will exceed short-term costs, the second because the long-term costs of ongoing developments threaten to become greater than the short-term benefits of the status quo.

Finally, the notion that a state will seek to change the system if expected benefits exceed expected costs does not mean that the benefits will in fact exceed the costs. As in many other areas of human activity, decisions are made under conditions of uncertainty. A group or state calculates its interests and acts on the basis of imperfect information; it may also lose control over the rush of events, and unanticipated consequences usually result. In fact, it is often the case that the actual costs of changing the system exceed the received benefits. As will be argued later, the ultimate beneficiaries of efforts to change international systems have more frequently than not been third parties on the periphery of the international system.

Although considerations of costs and benefits are ultimately subjective in nature, calculations regarding expected net benefits of changing the system are profoundly influenced by objective factors in the material and international environment. Whether it is profitable at one particular time or another is dependent on economic, military, and technological factors, as well as domestic and international political structures. A group or state will have an incentive to change the international system if modifications in one or more of these features make it profitable to do so.

A state system, like any other political system, exists in a technological, military, and economic environment that both restricts the behavior of its members and provides opportunities for policies of aggrandizement. Although it is impossible a priori to determine if a particular technological, military, or economic innovation will contribute to stability or instability in a system, it is possible to identify characteristics of innovations that tend to stabilize or destabilize an international system by decreasing or increasing the profitability of change. A major purpose of this chapter is to analyze types of innovations from the perspective of their contributions to the stability or instability of the system.

An important consequence of economic, military, or technological changes is that they increase (or decrease) the area it is profitable to control or over which it is profitable to extend protection and thereby encourage (or discourage) the creation or enlargement of political and economic organizations. It will be recalled that government, or, more broadly, governance, has been defined as the provision of collective or public goods in exchange for revenue. As will be argued in a moment, any development that increases the power and enlarges the opportunity of a state to increase its revenues will encourage political or economic expansion. In many cases, if not in most, the "benefited" groups are incorporated into the enlarged political or economic structure against their will.

In addition to positive economic gains, the profitability of changing the system may mean the denial of economic or political gains and opportunities to a competitor. That is, a state may seek to achieve control of strategic territory of little intrinsic economic value whose loss would cause income losses. For example, in the nineteenth century, Great Britain held many territories less for their direct economic value than for their strategic value in protecting revenue-producing assets (colonies). Thus the value of Egypt to the British Empire was that it protected the lifeline to India, the jewel in the imperial crown. The important point is that the economic, political, or strategic gain from controlling territory or protecting the property rights of citizens is judged to be greater than the associated costs.

The area over which it is profitable for the state to extend its protection of persons and their property rights is dependent on two basic sets of variables: (1) the costs of extending the protection and (2) the amount of income generated or safeguarded by the extension of protection. Thus, any development that decreases the cost of expansion or increases the amount of income will encourage a state to enlarge the area over which it extends protection, and vice versa. Therefore, in this study we shall examine the ways in which environmental factors and modifications in these factors affect the incentives of states to increase their control over the international system.

Whether or not a state will seek to change the international system depends ultimately on the nature of the state and the society it represents. In the first place, the incentive for a state to try to change the international system is strongly affected by societal mechanisms for distributing the internal costs and benefits of such an effort. Differing domestic social arrangements and definitions of property rights create varying incentives or disincentives for a society to overthrow the existing international system. These domestic arrangements provide the answer to an important question: Profitable (or costly) for whom?

In the second place, a state will attempt to change the international system only if it has some relative advantage over other states, that is, if the balance of power in the system is to its advantage. This superiority may be organizational, economic, military, or technological, or some combination of these elements. Most frequently this advantage, especially in the modern era, has been conferred by technological innovations in the areas of military weapons and/or industrial production. The advantage over other states provided by superior capabilities in these areas enables a state to seize the opportunities or overcome the constraints provided by the external environment in order to advance its economic, security, or other interests. As long as a state enjoys such an advantage, it will tend to expand and enlarge its control over the international system.

These two broad sets of factors (the society itself and the nature

of its material and political environment) that influence whether
or not a state will attempt to change the international system
obviously are not independent of one another. They can seldom
be separated from one another in reality; indeed, they interact
with and influence one another. For example, whereas environmental factors such as climate and geography lie outside of state
control, the technological environment is man-made, and a society
will develop technological capabilities in order to gain an advantage over other states. By the same token, external factors may
stimulate domestic changes in a state. In fact, although it is not
necessary to accept the so-called doctrine of the primacy of foreign policy, it may not be an overstatement to argue that the
exigencies of survival in the competitive international system constitute the foremost determinant of the priorities and organization
of domestic society. For analytical purposes, however, it is possible to distinguish between environmental and domestic factors
that create incentives or disincentives for particular states to seek
to change the international system.

In summary, the material environment (especially economic
and technological conditions) and the international balance of
power create an incentive or a disincentive for a state to attempt
to change the international system. Whether or not the state
makes this attempt depends on domestic factors such as the interests of groups, classes, and others in the society. In the succeeding sections of this chapter these environmental, international, and domestic factors affecting international political
change will be discussed.

ENVIRONMENTAL FACTORS THAT INFLUENCE CHANGE

Accretive factors such as economic growth and demographic
change are among the most important forces underlying international political change. A steady rate of economic growth or a
population shift may be the most significant cause of political
change over the long term. Frequently, however, the triggering
mechanism for change may be major technological, military, or
economic changes that promise significant gains to particular
states or major losses to other states in an international system,

gains that cannot be realized and losses that cannot be prevented within the existing international system. The resultant disequilibrium is a prelude to an effort on the part of potential gainers (or potential losers) to change the international system (Davis and North, 1971, p. 10).

An exhaustive listing of those environmental changes that influence calculations of costs and benefits would be an impossibility. However, several sets of environmental factors are of particular importance; throughout history, modifications in these factors have had a profound impact on the propensity of states to seek to change the international system. Three of these factors (the system of communications and transportation, the military technology, and the nature of the economy) and changes in them have significant influences on the benefits and costs of changing the international system, and they will be discussed in the following sections.

Transportation and communication

In many instances the great social and political upheavals throughout history have been preceded by major advances in the technology of transportation and communication (McNeill, 1954). Significant increases in the efficiency of transportation and communication have profound implications for the exercise of military power, the nature of political organization, and the pattern of economic activities. Technological innovations in transportation and communication reduce costs and thereby increase the expected net benefits of undertaking changes in the international system.

The single most important consequence of innovation in transportation is its effect on what Kenneth Boulding called the loss-of-strength gradient, that is, "the degree to which [a state's] military and political power diminishes as we move a unit distance away from its home base" (1963, p. 245).[2] Clearly, the factors affecting this gradient are complex and by no means solely tech-

---

[2] Despite its oversimplification, this concept is useful. For a sophisticated critique, see the work of Wohlstetter (1968, pp. 40–6). Quester used the concept in a manner similar to that of this book (1977, pp. 25–7).

nological. Geographic, medical, and even psychological factors are also involved (Sprout and Sprout, 1962, p. 288). Yet technological improvements in transportation may greatly enhance the distance and area over which a state can exercise effective military power and political influence. The most important technological innovations, in terms of their effects on military power, have been the thoroughbred horse, the sailing ship, the railroad, the steamship, and the internal-combustion engine. Among these innovations, perhaps the most important prior to the development of the internal-combustion engine was the development of the thoroughbred horse. Until the modern era, cavalry and the horse-drawn chariot dominated long periods of history.

The loss-of-strength gradient obviously has profound significance for political organization. The territorial expansion and integrity of a political entity are largely functions of the costs to a state or group of exercising military and political dominance over an enlarged area. Thus the ability of a political center to radiate its influence is affected significantly by the cost of transportation. The rises of great empires and the eras of political unification appear to have been associated with major reductions in the cost of transportation. This seeming correlation between innovation in transportation and the rise of empire has led one writer to observe that "empire is a matter of transportation. It begins, culminates and ends in the control of means of communication" (Tucker, 1920, p. 7).[3]

Improvements in transportation and communications encourage military expansion and political unification. Moreover, by facilitating the ability of an imperial or dominant power to extract and utilize the wealth of a conquered territory, such technological innovations create economies of scale and are advantageous to large states. They make it easier for central authority to suppress rebellion and to supervise subordinate local officials. As a consequence, unless countered by other developments such as increases in the efficiency of defense, improvements in transportation tend to encourage empire and political consolidation by

[3] For an impressive demonstration of this thesis, see the work of Hart (1949).

decreasing the cost and increasing the benefits of conquest (Andreski, 1971, p. 79).

The sensitivity of the scale of political organization to the costs of transportation partially explains why empires and great states, until the modern era, have tended to be centered around water transportation. The availability of water transportation accounts in part for the first great empires in the river valleys of the Middle East (Mesopotamia and Egypt), India, and China. A later generation of empires (Carthaginian, Roman, Byzantine, etc.) grew up around the Mediterranean Sea, and, of course, the greatest empire that ever existed, the British, was based on control of the seas. These advantages of sea power relative to land power prevailed until the innovation of the railroad in the nineteenth century, which facilitated the emergence of continental land powers (Germany, the United States, and Russia), and the innovation of the submarine, which destroyed the relative invulnerability of sea power.

At first glance the significance of efficient transportation and sea power in the rise and endurance of empires seems to be challenged by two of the greatest land empires that have existed, that of the Mongols and that of the Arabs. The Mongol empire was the greatest ever in terms of control of contiguous territory. It extended from the Pacific Ocean into eastern Europe and southward into the Middle East. The Arab empire extended from the Middle East across North Africa and north to the Pyrenees. Although the Arabs did create a fleet, this was of secondary importance and was not the major factor in their course of expansion; however, it did have important effects on Europe and on the Byzantine Empire.

Ibn Khaldûn, referring to the Arabs, long ago provided the answer to this apparent anomaly; a similar answer is applicable to the Mongols. Ibn Khaldûn pointed out that the desert, with its absence of topographical barriers, provided the Arabs with the equivalent of the sea; the cities of the desert functioned as seaports (Ibn Khaldûn, 1967, pp. 264–5). Similarly, for the Mongols the great steppes of central Asia provided a sea of grass (McNeill, 1974, p. 47). Underlying the expansion of both these powers lay a critical development: the perfection of the thoroughbred horse. As Bernard Lewis commented (1966, p. 55), following their mastery of the horse (and, to a lesser extent, domestication of the camel), the Arabs began to use the desert as a sea. Thus, for the Mongols and the Arabs, steppe power and desert power functioned as sea power.

Technological innovations in transportation and communication have also influenced the patterns of economic activities: the location of production, the organization of markets, and patterns of trade. In our own age, the compression of time and space that has resulted from development of the internal-combustion engine and electronic communications has facilitated the creation of a highly interdependent world economy. This world economy has, in turn, had a profound impact on the process of international political change.

Modern communications and technology have greatly decreased the significance of space, but the loss-of-strength gradient has not completely lost its force or relevance in the contemporary world. Although we live in a world dominated by intercontinental ballistic missiles, geographic position and distance continue to be relevant factors in international relations. In fact, three of the principal features of contemporary world politics relate to geography and transportation. The first is the central position of the Soviet Union on the Eurasian continent and the advantage over the United States that this entails in the arena of conventional military power. The second is the creation by the Soviet Union in the 1970s of air and sea intervention capabilities that have enabled the Soviet Union (Russia) for the first time in history to extend its influence far beyond its national borders. The third is the relative geographic isolation of the United States and the absence of powerful hostile neighbors (as compared with the Soviet Union and China). These factors are highly relevant in the determination of the national interests and foreign policies of the Soviet Union, the United States, and China.

Military techniques and technology

From earliest times, innovation and adoption of novel weapons and tactics have launched groups and states on the path of conquest. In many instances the critical development has been a new weapon or a new mode of transportation, such as the innovation of iron weaponry or of the heavy chariot. Changes in military capacity can also result from the development of new battlefield tactics or new modes of military organization. For example, the Roman armies that conquered an empire had few technological advantages over their opponents; their superiority lay in their tactics, their esprit, and the legion form of organization, as well as their overall sense of grand strategy (Luttwak, 1976). Therefore, one should be careful of a tendency to equate changes in military capabilities with weaponry and technology alone. On the contrary, technology was relatively static until the modern era, and technological changes were not as important as they are today in the balance of military power.

Military innovations are important when they increase or decrease the area over which it is profitable to extend military protection in exchange for revenue. They thus encourage or discourage economic and political expansion and the formation of larger or smaller political entities. All other things being equal, if a military innovation decreases the cost of changing the international system, it will increase the incentive for a state to make the necessary effort. Similarly, an increase in cost will create a disincentive to change and will tend to stabilize the status quo.

Military innovation gives a particular society a monopoly of superior armament or technique and dramatically decreases the cost of extending the area of domination, thus providing a society with a considerable advantage over its neighbors and an incentive to expand and to change the international system. The historical record is replete with examples of military innovations leading to imperial conquest and to massive changes in international systems (e.g., the tactical and organizational innovations of Gaius Marius, Philip of Macedonia, and Napoleon).

On the other hand, international political history reveals that in many instances a relative advantage in military technique has been short-lived. The permanence of a military advantage is a function both of the scale and complexity of the innovation on which it is based and of the prerequisites for its adoption by other societies. For example, a superiority based on a simple weapon may fade relatively quickly as the weapon is adopted by one's enemies. On the other hand, the adoption of a weapon and accompanying tactics may require a level of social discipline one's enemies cannot attain. The Roman monopoly of superior military technique lay less in the possession of particular weapons than in the character of the Roman citizen-soldier. In the modern world, the military superiority of Western civilization has rested both on the complexity of modern technology and on the character of Western science-oriented culture.

Another important consequence of military innovation is its impact on the relationship between offense and defense. Military innovations that tend to favor the offense over the defense stimulate territorial expansion and the political consolidation of international systems by empires or great powers (Andreski, 1971, pp. 75–6). Innovations such as the thoroughbred horse and the sailing ship that have increased the mobility and range of armies and fleets have encouraged conquest and the expansion of influence. Alternatively, innovations in fortifications and heavy armor that have favored the defense over the offense have tended to inhibit conquest and preserve the territorial status quo. Alternations between offensive superiority and defensive superiority constitute a prevalent theme in military history and analysis (Quester, 1977).

The great eras of empire building and political consolidation have been associated with military innovations that have given one or another society a massive offensive superiority over the defense. In the first millennium B.C. the Assyrians created the first "technology of empire," in which they combined the innovations of iron metallurgy, siege machines, and horseback riding with advances in organizational skills and thereby produced the first great upheaval in international affairs (Carney, 1973, p. 113). By drastically decreasing the cost and increasing the benefits of conquest, these technological and organizational changes made the unification of the Near East an economically attractive proposition for these ruthless and aggressive warriors. Similarly, the imperial unification of China by Ch'in was due to advances in the offense over the defense (Andreski, 1971, p. 76).

On the other hand, military developments that increase the

superiority of the defense over the offense tend to inhibit expansion and thereby stabilize the territorial status quo and hence the international system. An example of the effect of advances in defense can be found in the later Middle Ages, when major advances in the art of fortification favored the preservation of the Byzantine Empire. Similarly, the adoption and perfection of these techniques by medieval Europe were important factors in the survival of a fragmented feudal political structure. In the fourteenth century the invention of gunpowder and artillery produced a resurgence in offensive capabilities that opened a new era of territorial consolidation and introduced a new political form: the nation-state.

From the early modern era to the Napoleonic period the balance between defense and offense oscillated. However, the Napoleonic revolution in military affairs led to a significant predominance of the offense that resulted in a continuous political consolidation of Western and Eastern Europe. Then, with the innovation of the machine gun and trench warfare during World War I, the defense reasserted itself, accompanied by refragmentation in European politics in the 1920s.[4] The offense regained supremacy in World War II because of the development of modern tank warfare and tactical aircraft, and this renewed offensive supremacy favored the reconsolidation of political power in both western and eastern Europe. The effects of more recent developments (i.e., the advent of weapons of mass destruction) on the offense–defense equation will be considered later.

The notion that the offense is superior or inferior to the defense must be interpreted in economic terms; it is a relative matter, not an absolute matter. To speak of a shift in favor of the offense means that fewer resources than before must be expended on the offense in order to overcome the defense. Similarly, a shift in favor of the defense means that fewer resources are required by the defense and greater resources are required by the offense. Major changes in the relative costs of offense and defense have significant impact on the costs and benefits of seek-

---

[4] The battle tank and the military airplane were used in World War I, but they were relatively ineffective because their capabilities and the tactics for their employment had not yet been perfected.

ing to transform the international system. Thus the defense is said to be superior if the resources required to capture territory are greater than the value of the territory itself; the offense is superior if the cost of conquest is less than the value of the territory.[5]

The innovation or adoption of new military techniques can have differential impacts on different societies and hence on the international distribution of power. The introduction of a novel military weapon or technique into an international system may give a particular type of society a significant advantage over others and thereby encourage it to become expansionist. There have been many examples in history in which the resource endowment, geography, or social structure of a society have facilitated or inhibited the innovation or adoption of a new military weapon or technique. For example, in seventeenth-century Sweden, Gustavus Adolphus realized the potential of national professional armies; the nonfeudal social structure of Sweden was sufficiently malleable for him to reorganize society in the interest of power and thus launch Sweden on a career of imperialist expansion (Andreski, 1971, p. 37).

On the other hand, the social, political, or economic organization of a society may inhibit the adoption of a novel and more efficient technology. For example, the costs to powerful vested interests may be too high, thereby causing resistance to the adoption of new techniques. Aristocratic and privileged elites have frequently resisted the arming of lower strata; this was true in both early modern Europe and Japan. A set of values and beliefs counter to the social and organizational prerequisites for adopting a new technology can also cause resistance. This may account for one of the great historical mysteries – why the once-powerful Moslems failed to adopt artillery and supporting infantry at the time these military innovations were revolutionizing the battlefields of Europe. These innovations, along with the modern sailing ship, enabled the backward Europeans to conquer the world. Behind this costly failure of the Moslems was a social structure and tradition focused on horsemanship, with disdain for the foot soldier (Cipolla, 1965, p. 92).

---

[5] For an interesting use of this idea, see the work of Bean (1973).

In some instances societies have radically transformed their
social and political structures in order to absorb new forms of
economic and military techniques, as with the establishment of
feudalism in western Europe to create the necessary economic
and political infrastructure for a defense based on heavy cavalry
(White, 1964). The Meiji restoration in late-nineteenth-century
Japan is a more recent example; its reforms provided the basis
for the rapid industrialization of that society. And, of course,
modernization of lesser-developed societies in the contemporary
world involves first and foremost changes in traditional attitudes
and social structures in order to permit the adoption of modern
technology. The essence of this problem of technology transfer
was well stated by Carlo M. Cipolla, quoting S. H. Frankel:

"At first sight the problem might appear to be merely one of introduc-
ing new methods of production and the instruments, tools or machines
appropriate thereto. But what is really involved is a vast change in
social beliefs and practices. . . ." Technical knowledge is "the expression of man's response to the changing problems set by the environment and by his fellow men. . . . For meeting any new situation, new
thoughts, new aptitudes, new action will be required. But knowledge
has to grow: capital has to be created afresh on the basis of continuous
experiment, and new hopes and beliefs have to evolve. It is because all
these new activities are not independent of the existing institutions into
which they have to be fitted, and which have in turn to be adjusted to
them, that the process of change is so complex and, if it is to proceed
harmoniously, necessarily so slow" (Cipolla, 1965, p. 130).

It has long been a theme of writers on political geography that
military innovations have differential impacts on various types of
societies. In general, commentary has focused on whether a particular innovation has favored sea power or land power. If the
latter, then the innovation tends to lead to political consolidation
and territorial imperialism, as in the cases of Sparta, Rome, and
Russia. If the former, then the innovation tends to lead to overseas colonialism, economic expansion, and spheres of influence,
as in the cases of Athens, Great Britain, and the United States.
Thus the innovation of the railroad gave an advantage to Germany, whereas the steamship favored Great Britain. In the contemporary world, the question whether the advent of interconti-

nental missiles and nuclear weapons will ultimately benefit the United States (sea power) or the Soviet Union (land power) or some other power is a matter of considerable controversy. The basic point, however, is that military innovations seldom are neutral in their effects; they tend to benefit one type of society or another.

Military innovations also alter the significance of the economic base of state power. It is obvious that there is generally a positive correlation between the material wealth of a society and its military power; wealthier states tend to be more powerful. Military innovations, however, can drastically strengthen or weaken this relationship by changing the unit cost of military power or creating economies of scale.

A weapons innovation may decrease the cost of weaponry and thus lessen the importance of the economic base necessary to support military power, thereby perhaps being of advantage to less wealthy societies. For example, prior to the development of iron metallurgy and relatively inexpensive iron, the settled and prosperous civilizations of the Bronze Age were able to keep lesser-developed peoples at bay. The latter could not afford to manufacture sufficient amounts of the more expensive bronze weapons to field armies capable of overpowering the wealthier civilizations. However, the innovation of the less expensive iron transformed this military balance and shifted the locus of power to rising societies such as the Hittites and the Assyrians.

The relationship between military innovation and the economic base of power may be illustrated by one of the most critical strategic interfaces in the history of the world. The 1300-year conflict between the pastoral people of the central Asian steppes and wealthier agrarian societies began with the domestication of the horse. Throughout this period the mounted archers of the steppes more frequently than not had the military advantage. Despite the relative poverty of these pastoral nomads, their mobility and offensive superiority enabled successive steppe peoples to forge great empires and to pillage more advanced civilizations. This career of conquest finally ceased with the invention of artillery, a technology far beyond the capabilities of a pastoral economy (McNeill, 1967, p. 316). In time, therefore, these peoples were subdued by the economically and technologically advanced Great Russians, whose course of empire followed the river valleys of Eurasia.

Alternatively, military innovations may increase the unit cost of military power; that is, military power may become more capital-intensive (Andreski, 1971, pp. 87–8). The resulting increase in the cost of effective military power and of war tends to favor larger and more wealthy political organizations (Wallerstein, 1974, pp. 28–9). This was the case, for example, in the early modern period, when neither feudal lords nor city-states could finance large concentrations of the new forms of military power: artillery, standing armies, sailing ships, etc. This revolution in the nature and cost of war was a decisive factor in the triumph of the territorial nation-state over other political forms.

Beyond a certain point, the increasing cost of military power may inhibit political expansion and change. For example, the disunity of feudal Europe and the conservatism of the Byzantine Empire were largely functions of the fact that heavy cavalry, although it was very effective, was a very costly form of military power, and therefore the amassing of an offensive capability for expansionist purposes within Europe itself was prohibitively expensive. The resources required for political consolidation of the continent were beyond the capabilities of the current political actors; thus preservation of the territorial status quo in Europe was encouraged.

Finally, a military innovation may lead to economies of scale that encourage the formation of larger political entities; that is, the unit cost of producing military power declines with an increase in scale. As a consequence, larger political entities and larger military forces may become more cost-efficient than smaller entities and forces, and this relative efficiency may then provide an incentive for larger political entities to displace smaller ones (Bean, 1973, p. 220). In terms of the earlier typology of international political change, military innovations that introduce economies of scale tend to produce a systems change rather than simply a systemic change; in the next chapter this generalization will be applied to the formation of the European nation-state system.

Economic factors

A third environmental factor influencing the profitability of changing the international system is the economic system (i.e., the techniques and organizations for the production, distribution, and consumption of goods and services). The means of production and changes in the means of production are particularly important determinants of political behavior, as Marxists have emphasized. Political systems at both the domestic level and the international level also profoundly influence the patterns of economic activities. In fact, there is mutual and reciprocal interaction between the political system and the economic system (Gilpin, 1975).

In this study we shall argue that the interaction between economics and politics is a fundamental feature of the process of international political change. On the one hand, the desire for economic gain is a powerful motive for seeking to change the international system, and thus the distribution of power among groups and states is an important determinant of the pattern of economic activities and particularly of which actors benefit most from the domestic or international division of labor. On the other hand, the distribution of power itself ultimately rests on an economic base, and as sources and foundations of wealth change because of shifts in economic efficiency, location of industry, or currents of trade, a corresponding redistribution of power among groups and states necessarily occurs. The struggle for power and the desire for economic gain are ultimately and inextricably joined.

Economic factors and motives are universal elements in the behavior of states and in international political change. This is so because in a world of scarcity the fundamental issue in domestic and international politics is the distribution of the available "economic surplus," that is, the goods and services produced in excess of the subsistence needs of society.[6] Groups and states seek

---

[6] The notion of an economic surplus is highly controversial in economics. Classical economists assumed its existence and defined economics as the determination of the laws governing its distribution. Neoclassical economists, partially in response to the Marxist identification of the surplus with capitalist exploitation, denied its existence (every

to control and organize economic relations and activities in ways that will increase their own relative shares of this surplus. For this reason, several predominant ways in which this surplus is produced and distributed have profound implications for international politics and political change.

The notion that economic motives and factors play an important role and at times a decisive role in international relations is hardly a matter of dispute. The significance of economic constraints and opportunities in the foreign policy of a state is readily accepted by students of international relations. Political realists, for example, acknowledge that power must have an economic base and that the pursuit of wealth and pursuit of power are indistinguishable. As one realist writer put it, "the distinction between political and economic causes of war is an unreal one. The political motives at work can only be expressed in terms of the economic. Every conflict is one of power, and power depends on resources. Population itself is an economic quantity; its growth and movement are governed by economic conditions" (Hawtrey, 1952, p. 81). Indeed, the political struggles among states throughout history have most frequently centered on the control of fertile lands, material resources, and trade routes.

Although economic interests have always influenced the course of international politics, they are of greater consequence in the modern era. Whereas other ages were dominated by religious and political passions, today economic interests and calculations have an enhanced role in the determination of foreign policy. What is unique about the modern world is that the economic aspects of social life have become more differentiated from other aspects because of the rise of a market economy (Hicks, 1969, p. 1). As a result, the economic motive has become more disentangled from other motives and also has increased in importance (Polanyi, 1957). This greater relevance of economic factors is a significant feature differentiating modern interna-

factor of production is rewarded in proportion to its marginal contribution to the economy). For a discussion of the subject see Blaug (1978, pp. 254–6).

tional relations from premodern international relations. In the early modern era, economic factors became more important; this was signified by the prevalent doctrine of mercantilism, with its emphasis on trade and finance as sources of state power (Gilpin, 1977). The importance of economic factors in global politics has grown continuously with the expansion of a highly interdependent world market economy.

As John Harsanyi pointed out, the evolution of the economic system is of crucial importance for political change because it is the principal means by which the natural environment constrains and influences human action:

One of the reasons why explanation of social phenomena in terms of *economic* forces is often so fruitful lies in the fact that the economic system is one of the main channels through which the natural environment (in particular, the presence or absence of natural resources and of natural routes of communication) acts upon the social system (Harsanyi, 1960, p. 1941.).

Economic variables tend to be accretive. Although sudden and dramatic economic changes can and do take place, in general the influence of economic changes tends to be cumulative, building up over decades or even centuries. However, their additive nature does not lessen their impact. For example, a 2 or 3 percent rate of economic growth or decline sustained over a sufficient period of time will have a decisive effect on the power and interests of a society. Similarly, a moderate change in the ratio of food supply to population can in time produce enormous consequences. In fact, of all the causes of international political change, one of the most critical is the Malthusian pressure of population on arable land (Teggard, 1941). Other crucial accretive economic variables include the accumulation of capital, increasing technical knowledge, and changes in relative prices for the factors of production. As Lord Keynes wrote in the quotation that opens this book, these types of cumulative secular changes ultimately produce the great events of history.

In general, an economic change operates like technological and military changes to create an incentive (disincentive) if it increases (decreases) the benefits or decreases (increases) the costs of changing the international system. Obviously the types of economic changes that can alter the benefits and costs of changing the international system are numerous. On the benefit side, any development that increases the need for (and hence benefit from) larger markets, capital outlets, or sources of raw materials will encourage a state to expand its political or economic influence. On the cost side, any development that decreases the costs of economic transactions will also encourage the transformation of economic and political relations.

[Changes in three broad categories of economic factors tend to encourage a state to expand and to attempt to change the international system.] First, any development that increases economies of scale will create a powerful incentive for a society to expand. Relevant economies of scale may involve the size of the market, the scale of production units, or a decrease in transactions costs. If an economic change promises a higher return or reduced costs through an increase in the scale of economic organization, it creates a powerful incentive for a society to capture these efficiency gains through economic or territorial expansion.

For the present study, the most important changes in economies of scale are those that affect the production of collective or public goods (Cox, Reynolds, and Rokkan, 1974, p. 124). For example, a development that decreases the costs or increases the benefits of providing protection over an enlarged area will create a powerful incentive for some political entrepreneur to supply this good in exchange for the revenue involved (Frohlich, Oppenheimer, and Young, 1971, p. 6). Later in this book, our discussion of the rise of the European state system will provide a case in which changes in the efficient scale for providing public goods constituted a primary cause of change in the international system.

Another related economic factor that creates incentives for expansion is the internalization of externalities. Externalities are benefits (positive) or costs (negative) conferred on political actors for which payment or compensation is not made (Davis and North, 1971, p. 15). In the case of positive externalities, the political system seeks to increase its control over the international system in order to force the benefited party to pay revenues for the conferred benefits. In the case of negative externalities, the political system seeks to incorporate those individuals responsible for negative externalities and force them to desist from the activities or pay compensation for the costs inflicted on the political system. For example, frequently the expansion of a political entity such as a city or a state is motivated by a desire to force individuals benefited by the activities of the city or state to pay the cost of the benefits (externalities) (Cox, Reynolds, and Rokkan, 1974, p. 125).

A third economic factor that provides an incentive for expansion is a diminishing rate of returns. As classical economists, and particularly David Ricardo in his law of rents, pointed out, if economic growth is to continue, all factors of production necessarily must increase in equal proportion. If one factor of production (land, labor, or capital) remains constant, and if there is no technological advance, the rate of growth of output will decline. This simple idea was central to classical economics. In fact, the whole edifice of classical economics was based on the law of diminishing returns; its pessimistic implications led Thomas Carlyle to christen economics the dismal science. The law was also taken over by Karl Marx, and thereby it became embedded in one of the most important and most systematic efforts ever undertaken to formulate a theory of sociopolitical change.

In the modern era since the Industrial Revolution of the eighteenth century and the advent of modern technology, the law of diminishing returns has lost much of its power: Technological advances increase the productivity of existing resources; as a consequence, quantitative increases in all factors of production are not necessary for economic growth to continue. It was, of course, this revolutionary development of technological advances that gave us the phenomenon of sustained economic growth and in turn created the modern era of affluent industrial societies. However, the revolutionary consequences of modern technology for economic growth were unappreciated by the classical economists who first formulated the law of diminishing returns.

The critical role of economic factors in social life has encouraged a number of scholars to place them at the center of efforts to understand and construct theories explaining sociopolitical change. Among such economic theories of change, two are especially interesting and relevant to the present study. The first is the neoclassical institutional economics of the "new economic historians."[7] The second is Marxism. Although they differ in significant respects, these two intellectual perspectives share the basic idea that sociopolitical change can be explained solely in terms of endogenous economic factors; that is, the relevant variables for explaining changes are primarily economic and are contained within the operation of the economic system. The "new economic history" and Marxism do not take adequate account of external factors such as religion, political forces, and random events, but because they are the two outstanding attempts to develop an economic theory of international political change, they will be considered in detail for the insights, albeit limited, that they do provide regarding political change.

The new economic history.   The fundamental proposition of the new economic history as set forth by two of its foremost exponents is that the "birth, growth, mutation, and, perhaps, death of [social, political, and economic] . . . institutions" can be understood through simple tools of economic analysis (Davis and North, 1971, p. 4). Thus the starting point for this innovative school of thought is that social and political changes are responses to the desires of individuals to maximize or at least advance their interests. Just as individuals seek material and other goods in order to improve their private welfare, they also attempt to transform social institutions and arrangements for the same self-serving reason. Thus this economic theory of sociopolitical change attempts to explain historical and institutional developments primarily in terms of factors endogenous (i.e., internal) to the operation of economic systems.

The methodology of the new economic historians involves the application of microeconomics (the laws of markets) to the study of institutional and historical changes. They rely heavily on the so-called law of demand, which holds that people will buy more (less) of a good if the relative price falls (rises); people will also

[7] The use of the term "neoclassical institutional economics" to characterize the approach of the new economic historians follows the usage of Alexander Field (1979).

tend to buy more (less) of a good as their relative incomes rise (fall) (Becker, 1976, p. 6). Thus, any development that changes the relative price of a good or the relative income of an actor will create an incentive or disincentive to acquire more of the good. The good in question for these scholars is a desired social or institutional change.

Although the new economic historians use the concepts and methodology of neoclassical economics, they change one fundamental assumption. Whereas neoclassical economics assumes that tastes and constraints (e.g., the system of property rights) do not change, the new economic historians assume that they do. Their major objective, in fact, is to explain how and why tastes and constraints, especially sociopolitical arrangements or institutions, change over time. Whereas the neoclassicists focus on optimizing behavior under a given set of conditions, the new economic historians are interested in explaining why both the goals that individuals seek to optimize and the external constraints themselves change over time (North, 1977).

The approach of the new economic historians to the problem of change may be [summarized in three general points]. In the first place, they emphasize that social change may be explained in terms of endogenous economic factors, that is, the efforts of individuals to satisfy their welfare objectives. Second, the primary determinant of behavioral change is assumed to be changes in relative prices and incomes. Because the changing of sociopolitical arrangements, whatever its ultimate benefits, involves transition and enforcement costs to someone, any development that changes the magnitude and distribution of the costs and the capacity to pay these costs affects the propensity for institutional change to take place. Third, individuals and groups attempt to use government to change property rights in ways that will advance their own basic interests. Thus, whereas neoclassical economics neglects the nature of social institutions and their effects on the distribution of economic gain, this subject is central to the new economic historians.

The primary value of this approach to social change is the simple yet powerful idea that the law of demand is applicable to the choice and changing of social and political arrangements.

Thus, as we have argued earlier, an actor will seek to change a political system if his income (power) increases or if the cost of changing the system decreases. Moreover, the actor will continue to try to change the system until the marginal costs of further change equal the marginal benefits and the system may be said to have returned to a position of equilibrium, that is, "none of the actors has any reason . . . for wishing to change his behaviour" (Barry, 1970, p. 168).

Despite this useful insight, this approach to understanding political change has a number of serious limitations. First, although the rationalistic assumption that actors make cost/benefit calculations in seeking to change social systems is a powerful one, political actions frequently lead to important and unanticipated consequences. Actors seldom can predict the train of events they set in motion, and they frequently lose control over social and political forces. Second, many important determinants of social and political change are exogenous to (i.e., outside) the operations of the economic system. For example, in order to understand the nature of international political change, one must take into account noneconomic variables such as military techniques, domestic political factors, and especially the international distribution of power. Third, the new economic history tends to assume that social and political arrangements are changed primarily in order to increase economic efficiency and to maximize social welfare. Thus, property rights are said to be created or abandoned depending on their social utility and especially their contribution to the efficient economic organization of society. This liberal assumption regarding sociopolitical change takes insufficient account of the fact that an equal, if not greater, motivation for political change is the desire of groups, social classes, or states to increase their individual welfare at the expense of others and at the expense of economic efficiency itself.

There are two differing economic situations in which individuals, groups, and/or states will seek to change social institutions and arrangements (Roumasset, 1974). First, they may seek to increase economic efficiency and maximize economic welfare by taking advantage of productive opportunities made possible by advances in knowledge, technology, etc. Through increasing economies of scale, reducing transactions costs, or achieving other gains in efficiency, everyone may benefit in absolute welfare terms from sociopolitical change. Second, political actors may instead seek to change sociopolitical arrangements in order to redistribute benefits in their own favor, even though most or all may lose in absolute welfare terms. What is important to the proponents of change is their relative gain in wealth or power. A theory of change must be able to account for both types of change.

Marxism. The other economic theory of political change that we shall consider is Marxism. As Karl Marx described his purpose in the Preface to Volume 1 of *Capital,* "it is the ultimate aim of this work to lay bare the economic law of motion of modern society" (quoted by Deane, 1978, p. 128). He believed he had found the key to social and political change in the development of the means of production:

The general conclusion at which I arrived and which, once reached, became the guiding principle of my studies can be summarized as follows. In the social production of their existence men inevitably enter into definite relations, which are independent of their will, namely relations of production appropriate to a given stage in the development of their material forces of production. The totality of these relations of production constitutes the economic structure of society, the real foundation, at which arises a legal and political superstructure and to which correspond definite forms of social consciousness (quoted by Deane, 1978, p. 129).

In highly oversimplified terms, Marxism maintains that political change is the consequence of the contradiction between a static sociopolitical system and the evolving means of agricultural or industrial production. Each successive social system has its peculiar class structure, legal framework, and economic logic that rest on the foundation of the existing means of production. Eventually the evolution of productive forces results in incompatibility between the sociopolitical system and the means of production. Consequently, a sociopolitical revolution takes place to make way for a social and legal system compatible with the requisites for further economic progress.

According to Marx, the capitalist system is driven by the law of accumulation. He reasoned that capitalists are compelled by virtue of the profit motive and the private ownership of the means of production to maximize and accumulate capital. However, capital accumulates in the form of productive forces and as a capitalist economy matures, the rate of profit tends to decline, thereby retarding further capital accumulation and economic growth. These developments then lead to steady impoverishment of the working class, to rising levels of unemployment, and finally to a general crisis in the capitalist order. Thus the contradiction between the capitalist sociopolitical system and the forces of production in a mature capitalist economy causes the overthrow of capitalism by revolution.

Marx and his collaborator Friedrich Engels were theorists of domestic society; they had little interest in the operation of the international economy. Later Marxist writers adapted Marxist doctrine to the highly internationalized capitalist economies of the late nineteenth and early twentieth centuries. Although many Marxist theorists contributed important ideas to this extension of Marxist theory to the international realm, it was Lenin, in his powerful 1917 polemic *Imperialism – The Highest Stage of Capitalism,* who brought these various strands together and formulated a Marxist theory of international political change in the capitalist era.

Lenin argued that because there is a general tendency for the rate of profit to fall, advanced capitalist economies try to arrest this decline through colonial expansion and imperialist behavior. This inherent need of capitalist economies to expand and acquire overseas colonies in order to absorb surplus capital provides the dynamics of international relations among these economies. It accounts for imperialism, war, and international political change. The centerpiece of Lenin's theory of international political change is the so-called law of uneven development:

There can be *no* other conceivable basis under capitalism for the division of spheres of influence, of interests, of colonies, etc., than a calculation of the *strength* of the participants in the division, their general economic, financial, military strength, etc. And the strength of these participants in the division does not change to an equal degree, for under capitalism the development of different undertakings, trusts, branches of industry, or countries cannot be *even*. Half a century ago, Germany was a miserable, insignificant country, as far as its capitalist strength was concerned, compared with the strength of England at that time. Japan was similarly insignificant compared with Russia. Is it "conceivable" that in ten or twenty years' time the relative strength of the imperialist powers will have remained *un*changed? Absolutely inconceivable (Lenin, 1939, p. 119).

Lenin reasoned further that because capitalist economies grow and accumulate capital at differential rates, a capitalist international system can never be stable. He argued that because of the law of uneven development, the accumulation of capital, and the subsequent need for colonies, capitalist economies can never be stabilized for longer than very short periods of time. At any given moment in time, the distribution of colonies among capitalist states is a function of relative strength and development; the most advanced capitalist economy will have the largest share of colonies. As other capitalist states develop, they will demand a redivision of colonial territories and changes in the international system in accordance with the new distribution of power. These demands lead to wars of division and redivision of colonies among the capitalist economies; World War I was the first of such wars. Such imperialist wars, Lenin wrote, were endemic in capitalism and would continue until capitalism was overthrown.

According to Lenin, the law of uneven development with its fateful consequences had become operative because the world had suddenly become finite. For decades the European capitalist powers had expanded and gulped up the unappropriated territory of the globe. As the open and available space contracted, the imperialist powers increasingly came into contact and thereby into conflict with one another. He believed that the final drama would be the division of China and, with the final closing of the global undeveloped frontier, the intensification of imperialist clashes. In time, the intensive conflicts among the imperialist powers would produce revolts among their own working classes even as economic development of the colonies was weakening Western capitalism's hold on the colonialized races of the globe.

It is not necessary to accept Marxist theory to appreciate its
heuristic value. The law of the falling rate of profit, first noted
by classical economists and so central to Marxist theory, can be
regarded as a special case of the more general law of diminishing
returns discussed earlier. As formulated by classical and neoclassical economists, the law may be stated as follows:

An increase in some inputs relative to other fixed inputs will, in a given
state of technology, cause total output to increase; *but after a point the
extra output resulting from the same additions of extra inputs is likely to
become less and less.* This falling off of extra returns is a consequence of
the fact that the new "doses" of the varying resources have less and less
of the fixed resources to work with (Samuelson, 1967, p. 26).

Or, to put it more succinctly, "the output of any productive
process will increase at a decreasing rate if the quantity of one
cooperating factor of production is kept constant while that of the
others is increased" (Hirschman, 1971, p. 17). Thus, every factor
of production (land, labor, and capital) must increase together (in
the absence of technological advance) if any economy is to escape the threat of diminishing returns.

Three general conclusions follow from this universal law of
production. In the first place, the addition of a given factor (e.g.,
labor) of production to a constant (land) will increase output rapidly, thus accelerating the economic growth and power of a society. Second, in the absence of technological advance, output at
some point will increase at a decreasing rate, thus decelerating
economic growth unless the quantities of all factors are increased. Third, as a consequence of the law of diminishing returns, the economic growth of a society tends to follow an S
curve. Initially the society grows slowly, and then it grows at a
more rapid rate until it finally reaches a maximum rate of
growth; thereafter, growth takes place at a much slower rate
(Figure 3). This history of any growing society can be described
by an S curve. As will be argued subsequently, in most cases the
slowing in the growth rate is a prelude to an absolute decrease in
the rate of growth and therefore a prelude to the eventual economic and political decline of the society.

The law of diminishing returns was central to the thinking of

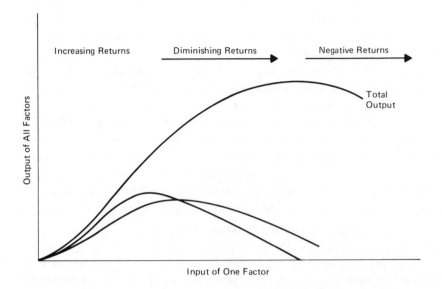

Figure 3. The law of diminishing returns. [Adapted from Heilbroner and Thurow (1978, p. 173).]

classical political economists and was incorporated into their several pessimistic laws. It was a foundation for Malthus's law of population, Ricardo's iron law of wages, and J. S. Mill's belief that industrial economies would one day reach a stationary state. Unappreciative of the revolutionary potential of modern technology, the formulators of the law assumed that economic growth would slow and eventually cease in a world of finite resources. Classical economics, thus oppressed by the law of diminishing returns, focused on the laws governing the distribution of the economic surplus.

According to classical economics, the critical limiting factor of production was arable land. The economic growth and wealth of society were constrained by the man/land ratio and the availability of good agricultural land. At some point, the density of population on the land and the decreasing quality of land brought into production would lead to decreasing returns to investment. These early economic thinkers thus reflected the experience of preindustrial history in which land was indeed the critical source of wealth and of power as well. Prior to the Industrial Revolution, economic growth in every civilization had eventually reached limits beyond which stagnation and eventual decline set in.

Marx and Engels, on the other hand, rejected the notion that economic growth was in any sense limited by fixed resources or natural endowments. For them, the fixed factor of production that inevitably would cause decreasing returns was the existing sociopolitical order. They argued that economic growth was limited only by human institutions and political organization rather than by nature. As Albert Hirschman observed, what Marx and Engels were in effect asserting with respect to the relationship of economic development and political change was the following:

At any one historical stage, the economy functions within a given political and institutional framework; on the basis of and owing to this framework, economic forces left to themselves can achieve some forward movement, but beyond a certain point further development becomes more difficult and eventually is held back by the unchanging political framework which, from a spur to progress turns into a "fetter"; at that point, political-institutional change is not only necessary to permit further advances, but is also highly likely to occur, because economic development will have generated some powerful social group with a vital stake in the needed changes (Hirschman, 1971, pp. 16–17).

Hirschman's generalization of the Marxist theory of political change contains three critically important insights. In the first place, every society in every age is governed by the law of diminishing returns. The society can grow and evolve in wealth and power within the existing social and political framework only to the point at which it begins to encounter diminishing returns; growth thereafter begins to falter. In the absence of technological advance and in the presence of population growth, fixed social arrangements and resources impose limits on every society, from primitive agricultural communities to contemporary socialist economies. If further economic advance is to take place, or even if economic decline is to be avoided, these fetters must be removed through political-institutional change and especially, although not necessarily, through territorial or economic expansion.

An important determinant of international political change is the fact that the economic surplus tends toward zero because of the onset of diminishing returns. Population growth, the depletion of high-quality land, and the scarcity of resources lead of necessity to a decrease in the economic surplus and consequent diminution in economic welfare and the power of the state.[8] The development of constraints on further internal economic growth of a society and the existence of external opportunities to arrest the operation of the law of diminishing returns thus constitute powerful incentives for states to expand their territorial, political, or economic control over the international system. Although the Industrial Revolution and modern technology have modified the operation of this law, they have not eliminated it as an important factor in international political change.

Second, economic growth tends to give rise to social and political groups that have an interest in undertaking actions that will remove the social and political fetters to further economic growth. The redistribution of power in society accompanying growth tends to bring particular groups into new positions of influence; they thus become the instruments of political change. In terms of our early discussion of the prerequisites for political change, these are groups that regard political change as profitable and therefore have an incentive to bear the necessary costs of seeking to change domestic or international society.

In domestic society, as a resource becomes scarce relative to the demands of society, the increasing cost of the resource creates an incentive for individuals, groups, or the government to pay the costs of innovations that will satisfy the unmet demand. The most important mechanism for stimulating this incentive is the creation and enforcement of new types of property rights: A right is conferred on the entrepreneur to enjoy the financial rewards of his endeavors (North and Thomas, 1973, p. 16). Thus the innovation of the patent system extended the notion of property rights to intellectual creations in order to encourage industrial invention.

[8] Until the modern era, a principal means employed in all societies to arrest diminishing returns and prevent economic decline was the practice of infanticide (Teggart, 1941, pp. 256–8).

In international society, groups and states may also seek international creation and recognition of certain property rights in order to reward productive types of endeavors. As has already been noted, the property rights of international investors tend to be respected in order to ensure the international flow of capital and technology. However, the more prevalent pattern historically has been for a society to use force to seize the scarce and increasingly costly resource, whether it be slave labor, fertile land, or petroleum. Although this response to diminishing returns has declined, it has by no means disappeared from world politics.

Third, as noted earlier, the law of diminishing returns (and Hirschman's elaboration of its signficance for political change) applies to international society as well as to domestic society. It helps to explain why both domestic groups and states seek to change social and political arrangements. It is especially useful in explaining the growth and expansion of political units, whether through the political incorporation of territory or through the creation of large-scale market economies. In short, the law of diminishing returns has a much greater range of applicability and political importance than either classical economists or Marxists appear to have appreciated.

The desire of groups and states to increase their shares of the economic surplus and the tendency for this surplus to decline as a result of the law of diminishing returns constitute powerful incentives behind expansion and international political change. Consideration of Hirschman's extension of Marxist theory leads to the conclusion that these economic motives and tendencies are universal rather than restricted to particular types of societies as Marxists contend. However, different types of economies may respond in very different ways to this economic stimulus; in a subsequent chapter we shall discuss this point in greater detail. However, the Marxist contention that capitalist societies, but not communist societies, have a tendency to expand and to try to change the international system by force does need further consideration at this point.

It is true, as Marxists argue, that capitalist economies have a strong propensity to expand economically. Capitalist economies do tend to prefer exports to imports; exports yield income and profits, whereas imports reduce them (Wiles, 1977, p. 522). Furthermore, the demand stimulant or Keynesian role of exports means that capitalist economies tend to take an export-biased (mercantilistic) view of trade. Finally, capitalist economies seek to maximize returns on capital, and therefore they have a powerful incentive to export surplus capital abroad if the rates of return abroad are higher than those at home.

International commerce plays a much different and less significant role in communist economies. In these economies the export of goods or capital is regarded as a claim on resources; at best, exports are considered to be a necessary evil required to secure essential imports, especially the capital goods and raw materials needed for industrial development. Although a communist economy may have security reasons to follow a mercantilist policy, its trade policy lacks a Keynesian or demand-stimulant dimension, and it is unlikely to have an incentive to export capital abroad. As Peter Wiles commented with respect to the only example we have of a multilateral communist trading system, "the Comecon itself is a device for assuring supplies, not outlets" (1977, p. 522).

These generalizations, however, do not validate Marxist theory regarding the association of capitalism, imperialism, and war. Although capitalist economies do possess a powerful incentive to expand, it does not follow that this expansion must take the form of colonial imperialism. Economic expansion through the market mechanism is also possible; there is a wide range of economic and noneconomic factors that are of significance in affecting the type of expansion. Furthermore, capitalist expansion by itself is not necessarily responsible for war; it may aggravate relations among states and even lead to minor conflicts, but major wars are due to the clash of more fundamental strategic and vital national interests.

The argument that capitalist economies have a powerful incentive to expand through the mechanisms of trade and investment does not support the position of some contemporary dependency theorists that capitalistic imperialism has purposely underdeveloped the so-called Third World. Although some capitalist countries obviously have exploited some lesser-developed economies, the major difference between capitalist and communist econo-

mies is that capitalist economies have a powerful economic incentive to develop other economies, but communist economies
do not. Whereas capitalist economies desire foreign trading
partners, communist economies are inward-looking. The former
export capital and technology and import foreign goods, thereby
assisting the development of other economies; the latter keep
their capital and technology at home and prefer local manufac-
turers. Ironically, both Marx and Lenin (in contrast to their
present-day followers) acknowledged that the historical role of
capitalism was to develop the world (Lenin, 1939; Avineri,
1969).

Communist societies do not eliminate the profit motive; rather,
they put it in the hands of the state (Hawtrey, 1952, p. 149).
The desire of a communist political elite to maximize the power
and wealth of the state can dwarf the capitalist profit motive.
Moreover, a communist economy is as subject to the law of
diminishing returns as is a capitalist society. Thus, although a
communist economy may take a different view of exports, the
need for imports of vital goods or raw materials required for
continued growth can become a powerful driving force behind
expansion in any type of economy. Moreover, because economic
relations under communism are subordinate to the state, it is
more likely than under capitalism that this expansion will take
the form of extending political control and influence over other
societies rather than through the market mechansim.

In conclusion, Marxism is inadequate as an economic theory
of political change. Like neoclassical institutional economics, it
neglects important political, technological, and other variables
exogenous to the operation of the economic system. Its almost
exclusive focus on class relations, the profit motive, and the
organization of production is too narrow to comprehend the
dynamics of international relations (Becker, 1976, p. 9). Marx
himself, as he grew older and as the revolution failed to materi-
alize, became aware of the narrowness of his economic dialectic
and began to speculate that the key to history might be not the
struggle of classes but that of races and nations (Feuer, 1969,
pp. 17–19).

THE STRUCTURE OF THE INTERNATIONAL SYSTEM

The structure of the international system itself greatly affects the capacity and willingness of a group or state to try to change the system. Structure means the form of the interrelationships of the states composing the international system. As Kenneth Waltz argued in his book *Theory of International Politics* (1979), a political structure is defined by (1) its ordering principle, (2) the specification of functions among units, and (3) the distribution of capabilities. Thus, according to Waltz's formulation, a domestic political structure is characterized by a hierarchical order based on authority, the specification of functions of differentiated units (executive, legislative, etc.), and the distribution of capabilities among groups and institutions. According to Waltz, an international political system, on the other hand, is characterized by an anarchic order of sovereign states, a minimum of functional differentiation among the actors, and the distribution of capabilities among states.

As Waltz demonstrated, the significance of structure is that actors "differently juxtaposed and combined behave differently and in interacting produce different outcomes" (1979, p. 81). This is because structure imposes a set of constraining conditions on actors. Whether it is a market or political system, structure influences behavior by rewarding some types of behavior and punishing others.[9] Through socialization of the actors and through competition among them, structure channels the behavior of actors in a system. Structure, therefore, affects the outcome of behavior regardless of the intentions and motives of the actors themselves (Waltz, 1979, p. 74).

International-political systems, like economic markets, are formed by the coaction of self-regarding units. International structures are defined in terms of the primary political units of an era, be they city-states, empires or nations. Structures emerge from the coexistence of states. No state intends to participate in the formation of a structure by which it and others will be constrained. International-political systems, like economic

---

[9] The limitations of applying the market analogy to international systems is treated by Russett (1968, pp. 131–7).

markets, are individualist in origin, spontaneously generated, and unintended. In both systems, structures are formed by the coaction of their units. Whether those units live, prosper, or die depends on their own efforts. Both systems are formed and maintained on a principle of self-help that applies to the units. To say that the two realms are structurally similar is not to proclaim their identity. Economically, the self-help principle applies within governmentally contrived limits. Market economies are hedged about in ways that channel energies constructively. One may think of pure food-and-drug standards, antitrust laws, securities and exchange regulations, laws against shooting a competitor, and rules forbidding false claims in advertising. International politics is more nearly a realm in which anything goes. International politics is structurally similar to a market economy insofar as the self-help principle is allowed to operate in the latter (Waltz, 1979, p. 91).

Structure is as significant a determinant of behavior in international politics as it is in economic markets and domestic political systems. Like the firm or political party, the state that fails to become socialized into the prevailing norms of the larger system pays a price and may be deprived of its very existence. The distribution of capabilities among actors has important consequences for the nature of international competition and hence for the behavior of states; whether that distribution is fairly equal, oligopolistic, duopolistic, or monopolistic (empire) affects the strategy of actors as it does in the market or political party system. In particular, the distribution of capabilities and the ways in which this distribution of capabilities changes over time are perhaps the most significant factors underlying the process of international political change.

The significance of the structure of the international system for the policies of states is, of course, the fundamental premise of political realism. According to this school of thought, a state is compelled within the anarchic and competitive conditions of international relations to expand its power and attempt to extend its control over the international system. If the state fails to make this attempt, it risks the possibility that other states will increase their relative power positions and will thereby place its existence or vital interests in jeopardy. The severe penalties that can be visited on states for failure to play the game of power

politics have exemplified the undeniable value of the realist position to an understanding of international relations.

An appreciation that the structure of the international system is
a significant determinant of the foreign policies of states does not
require acceptance of the deterministic realist formula of the
primacy of foreign policy or its identification of national interest
solely with the pursuit of power. Nor must one accept a structural
or systems-theory approach to international relations such as
Waltz's in order to agree that the distribution of power among the
states in a system has a profound impact on state behavior. Both
the structure of the international system and the domestic conditions of societies are primary determinants of foreign policy.

An understanding of how structure constrains and influences
the foreign-policy behavior of states is provided by the theory of
oligopolistic competition. The international system, like an oligopolistic market, is characterized by (1) interdependent decision
making and (2) sufficiently few competitors that the behavior of
any one actor has an appreciable effect on some or all of its
rivals. Because the behavior of other states and the effects of this
behavior on one's interests and competitive position are uncertain and unpredictable, a state (like a business firm) must maintain as wide a range of choice or options as possible. The implications of this oligopolistic situation for international politics and
the behavior of states have been well described by Benjamin
Cohen:

In a situation of competition, interdependence, and uncertainty, the
survival of any one unit is a function of the range of alternative strategies available to it. The oligopolistic firm with only one strategic option
leads a precarious existence: if that strategy fails to result in profit, the
firm will disappear. Likewise, the state with only one strategic option
can never feel truly secure: if that strategy fails, the state will disappear, be absorbed by others, or, more likely, be compelled to abandon
certain of its national core values. For both the firm and the state, the
rational solution is to broaden its range of options – to maximize its
power position, since power sets the limits to the choice of strategy
(Cohen, 1973, pp. 240–1).

Thus the oligopolistic condition of international relations stimulates, and may compel, a state to increase its power; at the least, it

necessitates that the prudent state prevent relative increases in the powers of competitor states. If a state fails to take advantage of opportunities to grow and expand, it risks the possibility that a competitor will seize the opportunity and increase its relative power. The competitor might, in fact, be able to gain control over the system and eliminate its oligopolistic rivals. Among states, as among firms, the danger of monopoly (empire) is omnipresent.

The structure of the international system is significant because of its profound effects on the cost of exercising power and hence of changing the international system. The number of states and the distribution of capabilities among them affect the ease with which winning coalitions or counterbalances of power can be formed. These structural factors determine the stability or instability of an international system, thus facilitating or inhibiting international political change.

During recent decades, scholars of international relations have debated the stability of varying types of international structures. The conventional wisdom is that multipolar systems are the most stable, and the long history of European balance-of-power system is cited as supporting evidence. The division of power and the flexibility of alignments found therein are said to create an uncertainty that induces caution in policymakers and facilitates adjustment of the system to potentially disruptive forces (Waltz, 1979, p. 168). Thus, a multipolar system (preferably of five powers, as was the case for the classic European balance of power) is believed to decrease the probability that nations will get locked into a zero-sum game that can be resolved only by conflict.

Recently this traditional position has been challenged by Waltz (1979). Drawing on oligopoly theory, Waltz sought to demonstrate that duopoly or bipolar structures are the most stable, and he cited as supporting evidence the durability of the contemporary superpower confrontation of the United States and the Soviet Union. Uncertainty and miscalculation cause wars, Waltz reasoned, and the virtue of a bipolar system resides in the "self-dependence of parties, clarity of dangers, certainty about who has to face them: These are the characteristics of great-power-politics in a bipolar world" (Waltz, 1979, pp. 171–2). As in an intrafirm duopoly, each antagonist need worry only about the other; they share an interest in preserving the status quo, and together they can control untoward events that might jeopardize international stability.

The inherent danger of a multipolar system, Waltz pointed out, is miscalculation: The train of events that precipitated a world war in 1914 when there were five great powers was essentially a series of miscalculations involving loss of control by the great powers over the actions of lesser powers on whom the great powers had become overly dependent. On the other hand, Waltz acknowledged that the inherent danger of a bipolar system is overreaction to events by one of the great powers (witness the American involvement in Vietnam, an area of no vital concern to the United States). Waltz reasoned that there is no structure that guarantees stability. There is only a dilemma: "which is worse: miscalculation or overreaction? Miscalculation is more likely to permit the unfolding of a series of events that finally threatens a change in the balance and brings the powers to war. Overreaction is the lesser evil because it costs only money and the fighting of limited wars" (Waltz, 1979, p. 172).

Waltz's argument that bipolar systems are more stable and less subject to abrupt transformations than multi-polar structures has an impressive logic to it. An especially useful contribution of his analysis is his point that "much of the skepticism about the virtues of bipolarity arises from thinking of a system as being bipolar if two blocs form within a multipolar world" (Waltz, 1979, p. 168). It will be argued subsequently that the bipolarization of a multipolar international system into two hostile blocs is extremely dangerous, as it creates a zero-sum game situation; this phenomenon of bipolarization into blocs in which one side or the other must lose in any confrontation has been the prelude to the great wars of history. The positive correlation between bipolarization of blocs and the outbreak of war forces consideration of whether bipolar or multipolar systems have a higher propensity to bipolarize into blocs. As Emile Durkheim pointed out in *The Rules of Sociological Method* (1894), it is impossible to predict change based on social structure, but certain types of structures and structural variables may increase the probability that change will take place (Nisbet, 1972, p. 44). Consideration of this question leads to three important qualifications of Waltz's argument regarding the stability of a bipolar system.

First, Waltz made an assumption that both of the great powers have an incentive to be vigilant and to maintain the duopolistic balance. Although this is a valid point, it may not occur; indeed, frequently one power fails to play its necessary role in a duopolistic balance. This was the case when Sparta failed to arrest the growth of Athenian power. Enumerating Athenian preparations for war, Sparta's Corinthian allies delivered the charge that Sparta failed to arrest Athenian expansion and permitted the balance to shift in Athens's favor:

For all this you are responsible. You it was who first allowed them to fortify their city after the Median war, and afterwards to erect the long walls, – you who, then and now, are always depriving of freedom not only those whom they have enslaved, but also those who have as yet been your allies. For the true author of the subjugation of a people is not so much the immediate agent, as the power which permits it having the means to prevent it; particularly if that power aspires to the glory of being the liberator of Hellas. . . . We ought not to be still inquiring into the fact of our wrongs, but into the means of our defense. For the aggressors with matured plans to oppose to our indecision have cast threats aside and betaken themselves to action. And we know what are the paths by which Athenian aggression travels, and how insidious is its progress. A degree of confidence she may feel from the idea that your bluntness of perception prevents your noticing her; but it is nothing to the impulse which her advance will receive from the knowledge that you see, but do not care to interfere. You, Lacedaemonians, of all the Hellenes are alone inactive, and defend yourselves not by doing anything but by looking as if you would do something; you alone wait till the power of an enemy is becoming twice its original size, instead of crushing it in its infancy. And yet the world used to say that you were to be depended upon; but in your case, we fear, it said more than truth. . . . against Athens you prefer to act on the defensive instead of on the offensive, and to make it an affair of chances by deferring the struggle till she has grown far stronger than at first. . . . if our present enemy Athens has not again and again annihilated us, we owe more to her blunders than to your protection. Indeed, expectations from you have before now been the ruin of some, whose faith induced them to omit preparation (Thucydides, 1951, pp. 38–9).

The second qualification relates to the meaning of stability. Waltz was certainly correct in arguing that multipolar systems composed of states with nearly equal powers are unstable in that they tend to be most prone to violence (viz., the Greek city-state system prior to the emergence of a Spartan–Athenian duopoly). There is, however, another meaning of stability/instability. This is the propensity in a system under particular sets of conditions for relatively small causes to lead to disproportionately large effects. The most frequently cited example of such an inherently unstable equilibrium is an egg balanced on one end – a slight breeze can cause the egg to topple. It is in this latter sense that a bipolar structure may be said to be more unstable than a multipolar system. If the delicate balance between the great powers is disturbed by a minor change, the consequences could be greater than would be the case in a multipolar system. This is the overreaction tendency that Waltz pointed out as characteristic of bipolar structures.

One of the most likely disturbing factors is entry of a newly powerful state into the system, either because of steady growth of a state in the system or because of entry into the system of a peripheral power, an entry caused, for example, by advances in transportation. It is easier for a multipolar system to make the necessary adjustment. Witness the capacity of the European balance of power to absorb (albeit with attendant upheaval) a succession of new powers over the centuries: Great Britain, Russia, and a unified Germany. In a bipolar system, even though the new state may not be equal to either of the two great powers, its strength added to the strength of one or the other great powers may tilt the balance and precipitate a major conflict. Although multipolar systems can become tripolar, the more usual occurrence is for bipolar systems to become tripolar, and as Waltz correctly observed, tripolar systems tend to be the most unstable of all (Waltz, 1979, p. 163). Thus the emergence of a powerful China, Japan, or united Europe would undoubtedly prove to be a destabilizing factor in contemporary world politics.

The third qualification of Waltz's analysis relates to his conclusions drawn from oligopoly theory. Challenging the conventional wisdom of political scientists regarding the greater stability of multipolar systems, Waltz wrote as follows:

Political scientists, drawing their inferences from the characteristics of states, were slow to appreciate the process [of American–Soviet accommodation]. . . . Economists have long known that the passage of time makes peaceful coexistence among major competitors easier. They become accustomed to one another; they learn how to interpret one another's moves and how to accommodate or counter them. "Unambiguously," as Oliver Williamson puts it, "experience leads to a higher level of adherence" to agreements made and to commonly accepted practices (Waltz, 1979, p. 173).

Thus a learning process takes place, and understood rules of the game evolve that facilitate control and management of the duopolistic competition (Kratochwil, 1978).

Cartel theory is applicable to this type of collusive oligopolistic behavior. There is a tendency in any oligopolistic structure for cartels to form, because the numbers are small and the firms (states) recognize their interdependence. The advantages of collusion include increased profits, decreased uncertainty, and the denial of entry to potential competitors. However, the history and the theory of cartels teach us that cartels and "collusive agreements tend to break down" (Mansfield, 1979, p. 348). There is a powerful incentive to cheat (although admittedly it is less in the case of duopoly) if the opportunity exists for a firm to increase its own profits. Contrary to Waltz's assertion that wars are caused by uncertainty and miscalculation, this book argues the opposite; it is perceived certainty of gain that most frequently causes nations to go to war (although these calculations, as Waltz rightly pointed out, may in fact be incorrect). Moreover, as Joseph Schumpeter pointed out long ago, oligopolistic firms tend to be highly innovative in their efforts to gain advantages over their competitors (Schumpeter, 1962, p. 96). Unless all oligopolistic firms or states are being equally innovative (this is difficult for a period of time), the balance of economic or military power shifts in favor of the more innovative firm or state, thus undermining the stability of the status quo.

In summary, one must reach the conclusion regarding the implications of oligopoly theory for international relations that Charles Kindleberger stated as the answer to all significant questions in economics (and, it should be added, in politics as well):

"It depends" (Kindleberger, 1959, p. 69).[10] Both bipolar and multipolar structures contain elements of instability, and the efforts by one or more states to improve their relative positions can trigger an uncontrollable train of events that can lead to international conflict and war. If the resultant war is of sufficient magnitude, it will cause a transformation in the system.

The most important factor for the process of international political change is not the static distribution of power in the system (bipolar or multipolar) but the dynamics of power relationships over time. It is the differential or uneven growth of power among states in a system that encourages efforts by certain states to change the system in order to enhance their own interests or to make more secure those interests threatened by their oligopolistic rivals. In both bipolar and multipolar structures, changes in relative power among the principal actors in the system are precursors of international political change.

Among the theories of international relations, two modes of theorizing have focused on the differential growth of power among societies as the key to political change. One is political realism; the other is Marxism. Although these two theories are often regarded as polar opposites, they have, in fact, remarkably similar perspectives on the nature and dynamics of international relations. Both political realism and Marxism explain the dynamics of international relations in terms of the differential growth of power among states. Both theories explain the most important aspects of international relations (war, imperialism, and change) as consequences of the uneven growth of power among states. Thucydides was perhaps the first political scientist to take note of this relationship when he wrote that "the growth of the power of Athens, and the alarm which this inspired in Lacedaemon, made war inevitable" (Thucydides, 1951, p. 15). Subsequent realists have made similar observations: "The great wars of history—we have had a world war about every hundred years for the last four centuries—" wrote Halford Mackinder in 1919, "are the outcome, direct or indirect, of the unequal growth of nations" (Mackinder, 1962, pp. 1–2). Lenin, in his *Imperialism,* stressed

[10] Or, more formally in the language of economics, there is no equilibrium solution to an oligopolistic situation. A valuable critique of the subject is Hart (1979, pp.9–15).

the critical significance of this phenomenon of uneven growth when he promulgated the law of uneven development.

However, political realism and Marxism differ from one another with respect to the underlying dynamic; realism stresses the power struggle among states, and Marxism stresses the profit motive of capitalist societies. Because the Marxist theory of international political change has already been discussed, the following discussion is restricted to realism.

The realist theory of international political change is based on what can be called the law of uneven growth, in contrast to the Marxist law of uneven development. According to realism, the fundamental cause of wars among states and changes in international systems is the uneven growth of power among states. Realist writers from Thucydides and Mackinder to present-day scholars have attributed the dynamics of international relations to the fact that the distribution of power in an international system shifts over a period of time; this shift results in profound changes in the relationships among states and eventually changes in the nature of the international system itself.[11]

Underlying the operation of this law and its significance is the fact that power by its very nature is a relative matter; one state's gain in power is by necessity another's loss. This creates what John Herz called "the security and power dilemma" (1951, p. 14). Each group, Herz pointed out, is concerned about being attacked or dominated by other groups. Each group strives, therefore, to enhance its own security by acquiring more and more power for itself. Although it can never attain complete security in a world of competing groups, by seeking to enhance its own power and security it necessarily increases the insecurity of others and stimulates competition for security and power. Herz concluded that one may speak of the struggle for survival as the inherent condition of international relations.

The realist law of uneven growth implies that as the power of a group or state increases, that group or state will be tempted to try to increase its control over its environment. In order to increase its own security, it will try to expand its political, eco-

[11] A modern, more restricted version of the law of uneven growth is the theory of power transition (Organski and Kugler, 1980, pp. 1–63).

nomic, and territorial control; it will try to change the international system in accordance with its particular set of interests.
Therefore, the differential growth of power among groups and
states is very important to an understanding of the dynamics of
international relations (see especially Doran, 1971; 1980).

The strong tendency of interstate oligopolistic competition to
stimulate states to expand their power is offset by the fact that
power and its exercise entail costs to the society; the society must
divert human and material resources from other social objectives. Power and security are not the only goals of the state; in
fact, they are seldom the highest goals. The presence of a multi-
plicity of goals that may conflict with one another means that a
state must weigh the costs and benefits of expanding its power
against other desirable social goals. The fact that the exercised
power thus has a cost has important implications for international
political change.

The critical significance of the differential growth of power
among states is that it alters the cost of changing the international system and therefore the incentives for changing the international system (Curry and Wade, 1968, p. 24). As the power of
a state increases, the relative cost of changing the system and of
thereby achieving the state's goals decreases (and, conversely,
increases when a state is declining). Regardless of its goal (security or welfare), a more powerful state can afford to pay a higher
cost than a weaker state. Therefore, according to the law of
demand, as the power of a state increases, so does the probability of its willingness to seek a change in the system. As John
Harsanyi observed, the explanation of political change must be
"in terms of the balance of power among the various social groups
pressing for the arrangements most favorable to their own interests (including their possible altruistic interests). At least this is
the type of explanation that any social historian or social scientist
would look for in his empirical research" (Harsanyi, 1969,
p. 535).

In summary, the structure of the international system and
shifts in that structure are critically important determinants of
state behavior. The structure of the system constrains behavior
and imposes a cost on any behavior that seeks to change the

international status quo. Similarly, the redistribution of inter-state capabilities may decrease or increase the cost of changing the international system. However, the tendency of a society to seek changes in the international system is dependent not only on decreased costs but also on domestic factors that influence the capacity and willingness of a society to pay these costs.

DOMESTIC SOURCES OF CHANGE

The character of a society is critical to its response to the opportunities for gain made possible by favorable environmental changes and shifts in the international distribution of power. Numerous writers in different ages have speculated on what makes some societies seize such opportunities and attempt to make changes in the international system, whereas others fail to try. Machiavelli, Montesquieu, and Ibn Khaldûn, as well as more contemporary social theorists, have sought to divine the connection between the internal composition of a state and the propensity of the state to expand. Through various approaches these thinkers have explored the ways in which national character, economic structure, and political culture influence the foreign policy of a state. Thus, explaining the outbreak of the Peloponnesian War, Thucydides told us that the critical factor was the contrasting characters of the Athenians and the Spartans. The former were energetic, democratic, inventive; they saw and seized the opportunities opening up by the development of sea power and long-distance commerce and consequently grew in wealth and power. The Spartans lacked initiative and failed to take advantage of the new opportunities for wealth and power; they were limited by their internal social and economic structure. Although Sparta had been the hegemonic power since the end of the Persian Wars, it fell behind as Athens grew. Eventually the Spartan fear of growing Athenian power led to the great war that weakened the city-state system and paved the way for Macedonian imperialism.

It is impossible to formulate in a systematic and exhaustive fashion the domestic determinants of the foreign policies of states. There simply are too many qualitative variables: personalities, national character, social structure, economic interests, political organization, etc. Moreover, as these factors change, so do the interests and power of the state itself. The rise and decline of social classes, the shifting coalitions of domestic interest groups, and secular economic-demographic changes, as well as other developments, can lead to far-ranging changes in the objectives of foreign policy and the capacities of states to pursue foreign-policy goals. Whether these domestic changes will encourage a state to expand territorially, withdraw into isolationism, or try to alter the international division of labor can be determined only by the historical record. Yet it is possible to make a few generalizations about these matters.

The most crucial aspect of a domestic regime related to international political change is the relationship between private gain and public gain. How do the growth of power and the expansion of the state affect the benefits and costs to particular individuals and powerful groups in the society? Do private and public interests tend to coincide or conflict? If the growth and expansion of the state and the interests of powerful groups are complementary, then there exists a strong impetus for the state to expand and to try to change the international system. If, on the other hand, the growth and expansion of the state impose a heavy cost on these groups and/or threaten their interests, then a strong disincentive exists.

Within the domestic society, social, political, and economic arrangements create incentives and disincentives for individuals and groups to behave in ways that contribute to or detract from the power of the state and that thereby affect its propensity to seek to enlarge its control over the international system. In the language of the new economic historians, one would say that a society will not grow in wealth and power unless its social organization is efficient. Individuals must be encouraged by incentives to undertake activities that will advance the power and wealth of the society. As two economic historians put it, "some mechanism must be devised to bring social and private rates of return into closer parity" (North and Thomas, 1973, p. 2). This is, in theory, the principal function of property rights, which distribute benefits and costs in a society. An efficient social organization is one in which property rights assure that private benefits exceed private costs to individuals undertaking socially profitable activities. In other words, the necessary condition within a state for it to attempt to change the international system is that domestic social arrangements must ensure that the potential benefits to its members of carrying out this task will exceed the anticipated costs to its members.

This, of course, was the central idea in Adam Smith's *The Wealth of Nations* (1937): In a competitive market economy the individual pursuing economic self-interest is led by an invisible hand to contribute to the economic growth and well-being of society. Motives other than those associated with economic gain have also been used by societies to encourage individuals to identify with and contribute to the common good. Religion and political ideologies promise rewards to the faithful. The religious fanaticism of the Arabian tribes converted to Islam and the fanaticism of Bolshevik revolutionaries in czarist Russia illustrate the point. The power of modern nationalism lies in the fact that individual identity and state interest become fused; the nationalist becomes the patriot willing to sacrifice his own life for the good of the state.

The notion that the internal ordering of the state has profound consequences for its political fortunes was a fundamental insight of classical political thinkers. The nature of the regime, Plato argued in *The Republic*, determined the true character of the citizenry, and this in turn influenced the success or failure of the polity. This observation may perhaps be best demonstrated by drawing on the insights of Polybius, the Greek historian of the second century B.C., who inquired why it was that Rome succeeded whereas other societies failed.

In Book Six of his history of the Roman Empire, Polybius began with an explanation of the success of the Romans, that is, the gaining and keeping of an empire (Polybius, 1962, p. 458). First, he acknowledged that historians have recorded as excellent the regimes or constitutions of Lacedaemonia, Crete, Mantinea, and Carthage, as well as those of Athens and Thebes. He dismissed the latter two because "their growth was abnormal, the period of their zenith brief, and the changes they experienced unusually violent. Their glory was a sudden and fortuitous flash, so to speak" (pp. 494–5). In his judgment, the folly of others and fortuitous ingenious statesmanship, rather than the intrinsic merits of these polities, led to their ephemeral, albeit brilliant, success.

Passing over the Cretan constitution as too base and Plato's ideal republic as too impractical, Polybius turned his attention to Sparta and Carthage. With respect to the Spartan constitution, he considered it excellent and appropriate "for securing unity among the citizens, for safeguarding the Laconian territory, and preserving the liberty of Sparta inviolate" (pp. 498–9). The Spartan customs of equality, simplicity, and communism "were well calculated to secure morality in private life and to prevent civil broils in the State; as also their training in the endurance of labours and dangers to make men brave and noble minded" (p. 499). However, the laws given to Sparta by Lycurgus, the lawgiver, had one vice: They made "no one provision whatever, particular or general, for the acquisition of the territory of their neighbours; or for the assertion of their supremacy; or, in a word, for any policy of aggrandizement at all" (p. 499). Although they were excellent warriors (like the later Romans), they had no economic or other incentive to expand. For this reason, in the view of Polybius, the Spartan constitution was deficient as a mechanism to encourage aggrandizement and domination.

The Carthaginian constitution, Polybius believed, displayed a different defect, although it was originally well contrived for the purposes of expansion. The division of power among the king, aristocracy, and people facilitated a well-ordered and self-aggrandizing polity. However, by the time Carthage entered its death struggle with Rome, it had passed its zenith and was in decay:

In Carthage therefore the influence of the people in the policy of the state had already risen to be supreme, while at Rome the Senate was at the height of its power: and so, as in the one measures were deliberated upon by the many, in the other by the best men, the policy of the Romans in all public undertakings proved the stronger; on which account, though they met with capital disasters, by force of prudent counsels they finally conquered the Carthaginians in the war (pp. 501–2).

The superiority of the Romans over the Carthaginians in war ultimately was founded on the Romans' interest in their land army, as compared with Carthaginian neglect of their infantry. The Carthaginians were devoted to the sea, and they employed mercenary forces on land; the Romans, on the other hand, employed native and citizen levies. As Polybius stated,

They [the Carthaginians] have their hopes of freedom ever resting on the courage of mercenary troops: the Romans on the valour of their own citizens and the aid of their allies. The result is that even if the Romans have suffered a defeat at first, they renew the war with undiminished forces, which the Carthaginians cannot do. For, as the Romans are fighting for country and children, it is impossible for them to relax the fury of their struggle; but they persist with obstinate resolution until they have overcome their enemies (p. 502).

In short, the difference between defeated Carthage and victorious Rome resided in the realm of incentives.

In the opinion of Polybius, the success of Rome was due to "the pains taken by the Roman state to turn out men ready to endure anything to win a reputation in their country for valour" (p. 502). The driving force behind Athenian aggrandizement was individual economic gain; for Rome, it was the achievement of individual glory.[12] Polybius went on to show how, through funeral laudations for illustrious men and other commemorative devices, the Romans celebrated those men who had well served the state as an inspiration for ambitious youth: "the chief benefit of the [funeral] ceremony is that it inspires young men to shrink from no exertion for the general welfare, in the hope of obtaining the glory which awaits the brave" (p. 502). Similarly, in economic affairs and religion, men were conditioned to serve the good of the state and were rewarded on earth and in the hereafter. Polybius believed the Roman constitution to be far "superior and better constituted for obtaining power" than were those of Sparta and Carthage (p. 501).

Polybius's observations regarding the character of the society and its implications for the foreign policy of the state lend them-

---

[12] Roman soldiers in the later Republic were also rewarded in more tangible ways, such as the distribution of land for military service (Andreski, 1971, p. 55).

selves to several generalizations. In the first place, the internal
ordering of a society is a critical determinant of its capabilities and
of its capacity to overcome environmental constraints and take
advantage of environmental opportunities. Classical writers acknowledged this fact in their recognition of the importance of the
lawgiver: a Cyrus, Solon, or Lycurgus. We Americans pay hom-
age to the same notion in our reverence for the Founding Fathers
and the ways in which the American Constitution was framed to
facilitate conquest of the continent. As many writers have noted,
important aspects in such lawgiving are found in the long-term
effects of internal social, economic, and political arrangements on
individual incentives and in the propensity of societies to grow in
wealth and power. The problem of the lawgiver, in the words of
Gordon Tullock, "is to so arrange the structure that the [citizen] is
led by self-interest into doing those things that he 'ought' to do"
(Tullock, 1965, p. 119). Or, as Montesquieu put it several centuries ago, "At the birth of societies, the leaders of republics create
the institutions; thereafter, it is the institutions that form the
leaders of republics" (1965, p. 25).

This generalization helps explain the oft-repeated observation
that the unification and internal reordering of a society by a
newly dominant political elite, social class, or religion are frequently (but not always) the prelude to its rapid growth and
expansion. The effect of changes in elites, beliefs, or organization
is to channel the energies of society toward achievement of the
common political, economic, or religious (or ideological) objectives of the renovated society (Huntington, 1968, p. 31). The
great changes in the history of the world have been engineered
by those political or military leaders and elites who have grasped
the significance of new possibilities and reordered their societies
to take advantage of such opportunities. It is this phenomenon
that writers have in mind when they observe that the rise of a
new elite and the stirring of religious (or ideological) passion are
frequently accompanied by outward expansionism.

Second, the influence of domestic sociopolitical arrangements
on individual initiative is of great importance. Thus the virtue of
the Roman constitution was its effect on the character and the
incentives of Rome's citizen-soldiers. Through moderation of in-

ternal strife, glorification of self-sacrifice, and distribution of the fruits of empire, private and public ambitions in the early Republic were made to coincide. Rome's citizen-soldiers fought hard because they had a personal stake in the system and the fortunes of Rome. "No wonder," Polybius wrote, "that a people, whose rewards and punishments are allotted with such care and received with such feelings, should be brilliantly successful in war" (Polybius, 1962, p. 492). It was for this reason that classical and early modern writers (Machiavelli and Montesquieu, in particular) believed republics with citizen armies were naturally expansionist and superior to other forms of political organization. Centuries later, Machiavelli was to echo the argument of Polybius:

> It is only in republics that the common good is looked to properly . . . and, however much this or that private person may be the loser on this account, there are so many who benefit thereby that the common good can be realized in spite of those few who suffer in consequence. . . . as soon as tyranny replaces self-government . . . it ceases to make progress and to grow in power and wealth (quoted by Wolin, 1960, p. 234).

Even more recently, writers have taken note of the fact that the greatest powers of the nineteenth and twentieth centuries have been democracies, Great Britain and the United States, respectively.

Finally, the nature of domestic arrangements confers on a society a relative advantage or disadvantage with respect to its capacity to adapt itself to specific environmental changes and opportunities. Thus, as Polybius observed, the great advantage of the Romans over their opponents was their capacity to learn from others and to adapt themselves to changing circumstances: "No nation has ever surpassed them in readiness to adopt new fashions from other people, and to imitate what they see is better in others than themselves" (Polybius, 1962, p. 480). Much the same thing could be said about Americans in the nineteenth century and Japanese in the late twentieth century.

As circumstances change over time, however, so may the requirements for political, economic, and military success. Social arrangements that are efficient and provide an advantage under one set of circumstances, as Polybius told us in the cases of Sparta and Carthage, can produce a disadvantage under a new set of environmental conditions. Unfortunately, as a society ages it becomes decreasingly able to learn from others and to adapt itself to changing circumstances. Tradition and vested interests inhibit further reordering and reform of the society. History records many societies whose social, economic, and political systems were well adapted to one set of environmental conditions but were entirely unsuited to a changed international environment.

The important point, as the classicist T. F. Carney pointed out, is that "a society's institutions and values, its structure of rewards and opportunities, advance particular personality types from among the personality pool comprised by its population" (Carney, 1973, p. 129). In an international environment that placed a premium on military power, the Roman rewarded military virtues. Modern democratic societies, on the other hand, tend to reward the profit seeker and economic maximizer. It is the congruence between the prevailing conditions in a given historical epoch and the personality types fostered by a society that largely determines the success or failure of a society in the power struggles among states.

Although the insights of Polybius were based on his observations of successful and unsuccessful military-based empires in the ancient world, they have a universal validity. The most critical factor in the growth of power of a society is the effect of the political and economic order on the behavior of individuals and groups. In the premodern world, the most significant effect was on the military efficiency of the society (i.e., on the incentives of individuals to contribute to the military power of the state). In the modern world, the effect of state policies on the incentives of individuals to contribute to the economic growth of the society is of great importance.

The key to economic growth, as Douglass North and Robert Thomas reasoned in their pioneering book *The Rise of the Western World* (1973), is an efficient economic organization. "Efficient organization," they wrote, "entails the establishment of institutional arrangements and property rights that create an incentive to channel individual economic effort into activities that bring the private rate of return close to the social rate of return"[13] (North and Thomas, 1973, p. 1). What this implies is that economic growth will be retarded unless individuals are "lured by incentives to undertake the socially desirable activities. Some mechanism must be devised to bring social and private rates of return into closer parity" (p. 2). A discrepancy between private and social benefits or costs means that a third party receives some of the benefits or incurs some of the costs. "If the private costs exceed the private benefits," individuals are less willing to undertake socially desirable activities (p. 3).

The primary mechanism for reconciling private and social benefits or costs is society's definition of property rights. Thus, inventors are given patents (intellectual property) that reward them for incurring the costs of undertaking socially desirable innovations. On the other hand, environmental polluters have no incentive to bear the costs of preventing pollution; they prefer to shift the costs of pollution to society (the free-rider problem). For numerous reasons a society may fail to develop a set of property rights that reconcile private and social returns and thereby encourage economic growth. First, there is no technique available to counteract the free-rider problem and to compel third parties to bear the costs of providing a public good. For example, commerce was inhibited until military techniques became available to protect honest traders against pirates and robber barons. Second, the costs of enforcing property rights may exceed the benefits to individuals or groups; even if the means are available to wipe out pirates, this will not happen until someone finds the benefits of such action to outweigh the necessary costs. In brief, if the exclusiveness of benefits and accompanying property rights can be enforced, "everyone would reap the benefits or bear the costs of his actions" (North and Thomas, 1973, p. 5); they would undertake those activities fostering economic growth (innovation, accumulation of capital, etc.). Why it was that the

[13] "The private rate of return is the sum of the net receipts which the economic unit receives from undertaking an activity. The social rate of return is the total net benefit (positive or negative) that society gains from the same activity. It is the private rate of return plus the net effect of the activity upon everyone else in the society" (North and Thomas, 1973, p. 1).

modern West created such an efficient set of institutions and led
the world in economic growth is discussed in the next chapter.

CONCLUSION

In this chapter we have analyzed the environmental, international, and domestic factors that influence a state either to support the status quo or to attempt to change the international
system. These factors and changes in these factors determine the
costs and benefits to particular groups and states in trying to
change the system. The relative importance of different types of
factors (economic, military, or technological) have differed considerably over time; in all ages, however, the most important
factors have been those that alter the relative power of states in
the system. Although numerous factors have been identified that
create incentives or disincentives to change the international
stystem, whether or not change will in fact take place is ultimately indeterminant.

3

Growth
and expansion

Assumption 3. A state will seek to change the international system through territorial, political, and economic expansion until the marginal costs of further change are equal to or greater than the marginal benefits.

As the power of a state increases, it seeks to extend its territorial control, its political influence, and/or its domination of the international economy. Reciprocally, these developments tend to increase the power of the state as more and more resources are made available to it and it is advantaged by economies of scale. The territorial, political, and economic expansion of a state increases the availability of economic surplus required to exercise dominion over the system (Rader, 1971, p. 46). The rise and decline of dominant states and empires are largely functions of the generation and then the eventual dissipation of this economic surplus.

If this relationship between the growth of power of a state and its control over the international system were linear, the result would be the eventual establishment by one state of a universal imperium. That this has not yet happened is a result of the fact that countervailing forces come into play to slow and eventually arrest the impulse to expand. Because of the influence of these

106

countervailing forces, as a state increases its control over an international system, it begins at some point to encounter both increasing costs of further expansion and diminishing returns from further expansion; that is to say, there are decreasing net benefits to be gained from further efforts to transform and control the international system. This change in the returns from expansion imposes a limit on the further expansion of a state.

The expansion of a state and of its control over the system may be said to be determined in large measure by a U-shaped cost curve (Bean, 1973, p. 204; Auster and Silver, 1979, p. 28). The initial phase of expansion is characterized by declining costs due principally to economies of scale. However, as the size of the state and the extent of its control increase, at some point it begins to encounter decreasing returns to scale. The increasing cost of expansion relative to the benefits eventually limits the size and expansion of the state and its control over the system. The point at which this crossover will occur is an empirical question dependent on technical and other circumstances (Mansfield, 1979, p. 162).

At the point at which expansion and efforts to change the system cease to be profitable, the international system may be said to have returned to a state of equilibrium, as the marginal costs of further expansion are equal to or greater than the marginal benefits of expansion. As a consequence of the interplay of these forces promoting and retarding expansion and growth, the expansion of a state and of its control over an international system is best described by a logistic or S curve.[1] Thus, a would-be expanding state at first increases its power and control over the system; the power of the state and the expansion of its control reinforce one another with the enhanced flow of resources into the coffers of the state. Eventually, countervailing forces come into play to slow down and finally arrest the expansion of the state, and the system returns to a condition of equilibrium.

The phenomenon described in the preceding paragraphs is universal. From the earliest civilizations, states and empires

[1] This task has been carried out by Hornell Hart, who fitted the territorial growths of ancient and modern empires to a logistics curve (Ogburn, 1949, pp. 28–57). For a more recent effort, see the work of Taagepera (1968).

have sought to expand and extend their dominance over their neighbors in order to increase their share of the economic surplus. However, the precise mechanisms they have employed have differed, depending on the nature of the state, the environment, and what Samir Amin called the "social formation" (1976, p. 16). These several factors have profound influences on the behavior of groups and states and hence on the process of international political change.

The type of social formation is extremely important because it determines how the economic surplus is generated, its magnitude, and the mechanism of its transfer from one group or society to another (Amin, 1976, p. 18); it influences the distribution of wealth and power within societies as well as the mechanism for the distribution of wealth and power among societies. The following discussion reformulates Amin's conception of social formation so as to facilitate an understanding of international political change.

According to Amin, a social formation combines modes of industrial and agricultural production within societies and organizes economic relationships among societies. There are, he pointed out, five basic modes of production: (1) the primitive-communal mode of primitive societies, (2) the tribute-paying mode characteristic of feudalism and certain types of empires; (3) the slave-owning mode; (4) the simple petty-commodity mode; (5) the capitalist mode. In every social formation, one or another of these modes of production tends to predominate and gives a society its peculiar character. Social formations also differ significantly with respect to their dependence on or involvement in long-distance trade, which affects the transfer of wealth among societies.

In contrast to Amin's elaborate formulation, in this study we identify three categories of social formations. In the first place, there are the localized social formations of the primitive-communal, feudal, and simple petty-commodity types. These economies are characterized by inability of the society to generate a sufficiently large economic surplus to invest in political or economic expansion; frequently these economies do not operate much beyond the subsistence level. This is the situation, for example, with most tribal societies; it was the condition in feudal

Europe prior to the revival of long-distance trade in the twelfth and thirteenth centuries. Because these localized types of society seldom play important roles in international political change, they will not be considered in detail here.

It must be noted that localized social formations can undergo transformations that can launch them on imperial careers. Two outstanding examples are the Mongols and Arabs, who created vast empires. A third example is provided by the rise of several black African empires in the early modern period following the opening of trade with Europe, which led, for the first time, to the generation of substantial economic surplus. Also, unique circumstances have enabled one type of relatively localized social formation to play an important role in the history of international relations: the city-state. In the river valleys of ancient civilization, classical Greece, and Renaissance Italy, city-state systems flourished and displayed all the characteristics of larger international systems. In every case, however, these city-state systems were eventually absorbed by expanding land empires. Only one independent city-state survives in the contemporary world: Singapore.

The second category of social formation is the empire or imperial system. Amin distinguished three types of imperial social formations based on the predominant mode of production: tribute empires, slave-owning empires, and empires based on long-distance trade. Although these three types of empires have important differences, they have in common the fact that the economic surplus is generated by agriculture and is siphoned off through direct or indirect means for the benefit of a warrior, religious, or bureaucratic elite. For these reasons, the dynamics of the rise and decline of all three types of traditional imperial systems are sufficiently similar to be treated as one.

Finally, the third category of social formation is the modern industrial nation-state. Amin referred to "capitalist formations," thereby emphasizing the private ownership of the means of production, with profit as the characteristic form of economic surplus. Amin's formulation, however, is too circumscribed. The "industrial nation-state" is a more apt characterization of the modern social formation, whether it be capitalistic or communistic. This is not to deny that capitalism has important features and dynamics that distinguish it from communism. The more important consideration, however, is that under both capitalism and communism the economic surplus is generated by industrial production, and this common characteristic has significant implications for the behavior of the society in international relations.

The social formation is significant in that it strongly affects the generation and distribution of wealth and power among groups and states and hence plays an important role in the dynamics of international systems. The distinguishing features of premodern and modern international relations are in large measure due to significant differences in characteristic social formations.[2] The displacement of empires and imperial-command economies by nation-states and a world market economy as the principal forms of political and economic organization can be understood only as a development associated with the change from an agricultural formation to industrial formation. The effects of these interrelated transformations on the nature of international political change are examined in the following sections of this chapter.

THE CYCLE OF EMPIRES

Although scholars acknowledge the contemporary primacy of the nation-state in referring to international relations, the predominant form of political organization before the modern era was the empire. Although city-states, feudalism, and other forms of localized social formations existed and frequently were of decisive importance, the history of interstate relations was largely that of successive great empires.[3] The pattern of international political change during the millennia of the premodern era has been described as an imperial cycle (Rader pp. 38–68, 1971; Rostow,

[2] The idea that modern society differs fundamentally from premodern ones is an idea that engaged the attention of such nineteenth-century writers as Auguste Comte, Karl Marx, and Herbert Spencer. This belief has been revived by a number of recent writers, although there is intense controversy today, as in the past, regarding the nature and causes of this difference.

[3] By "empire" we mean an aggregation of diverse peoples ruled over by a culturally different people and a political form usually characterized by centralization of power in an emperor or sovereign.

1971, pp. 28–9). World politics was characterized by the rise and decline of powerful empires, each of which in turn unified and ordered its respective international system. The recurrent pattern in every civilization of which we have knowledge was for one state to unify the system under its imperial domination. This propensity toward universal empire was the principal feature of premodern politics, and as earlier scholars of international relations have emphasized, it contrasts dramatically with the pattern of the modern European balance of power.[4]

During the imperial era, the governance of an international system (what some today would call the international order) was provided by these imperial structures. Because each empire tended to represent, or at least to be dominated by, a particular civilization and religion, empires held few values and interests in common; they evolved few rules or institutions to govern their relations. The principal ordering mechanisms were territorial control and spheres of influence. These imperial orders constituted merely a system of states, not what Hedley Bull (1977) characterized as an international "society." International conflict was at once economic, social, political, religious, and civilizational. This was true until the Treaty of Westphalia (1648) and the subsequent triumph of Western civilization over its Islamic and other rivals.

The principal determinant of this cycle of empires was the underlying agriculture-based social formation. During this imperial era, before the advent of modern industry, the wealth of societies and the power of states rested on the exploitation of peasant and slave agriculture. Before the massive increases in agricultural productivity of the modern world, the size of the economic surplus from agriculture and imperial tribute was principally a function of the extent of territorial control. Therefore, other things being equal, the greater the territorial extent of an empire and of its political control, the greater the taxable surplus and the greater the power of the empire. As in all things, however, this was true up to the point at which the extension of

---

[4] This was the view, for example, of such diverse writers as Edward Gibbon, Montesquieu, and A. H. L. Heeren. Later writers who have made the same point include Leopold von Ranke, Arnold Toynbee, and Ludwig Dehio.

control began to encounter diminishing returns and expansion ceased to be profitable.

A fundamental feature of the era of empires was the relatively static nature of wealth. In the absence of significant technological advances, agricultural productivity remained at a low level, and the primary determinant of economic growth and wealth was the availability of land and the man/land ratio. For this reason, the growth of wealth and power of the state was primarily a function of its control over territory that could generate an economic surplus. With only limited and intermittent periods of real economic growth, the dynamics of international relations were provided by the continuous division and redivision of territory and the conquest of slaves (or a docile peasantry) to till the land. Thus, when agriculture was the basis of wealth and power, growth in power and wealth was nearly synonymous with conquest of territory.

Imperial economies tend to be command economies in which the state has control over and disposition of the society's goods and services. Because empires are created by warriors, bureaucracies, and autocracies in their own interests, the primary function of the imperial economy is to advance the wealth and power of these dominant elites. The economy and economic activities are subordinate to the perceived security and economic interests of the state and the ruling elite. A major function of economic exchange is to enhance the war-making capability of the state. The Assyrians of antiquity exemplified this type of economy.

Although the generation of an economic surplus during the imperial era was dependent on agriculture, its distribution was frequently influenced by commerce and international trade. At least since the time of the expeditions of the Greeks under Agamemnon against Troy, the control of trade routes has been an objective of states and a source of great wealth and power. The great and enduring empires frequently have arisen at the crossroads of trade, and struggles over control of the principal arteries of commerce have been constant sources of interstate conflict. Changes in the control of these trade routes and changes in the locations of the routes themselves have played decisive roles in the rise and decline of empires and civilizations. It was with good reason that Brooks Adams in his provocative study *The Law of Civilization and Decay* (1943) considered changes in trade and trade routes to be the key to history.

The history of the Middle East attests to the significant impact that shifts in trade routes have had on international relations. From the time of the earliest empires in this region, shifting control over the caravan routes of Asia has given rise to a succession of empires. Even under Rome the economic center of gravity of the empire remained in the eastern Mediterranean basin. The Byzantine Empire or later Roman Empire survived for 1,000 years after the collapse of the western Roman Empire into barbarism; it survived largely because it retained its hold on these trade routes until the rise of the Ottoman Turks. The economic growth of western Europe and the discovery of the New World and of new ocean routes to Asia resulted in the eventual decay of the Middle East and shifted the locus of world power away from the Mediterranean basin.

Historically, taxation of trade was a major source of state revenue; this accounts for the importance of trade in the distribution of the economic surplus and hence of power. In contrast to other sources of state revenue, such as taxation of land or internal trade, international trade is relatively easy to administer and tax. This critical role of trade revenue in the formation of empires was analyzed by Max Weber in the following terms:

Scholars have often overlooked one constant that has been historically important in the development of strong, centralized patrimonial bureaucracies – trade. We saw previously that the power positions of all rulers transcending the level of the primitive village headman were based on their possession of precious metals in raw or finished form. They needed this treasure above all for the maintenance of their following, the bodyguards, patrimonial armies, mercenaries and especially officials. This treasure was supplied through the exchange of gifts with other rulers – this was in fact often an instance of barter –, through the ruler's own regular trade (in particular, the coastal intermediate trade), which can lead to a direct monopolization of foreign trade, or finally through other uses of foreign trade. This was done either directly in the form of taxation through tariffs, tolls and other tributes, or indirectly through market-privileges and the founding of cities, which were princely prerogatives that yielded high ground-rents and subjects capable of paying high taxes. Throughout history, this last type of utilizing trade was systemically undertaken; as late as the beginning of modern times, Polish seigneurs founded countless towns and settled them with Jews emigrating from the West. Typically, patrimonial political structures persist and expand territorially, although their trade is relatively moderate or outright weak in comparison to their size or their population – see the case of China and of the Carolingian empire –, but the genesis of patrimonial political rulership is infrequent without trade playing a considerable role; it has happened – witness the Mongolian empire and the kingdoms of the Teutonic Migration –, but nearly always according to the pattern that tribes who live adjacent to territories with a highly developed money economy invade these, take possession of their precious metals and found new polities on these territories. The royal trade monopoly can be found all over the world, in Polynesia just as much as in Africa and in the ancient Orient (Weber, 1968, p. 1,092).

The dynamics of the cycle of empires were built on the economic reality of primitive agriculture and taxation of trade. Although empires might break up, as did the Roman, when one group or another sought to suboptimize (i.e., increase its own gains at the expense of the whole), the more prevalent pattern was the overthrow and conquest of the imperial civilization by outside barbarians. In this recurrent struggle, the empire initially had the advantage of a large economic surplus and usually superior military technique. The barbarian, although at a lower level of economic development, was able to counter the advantages of the more advanced civilization because "the surplus available for war in a barbarian economy constitutes the whole resources at that economy's disposal aside from minimum requirements for food and other 'necessities' " (Rader, 1971, p. 55). It frequently happened that with sufficient time the barbarians surpassed the empire in military capabilities as well:

An explanation of the empire cycle now appears. As the empire and the barbarian meet, the barbarian gradually learns the civilized method of war making. Only steady technical progress in military affairs can keep the empire a step ahead of the barbarian. On the other hand, as the barbarian learns to defend himself against imperial slave expeditions, the slave inflow falls, causing slave incomes at home to rise in order to preserve population equilibrium. Nevertheless, even with no slaves at all, the soldiers of the empire are not likely to be as healthy as the barbarians. Some empires may recruit their soldiers from barbarian lands, but this has the disadvantage of hastening the day when the barbarians can make war as skillfully as can the empire. Eventually, the barbarian is knowledgeable enough to use this superior strength. Small armies of barbarians are able to conquer areas of relatively large population. The empire passes over to plunder and perhaps some barbarian leaders set themselves up as rulers. The outside culture is imposed; the cities which were constructed on tribute disappear, and a "dark" age reigns. So long as the cost of conquest by nearby empires or by a given region is in excess of the tribute from empire, the barbarian economy remains intact. Only the advent of a technical improvement can give one region an advantage over another. When this finally occurs, that region spreads its domination, likely as not enslaves those who are conquered, and constructs a new capital city. There are available cities with substantial resources, which can be the basis of real economic surplus beyond a totally decentralized economy. The empire is reborn under new masters and the cycle begins again (Rader, 1971, pp. 56–7, footnote).

During the cycle of empires, the rise and decline of dominant states were governed principally by (1) the tendency for the cost of the best military techniques to increase with time and (2) the fact that the financial burdens of scale were large relative to the cost of the best armaments (Elvin, 1973, pp. 20–1). For the empire to survive, the economic surplus had to increase faster than the cost of war. In an age of static or low economic growth, this was difficult to achieve over a long period of time; although state revenue might be increased through territorial expansion, at some point this method encountered diminishing returns as territorial expansion added to the financial burden. Under these circumstances of increasing costs, the empire either fragmented or was forced to reduce its territorial control and financial burdens. If it was unable to retrench successfully and thereby bring costs and resources into equilibrium, the empire declined and eventually was succeeded by the next cycle of empires.[5]

---

[5] In a subsequent section this process will be discussed in greater detail.

THE MODERN PATTERN

The cycle of empires was broken in the modern world by three significant interrelated developments: the triumph of the nation-state as the principal actor in international relations; the advent of sustained economic growth based on modern science and technology; the emergence of a world market economy. These developments reinforced one another and in turn led to displacement of the cycle of empires by the European balance-of-power system and, later, a succession of hegemonies in the nineteenth and twentieth centuries.[6] In place of the imperial cycle and imperial control of the international system, the dominant nation-states have balanced one another, or one state has achieved preeminence over the other states in the system. Thus the principal entities, modes of interaction, and mechanisms of control were transformed. An explanation (or at least a first approximation thereto) of this sytems change is the principal purpose of the following sections.

The triumph of the nation-state

The predominant feature of modern international relations has been the emergence of the nation-state as the dominant form of political organization. In the premodern era, the multiethnic empire and localized social formations (tribes, city-states, and feudal entities) constituted the principal actors or entities in international relations. In the modern world, the nation-state has eclipsed every other type of political actor. The reasons for this systems transformation are, of course, extremely complex, provoking intense debate among scholars (North and Thomas, 1973; Anderson, 1974; McNeill, 1974; Wallerstein, 1974; Tilly, 1975). Our discussion here draws heavily on the arguments of Joseph Strayer (1970) and of Douglass North and Robert Thomas (1973) that the nation-state succeeded because it was the most efficient form of political organization for the set of environmental conditions that developed in early modern Europe.

As Strayer put it, the modern state was a political innovation

---

[6] Hegemony, from the Greek, refers to the leadership of one state (the *hegemon*) over other states in the system.

that solved the dilemma faced by the predominant forms of premodern political organization, especially empires and city-states (1970, pp. 11–12). On the one hand, although empires were militarily strong, they were able to enlist and secure the loyalty of only a small fraction of their inhabitants. This lack of identification between the public good of the empire and the private objectives of most citizens was a source of serious weak- ✓ ness; it accounts for the ultimate fragility of empires in the face of internal revolts and external pressures. On the other hand, whereas city-states enjoyed the passionate loyalty of their citizens, they were severely limited in their capacity to generate power; they could not easily incorporate new territories and populations and thereby add to their power. Thus the city-state became either the nucleus of an empire (Rome) or the victim (Greek *polis*) of an empire. As for feudalism, based on a warrior elite and docile serfs, it was characterized both by fragmented political structures and by loose ties of loyalty. Its weakness lay in its failure on both accounts; both scale and strong loyalties were absent. In brief, premodern political forms were plagued ✓ by the inevitable trade-off between scale and loyalty.

The modern nation-state solved the dilemma posed by this trade-off and in doing so triumphed over its political competitors: the city-state, empire, and feudalism. It was able to join large scale with intense loyalty. As Strayer wrote,

The European states which emerged after 1100 combined, to some extent, the strengths of both the empires and the city-states. They were large enough and powerful enough to have excellent chances for survival – some of them are approaching the thousand-year mark, which is a respectable age for any human organization. At the same time they managed to get a large proportion of their people involved in, or at least concerned with the political process, and they succeeded in creating some sense of common identity among local communities. They got more out of their people, both in the way of political and social activity and in loyalty than the ancient empires had done, even if they fell short of the full participation which had marked a city such as Athens (Strayer, 1970, p. 12).

One reason for this achievement and the systems change it entailed has been explained, at least in part, by North and Thomas (1973). The fragmented feudal system of political organization that the nation-state system displaced was the consequence of a peculiar set of economic, political, and military conditions, especially the absence of long-distance trade and the weakness of central political authority. The late Middle Ages were a time of intense personal insecurity, with marauding lawless bands and robber barons alike plundering the weak. Because of the prevailing social conditions and the existing military techniques (the fixed castle and the mounted knight), the localized economy and government of the feudal manor and kingdom were the most efficient mode of economic and political organization (North and Thomas, 1973, p. 19). The lord and his knights supplied protection and welfare (what there was of it) in "exchange" for the labor services of the peasantry. The king (little more than a feudal lord himself) sought to keep the peace and keep his kingdom intact with scarcely adequate resources.

The creation of a market economy and a revolution in military affairs between 900 and 1700 transformed the optimum scale of political organization. On the one hand, the growth of trade and the reemergence of a money economy expanded the revenues available to governments. On the other hand, a series of military innovations (the crossbow, the longbow, the pike, gunpowder, and, most of all, the rise of professional armies) meant an increase in the cost and optimum size of the most efficient military unit (North and Thomas, 1973, p. 17). As a consequence, a halting but ultimately self-reinforcing process took place that led to the displacement of feudal organization by the modern nation-state. First, the revival of trade meant a vast increase in taxable revenue provided that new forms of property rights for traders could be created and also protected. Second, the new types of military weaponry and organization greatly increased the economies of scale and expanded the effective range of military power; these military innovations were extremely costly to finance and were beyond the means of most feudal lords and the traditional resources of the king, thus causing a fiscal crisis for the feudal mode of social organization.

This fiscal crisis of feudalism, as Joseph Schumpeter argued, was produced by the disjuncture between the ever-mounting cost of government, especially warfare, and the inadequate tax base of feudal government (Schumpeter, 1954a, p. 14). The technological revolution in warfare greatly increased the cost of the most efficient weaponry, and the fragmented, inefficient feudal form of economy that preceded the development of a market economy was unable to generate sufficient revenues to pay for the new modes of military power. As a consequence, feudal political organizations were decreasingly able to protect themselves and thus to survive in the changed economic and military environment.

Under this new set of economic and military conditions, it paid some entrepreneurs to provide protection for persons and property rights in exchange for enlarged revenues collected on a much larger scale than previously. However, the changing of economic and political arrangements is a costly affair, as individuals must be forced to alter their behavior in ways contrary to what they regard as their interests. This task of organizational innovation was beyond the military and financial capabilities of the feudal lords. The feudal mode of organization could not adapt to the new set of conditions. Feudal lords had little incentive to expand and protect trade because they lacked the organizational means to collect the revenue generated by increased trade. The protection of economic activities through use of the expensive new military techniques and the collection of the revenues generated by the expansion of trade necessitated a far larger form of political organization than ever existed under feudalism. In short, the new economic and military environment made it possible and profitable to create a new type of economic and political structure that usually was larger.

A fierce struggle began among rulers for revenues to finance the new forms of military power. The transformation of the economic and military environment triggered a Darwinian struggle among political entrepreneurs in which only the strong would survive; the survivors would eventually create the nation-states of Western Europe:

As the demands of a growing market economy thus imposed pressure to establish larger units of government, the multitude of local manors faced the choice of enlarging their own jurisdictions over neighboring manors, combining with other manors to do so, or of surrendering certain of their traditional political prerogatives. Beginning with the rise of the market, throughout Western Europe more and more of the functions of government were assumed by regional and national political units in a growing groundswell leading eventually toward the creation of nation-states.

At this point we can usefully pause in our historical narrative to offer an analogy from economic theory. Take the case of a competitive industry with a large number of small firms. Introduce an innovation which leads to economies of scale over a substantial range of output so that the efficient size for a firm is much larger. The path from the old competitive equilibrium to a new (and probably unstable) oligopoly solution will be as follows. The original small firms must either increase in size, combine, or be forced into bankruptcy. The result is a small number of large firms of optimum size, but even then the results are unstable. There are endless efforts toward collusion and price fixing, but equally ubiquitous are the advantages that will accrue to an individual firm which cheats on the arrangement. The result is periods of truce interrupted by eras of cut-throat competition.

When we translate the above description to the political world of this era we have an exact analogy. Between 1200 and 1500 the many political units of Western Europe went through endless expansions, alliances and combinations in a world of continual intrigue and warfare. Even as the major nation-states emerged, the periods of peace were continually interrupted. In short it was an era of expanding war, diplomacy and intrigue. The magnitude of the increasing cost was staggering. A year of warfare represented at least a fourfold increase in costs of government – and most years were characterized by war, not peace. Monarchs were continuously beset by immense indebtedness and forced to desperate expedients; the specter of bankruptcy was a recurring threat and for many states a reality. The fact of the matter is that princes were not free – they were bound to an unending runaway fiscal crisis (North and Thomas, 1973, p. 95).

At the same time that the feudal form of economic and political organization was inefficient and too small, the other traditional form of organization (the empire) proved to be too large for the prevailing modes of transportation and military techniques.[7] At least in continental Europe, large-scale territorial

---

[7] In effect, the new forms of military power created no economies of scale whose exploitation would necessitate an organization larger than the traditional nation-state within Europe. However, they did permit the creation of mercantile empires outside the European political framework in Asia and the New World.

conquest and empire building became prohibitively expensive; the effort to demonstrate otherwise ruined Spain and the Hapsburgs. The fragmented topography of Europe created barriers to communication and made political unification of the Continent difficult. The existence of comparable levels of development among the several emergent European states and rapid rates of diffusion of technology and organizational techniques among them prevented any state from acquiring a massive advantage over its neighbors (Montesquieu, 1965, p. 39).[8] Finally, that uniquely European institution, the balance-of-power system, kept expansionist powers in check. As a consequence, the several attempts to unify Europe under a universal imperium failed.

The nation-state proved to be the optimum size for political organization under the new set of military and economic conditions. Although the cost of the best military techniques had incrased as in the past, the financial burdens of scale had decreased because of advances in organization and transportation (Elvin, 1973, p. 21). Additionally, the increased rate of economic growth and the expansion of the tax base meant that state revenues could rise faster than the costs of the best military techniques. For these reasons the nation-state displaced the feudal, city-state, and imperial forms of organization; it was simply more efficient, given the changed economic and military environment.

Although the state as an institution has a long history, the modern nation-state is qualitatively different from its predecessors in the premodern era.[9] In the first place, there is a strong central authority that is differentiated from other social organizations, and it exercises control over a well-defined and contiguous territory. The sovereign has a monopoly over the legitimate use

[8] As oligopoly theory tells us, the intense political rivalries of these European states gave a major stimulus to technical innovation. In contrast to the relatively static empires of Asia (political monopolies), European states were forced to innovate new forms of military technology and social organization simply to stay ahead of their competitors (McNeill, 1974, pp. 124–6). The impetus given by this oligopolistic competition to European energies was a factor in their supremacy over older civilizations.

[9] The general characterization of the nation-state presented here obviously has exceptions. It is, in Max Weber's terms, an ideal type. The primary sources from which this description has been drawn include the following: Bendix (1973), Gilbert (1975), Hawtrey (1952), Hicks (1969), North and Thomas (1973), Schumpeter (1954a), Strachey (1964), and Tilly (1975).

of force and is served by a bureaucracy and single set of laws that reach down into the everyday lives of the people. In contrast, the Roman state restricted its interests to the army and finances (Hintze in Bendix, 1973, p. 164). Second, the society and the economy of the modern state are characterized by a complex class structure and division of labor; earlier societies, based on simpler economies, tended to be composed of an elite and a mass, or else of functional estates. Third, the ideology of nationalism fosters internal cohesion and intense loyalty to the state; the identification with and commitment to the welfare of the state by its populace seldom occurred in earlier societies, with the exception of tribes and city-states.

The essence of the modern state is that it consists in a set of laws, beliefs, and institutions for creating and using power. It is consolidated and organized internally in order to increase its power externally (Collins, in Bendix, 1973, p. 59). The modern state, in contrast to premodern empires, tends toward intensive rather than extensive development (Hintze in Bendix, 1973, pp. 163–4). Through its taxation and conscription policies the modern state has the capacity to mobilize the wealth and services of its citizenry to advance the power and interests of the state. As noted earlier, however, whether these interests are defined as the aggrandizement of a Louis XIV or as the welfare of the people is dependent on the nature of the society; no attempt is being made here to reify the state and set it apart from the society to which it is ultimately responsible.

A fundamental and novel feature of the modern state is its role in the economy. Although there were important exceptions, the economic function of the premodern state was primarily to facilitate exploitation of the masses by the elite and to protect society from being exploited by foreign conquerors. In contrast, the primary function of the modern state has become the promotion of economic development through creation of an internal technical infrastructure, removal of obstacles to the formation of a unified domestic market, and intervention in the economy in more direct ways. In effect, the state (representing the emergent middle class and its interests), as Schumpeter argued, liberated people to work and create wealth that could then be taxed for purposes of

domestic welfare and national power (Schumpeter, 1954a; Hawtrey, 1952, p. 57).

The nation-state triumphed over other forms of political organization because it solved the fiscal crisis of feudalism (Schumpeter, 1954a, p. 14). As mercantilist writers appreciated, the
success of the nation-state was due to its war-making capability
and its fiscal capability; the military evolution and fiscal evolution of the modern nation-state were part and parcel of the same
historical development. This fact accounts in large measure for
the continued viability of the nation-state. For the past several
centuries it has transcended all other forms of political organization. Contrary to the oft-repeated idea that the nation-state is
disappearing as a form of political organization, it is encompassing more and more of mankind. The process of state formation
that began in western Europe is still transforming the rest of the
globe as one people after another demand their own state in
order to secure what they regard as their rights.

The breakthrough to economic growth

The second major change in the character of international relations in the modern era has been the greatly enhanced role of
economic growth and technological advance in the international
distribution of wealth and power. In the imperial age, various
societies had known periods of economic growth (i.e., an increase
in wealth per capita), but their magnitudes and durations were
modest. In these preindustrial societies, social, political, and especially technological constraints placed severe limits on the
capital accumulation and productive efficiency necessary for
long-term economic growth. Although these limits began to disappear in the early modern era, it was the enduring technological breakthroughs associated with the Industrial Revolution that
first caused the great, unprecedented advances in wealth and
power. Economic growth became cumulative and self-sustaining
because modern industrial technology made it possible for certain societies to escape, at least for a time, the classic Malthusian
problem of diminishing returns.

Modern economic growth strengthened the relationship between wealth and power, and in doing so it profoundly altered the nature of international relations. As already noted, the cycle of empires was generated largely by the tendency for the costs of the best military techniques to rise faster than state revenues, causing the state either to fragment or to fall behind its rising rivals. The breakthrough to economic growth overcame this limit. A growing economy could afford the best military techniques and stay ahead of its rivals with lower rates of economic growth. Henceforth, the relative rates of economic growth among societies, the sizes of the economic bases of the societies, and the proportions of total outputs devoted to defense would increasingly determine the power and position of states in the international system (Elvin, 1973, p. 18).

In the premodern world, wealth and power did not necessarily coincide. On the contrary, as McNeill demonstrated in *The Shape of European History* (1974), throughout the premodern era the more wealthy and more economically advanced societies were frequently destroyed and plundered by economically less advanced societies. These rougher peoples were more powerful militarily because they had numerical superiority or had developed a radical new form of military organization and technology or simply were a more hardy and martial breed. Moreover, as was pointed out earlier, in barbarian societies, although the economic surplus available for war was relatively small, it constituted all the resources of the society above the subsistence level.

When agriculture was the basis of wealth, demographic changes, innovations in military or political organization, and random technological developments were frequently the foremost factors underlying political change and the uneven growth of power among states. The accumulation of wealth through exploitation usually followed rather than preceded military conquest; through the exacting of tribute, plunder, and enslavement of conquered peoples, the militarily powerful acquired wealth. Although the advent of modern industry obviously did not end the exploitation of the weak by the strong, it did enhance the direct relationship between wealth and power. Economic wealth and military power became increasingly synonymous.

The frequent separation of wealth and power had continued as late as the seventeenth century. After the Thirty Years' War and the decline of the Hapsburg hegemony (Spain and Austria), the centers of political-military power were France and Sweden, whereas England and Holland were the expanding economic and commercial centers of Europe. Mercantilists who appreciated the increasing economic dimensions of power recognized that a change was taking place. Treasure was needed to purchase arms, hire soldiers, and finance foreign campaigns; to obtain treasure, a nation had to have a favorable balance of trade. But it was not until the Industrial Revolution that economic and military power became securely united in the modern world.

Although, the Spanish Empire was the last in which massive accumulation of wealth followed conquest, the relationship between wealth and power began to change in the late medieval period. It was then that Europe began to surpass its rival civilization in economic growth (Jones, 1981). The supremacy of Europe was based on its technological mastery of sea power, its perfection of artillery, and its social organization, as well as its overall economic superiority (Cipolla, 1965).[10] In its early phase, European imperialism brutally plundered the non-European societies of their precious metals and luxury goods. Then, with the advent of modern industry, technological advance and economic efficiency became the most efficient means to gain wealth and power. Thus, there took place a shift in the relative importance of productive technology and control of territory as factors in the uneven growth of wealth and power among political entities (McNeill, 1967, p. 299). Although both economic development and territorial control (or at least access to territory) were and continue to be the bases of wealth and power, the Industrial Revolution greatly enhanced the relative importance of productive technology in the generation of wealth and power. As Friedrich List (1856, p. 208) put it, "the power of creating wealth is then vastly more important than wealth itself."

As several writers have argued, the reason for this change in the basis of state power was that the western European nation-state succeeded for the first time in history in creating a rela-

[10] A major factor contributing to this supremacy was "the extraordinary bellicosity of Europeans" (McNeill, 1954, p. 29).

tively efficient economic organization (North and Thomas, 1973, p. 157; Anderson, 1974, p. 399). Through trial and error, Europeans created and protected a set of property rights and a concept of human freedom that narrowed the gap between the private and social rates of return; consequently, individuals (though obviously a privileged number) were induced to undertake productive economic activities. In contrast to the situation with its predecessors, a major objective of the modern state has been to use its authority to favor the activities of those individuals who contribute most to economic development (Hawtrey, 1952, pp. 18–19). To give an example, the creation of the first patent law in the seventeenth century (the concept of intellectual property) gave individuals an incentive to engage in inventive activities and thereby set the stage for the Industrial Revolution (North and Thomas, 1973, pp. 155–6).

The initial creation of an efficient economic organization and the breakthrough to sustained economic/technological development took place in the Netherlands and shortly thereafter in Great Britain. In these countries, "a fortunate conjuncture occurred between the interests of the state and the interests of the progressive sector of society" (North and Thomas, 1973, p. 132). In these societies the rising middle classes refashioned social and economic arrangements in order to take advantage of the new opportunities for gaining wealth that environmental changes had created. They invented new forms of property rights and economic institutions that facilitated economic growth and technological advance. As is the case with any successful innovation, this new institutional framework for economic growth was subsequently adopted with various modifications and improvements by other European countries, the United States, Japan, and more slowly today by the so-called developing countries. As a consequence of this economic and technological transformation, the German historian Otto Hintze observed that the primary determinant of the wealth and power of a state in the modern world is the internal efficiency and ordering of the society itself: "The characteristic feature of modern international relations is not the states' drive toward unlimited expansion of their power, but is rather their drive to round off their territory in a more favorable way and to consolidate more firmly" (quoted in Gilbert, 1975, p. 432).

From the seventeenth century onward the character of modern statecraft was profoundly affected by the discovery that economic growth contributed to the national interest and power (Hicks, 1969, pp. 61–2). Mercantilism and its identification of the pursuit of power and plenty as desirable and inseparable goals provided the initial acknowledgment of the changing relationship between the economy and the state (Viner, 1958, p. 286). Expansion of exports and manufactures and achievement of a favorable balance of payments became major goals of state policy. Statesmen became increasingly preoccupied with the international economy and the position of the state in the international division of labor. This concern was a response to the third characteristic of modern international relations: the creation of a world market economy.

The creation of a world market economy

In the modern era, both the domestic and international economies that have replaced the previous localized and imperial economies have become increasingly integrated into a complex web of market relations in which relative prices determine the flow of goods and services among groups and states. Although the more recent rise of socialist and communist-type economies has partially slowed, if not reversed, this trend toward economic interdependence, the world market economy remains a principal feature of the international system in the final decades of the twentieth century.

A market economy constitutes a significant change from more traditional types of economic exchange in both domestic and international terms. Previously, three types of economic exchange were predominant. First and most prevalent was localized exchange. This type of exchange was highly restricted in terms of goods and geographic scope; in general, it was barter trade. Second, there were the command economies of successive great empires; in these planned economies, the production, distribution, and prices of commodities were controlled by the state bureaucracy. Third, there was the long-distance trade in high-value goods. The caravan routes of Asia and Africa were the principal loci of this trade. Although this trade may be said to have constituted a world market, in comparison with modern world trade it involved only a narrow range of goods (spices, silks, slaves, precious metals, etc.) and was based on the absolute advantages of different geographic regions in the production of particular goods.

Stated in simple terms, a market economy involves a market-place wherein goods and services are exchanged to maximize the returns to individual buyers and sellers. Although markets can exist with respect to all types of commodities (goods, labor, capital, etc.), the nature of the market depends on two characteristics: openness and competition. This means that markets may differ with respect to the freedom of individuals to enter and with respect to the extent to which particular buyers or sellers can influence the terms of the exchange. A perfect or self-regulating market is one that is open to all potential buyers and sellers and in which no individual can determine the terms of the exchange. The relative prices of various commodities tend to govern this flow, and a tendency exists for all factors of production (land, labor, and capital), depending on their mobilities, to be rewarded equally throughout this market.

At least in theory, and occasionally in practice, a market system is not subordinate to society or the state. Although the parameters of exchange are set by the larger goals and needs of the society, market forces operate by a logic of their own. The market is composed of individuals seeking to enhance their own objectives, and the outcome of exchange in a self-regulating market is determined by economic "laws," such as those of comparative advantage and of supply and demand, subject to constraints set by the society's values and the security interests of the state. Thus, under a market system, the economy constitutes a more or less autonomous sphere.

The rationale for a market system is that it increases economic efficiency and maximizes economic growth. The objective of economic activity is not explicitly to enhance the power and security of the state (though it usually does so nevertheless) but ultimately to benefit consumers. It holds, if you will, that it is more blessed to consume than to produce. Thus, Smith and other proponents of the market system have tended to deemphasize the security and other costs of the market system. However, disruption of the society's traditional values and increased vulnerability to external influences are frequently among the costs of increasing market interdependence among national economies.

A market system of exchange is a radical departure indeed from the ways in which societies had traditionally organized their economies. Societies throughout history placed much greater emphasis on security values, such as military power, social stability, and self-sufficiency, than on rises in real income through an unfettered market mechanism. This was the case with feudal societies, ancient empires, and tribal kingdoms. There were, of course, exceptions. The city-state systems of classical Greece and the Hellenistic Mediterranean economy, for example, did contain a peculiar set of conditions that enabled markets to break free from social and political constraints. But their durations were brief on the scale of historical time.

Societies freely enter into extensive market relations only when the perceived gains are much greater than the perceived costs or when the market relations are forced on them by a superior society. Therefore, it is not surprising that the champions of an interdependent world market economy have been politically the most powerful and economically the most efficient nations. Both elements, hegemony and efficiency, are necessary preconditions for a society to champion the creation of an interdependent market economy. Hegemony without efficiency tends to move toward imperial-type economies, as is the case in the Soviet bloc. National economic efficiency without a corresponding political-military strength may not be able to induce other powerful societies to assume the costs of a market system. Thus the economically efficient but militarily weak Japanese continually fear exclusion from foreign markets by tariff barriers. Because the precondition of combined political hegemony and economic efficiency has infrequently existed, it is not surprising that market systems have been few in the past and that the two great champions of market systems in the modern world have been

Great Britain in the nineteenth century and the United States in the twentieth.

The association of the global market system with the political and economic fortunes first of Great Britain and then of the United States provides one clue to the reasons why the market system of exchange emerged in the modern era and in time became the predominant mode of organizing international economic relations. However, it is not enough to focus on these two economies and their interests. The market system (or what today we call international economic interdependence) runs so counter to the great bulk of human experience that only extraordinary changes and novel circumstances could have led to its innovation and triumph over other means of economic exchange.

The rise of a world market economy was the result of a number of factors: dramatic and rapid improvements in communications and transportation; the political success of the rising middle class; the discovery of the New World. Three other factors should also be emphasized because of their impact on the nature of international relations: the monetarization of economic relations; the "innovation" of private property; the structure of the European state system.

The monetarization of an economy has a revolutionary effect on politics because it deepens and extends the market. A monetarized market greatly accelerates the accumulation of wealth, the expansion of international commerce, and the centralization of political power; it dissolves traditional social relations and encourages the creation of larger and more complex forms of social, economic, and political organization. It makes possible an extensive and more efficient division of labor (Clough, 1970, p. 165). It facilitates the mobilization of wealth for war and thereby increases the scale of military power and warfare. Money itself becomes a form of power.[11] For all these reasons, the introduction of a monetarized market economy into an international sys-

---

[11] As Ralph Hawtrey has shown, the power of society is dependent not so much on the quantity of its wealth as on the mobility of its wealth. Mobility refers to the availability of taxable wealth to the state, especially for military purposes. It is vitally affected by the transportation system, the concentration of wealth in economic centers, and the degree of monetarization of the economy (Hawtrey, 1952, pp. 60–3).

tem has far-reaching consequences for political and military relations as well as economic relations (Andreski, 1971, pp. 84–7).
The monetarization of the ancient Greek economy, for example,
transformed all aspects of international relations, as revealed in
the following observation:

The consequences of the spread of money and markets are, clearly,
enormous. Even warfare is affected. The Greeks who fought the Trojan
War took ten years to do so, because their forces had to scatter and live
off the countryside. By the time of the great Peloponnesian War, however, the market and its sutlers (merchants following an army to buy up
booty for resale elsewhere) had coped with the logistical problems of
servicing major concentrations of manpower. The scope and scale of
warfare changed in consequence (Carney, 1973, p. 25; footnote deleted).

In similar fashion, the flow of New World gold and silver into
Europe in the sixteenth and seventeenth centuries and the gradual diffusion of the market system had a profound economic,
political, and security impact (Clough, 1970, p. 193). The vast
expansion of the money supply led to increasing monetarization
of the economy and vast expansion of the market exchange system. The demand for money grew apace, and the accumulation
of bullion became a major preoccupation of the state.

In particular, the monetarization of the European economy
financed the revolution in military affairs and the modern
nation-state. Both the rise of professional armies and the creation of supporting national bureaucracies required money, and
lots of it. The nature of war changed; war was transformed from
a clash between societies to an instrument of national policy for
emerging nation-states in pursuit of their various national interests (Clark, 1958). The monetarization of economies and the rise
of the nation-state as essentially a war-making machine went
hand in hand. On a world scale, the rise of a monetarized market
economy and the mobilization of wealth it made possible were
major factors in the military triumph of the West over earlier
civilizations (Clough, 1970, pp. 165, 192–5).

A further reason for the rise and spread of a market economy
and for its impact was a decrease in transactions costs, especially
the costs of defining and enforcing property rights. In the pre-

modern era, the non-price-based allocation of goods and services was more efficient because the costs of enforcing property rights exceeded the benefits. For this reason, reciprocity and distributive forms of exchange predominated. Improvements in transportation, the revolution in military affairs, and the growth of the money supply decreased the costs and increased the benefits of creating new forms of property rights. This development, in turn, made it possible to organize economic transactions in terms of free competitive markets (i.e., the exchange of property rights over goods and services on the basis of price). The greater efficiency of this form of exchange led to stimulation of economic growth and displacement of premodern non-price-based systems of exchange (North, 1977, p. 710).

The diffusion of the market economy throughout western Europe and the enforcement of private property rights throughout the world vastly increased the role of economic factors as important elements of national power; this enabled the Europeans to mobilize their resources in the interest of growth and power, surpassing all other civilizations. Subsequently, the incorporation of more and more countries into the global market economy through the universal recognition of European private property rights (rights protected by Western military power) meant that the market became an increasingly important nexus of international relations. As a consequence of these developments, the position of a state in the world market (the so-called international division of labor) became a principal determinant, if not the principal determinant, of its status in the international system.

In the new international environment created by the advent of sustained economic growth and a world market economy, the tendency of states to expand as their power grew underwent a profound transformation. Whereas in the premodern world, expansion principally took the form of territorial expansion, political expansion and economic expansion have tended to characterize growing states in the modern world. The primary objectives of increasing numbers of states have been to extend their political influence over other states and to increase their dominance over the world market economy. Through specialization and international trade an efficient state could gain more than through territorial expansion and conquests. The expanded market and the diversity of available resources made possible by trade were spurs to the growth of wealth and power of those states best able to take advantage of the change in world conditions. For these states, trade proved to be more profitable than imperial tribute (Lane, 1942, p. 269).

A further condition that was necessary for the emergence of a world market economy was the structure of the international political system. An economy exists within a social and political framework that both permits and proscribes certain types of economic activities; the economy, at least in the short run, is subordinate to the larger social and political goals of the society. It does not exist in an autonomous sphere governed solely by economic laws. In the words of E. H. Carr, "the science of economics presupposes a given political order, and cannot be profitably studied in isolation from politics" (1951, p. 117).

In the modern world, the emergence of a world market economy was dependent on the pluralistic structure of the European (and, subsequently, the global) political system. In the premodern era, flourishing international markets such as those of Greece and the Hellenistic period were eventually displaced by expanding imperial economies (Hicks, 1969, p. 41). But in the modern period, the failure of the several efforts to unify Europe politically permitted the expansion of a market-type international economy. The absence of an imperial power to organize and control production and exchange gave free rein to market forces.[12] As a consequence, the market system has come to encompass more and more of the globe since its beginning in the seventeenth century.

The first phase of this emerging world market economy was the mercantilist era of the seventeenth and eighteenth centuries. Mercantilist doctrines and policies were responses to the increasing importance of commerce and overseas colonies to the power of the emerging European nation-states. The conflicts of this era

[12] This interpretation of the rise of a market economy was put forth by two contemporary authors with very different ideological perspectives. Jean Baechler (1971) used this idea to support the superiority of capitalism over other forms of economic organization. Immanuel Wallerstein (1974) presented a quasi-Marxist critique of capitalism.

largely revolved around the efforts of one state or another to gain control over the new sources of wealth in Asia and the New World (Gilbert, 1961, pp. 20, 46). This era came to a close with the British defeat of France in the Napoleonic wars and the creation of the Pax Britannica, which ushered in the second phase of the modern world market economy. In an earlier work, we set forth in brief terms the nature of and reasons for this change:

Throughout the late seventeenth and eighteenth centuries, the five littoral states of Western Europe – Portugal, Spain, the Netherlands, France, and Britain – fought over the economic exploitation of Asia and America. One by one, these contenders for control of overseas mercantilistic empires and for European hegemony were eliminated until only France and England remained. The former, supreme on the continent of Europe, was the dominant power at that time. The latter, dominant on the high seas, was the rising challenger.

Although both powers were growing in wealth and power, after 1750 British power had begun a more rapid advance due to the accelerating pace of the Industrial Revolution and to British control of access to America and Asia. Favored by rich veins of coal, deposits of iron, and an enterprising population, Britain began to take the lead in the technologies of the first phase of the Industrial Revolution – textiles, iron, and steam power. The growth of the British economy and the relative decline of French power caused increasing disequilibrium between France's dominant position and her capacity to maintain it. Eventually this struggle between a declining France and a rising Great Britain gave rise to the wars during the period of the French Revolution and Napoleonic era.

At issue in the clash between industrial Great Britain and Napoleonic France were two fundamentally opposed systems for organizing the world's economy – and ultimately, of course, for dominating the globe. Whereas the ideal of the older mercantilism had been the integration of national economies with colonial dependencies, the struggle between England and France reflected the commercial and productive potentialities of the Industrial Revolution. Great Britain, in command of the sea and leading in the productive technologies of the Industrial Revolution, desired the creation of a world economy centered on her industrial and financial core.

The objective of Napoleon, on the other hand, through the instrumentality of the Continental System, was to develop the economy of Continental Europe, with France as its main center. As the dominant power of an integrated regional economy, France would be able to arrest her own decline and destroy England's lucrative commerce with the continent; eventually a unified Europe under French leadership could itself take to the sea. This regionalization of the world economy under France would destroy the economic basis of British power and restore French grandeur. But with the final defeat of Napoleon at Waterloo, the last French effort to challenge British economic and political predominance came to an end. From then until the latter part of the nineteenth century, no nation would have the economic and territorial base to challenge British world hegemony.

The *Pax Britannica,* which determined the general structure of international relations until the collapse of the system under the impact of World War I, transformed the conduct and general features of international economic relations. At its height (1849–80), the *Pax Britannica* emphasized an open, interdependent world economy based on free trade, nondiscrimination, and equal treatment rather than one based on the control and possession of colonies. Although Great Britain and several other European powers retained the remnants of colonial empires, the conquest of territory and colonies declined in importance. Behind the shield of British command of the seas, British trade and investment had relatively free access to the world's markets and sources of raw materials.

The political order identified with the *Pax Britannica,* which constituted the necessary condition for the British strategy of portfolio investment, had two critical elements. The first was the redistribution of territory following the Napoleonic wars. The territorial settlement reached at the Congress of Vienna and the related negotiations may be divided into two parts. First, the redistribution of territory on the continent of Europe checked the ambitions of Russia in the east and France in the west. Second, the overseas conquests of the continental powers were reduced and Great Britain acquired a number of important strategic bases abroad. As a consequence, the four major powers on the continent were kept in check by their own rivalries and by Britain, which, having no direct interests at stake on the continent, could play a balancing and mediating role.

The second major element of the *Pax Britannica* was British naval supremacy. It was able to exercise a powerful and pervasive influence over global politics owing to a fortuitous juncture of other circumstances. Britain's geographic position directly off the coast of continental Europe and her possession of naval bases strategically located throughout the world enabled her to control continental Europe's access to the outside world and to deny overseas colonies to her European rivals. Among these strategic control points were what Admiral Lord Fisher called "the five keys" which "lock up the world": Gibraltar, Singapore, Dover, the Cape of Good Hope, and Alexandria. As a consequence, from 1825, when Great Britain warned Russia not to take advantage of the revolt of Spanish America, until the latter part of the century, the greater part of the non-European world was either largely independent (at least, politically) of European rule or else under British rule. It was in the British interest and was within British power to prevent both the reemergence of mercantilism and the struggle on the part of the European powers for exclusive overseas empires. Controlling the seas and access to the globe, the British had little need for the possession of overseas colonies in order to exploit the world's markets and riches.

In effect, as noted above, two complementary subsystems emerged from the Napoleonic wars and the subsequent peace treaties. Outside Europe there was the maritime realm, governed by British naval power. On the continent, the status quo was preserved partially by the British in their role as balancer, but principally by the distribution of power among the major states. The central features of this continental equilibrium were: the fragmentation of German power among scores of minor principalities, a growing but still relatively small Prussia, and a conservative, multi-ethnic Austro-Hungarian Empire. Thus, politically fragmented, largely agrarian, and lacking good land transportation, continental Europe was relatively stable until the unification of Germany under Prussian hegemony by the force of arms and the railroad.

The British possessed the further advantage of being able to preserve their global hegemony and the status quo at a minimal cost. Given their geographical position, they could bottle up the continent with relatively few ships; only with the re-emergence of the French navy and, more importantly, with the German navy in the latter part of the century could a continental naval power threaten British supremacy. Outside the continent there were really no challenging states until late in the century when the United States and Japan became important naval powers. With the rise of these challenging naval powers, maintaining hegemony would become a heavy economic burden for the British. But until then, as Susan Strange has put it, the British empire was like a Model-T Ford: "It was comparatively easy to assemble and comparatively cheap to run."

In addition to these political and strategic factors, another necessary condition for the British strategy of portfolio investment was a technological revolution in transportation. Communications and transportation by land and by sea were revolutionized with the invention of cheap steel and the application of steam power to sea and land transport. The steamship decreased the time, cost, and risk of marine transportation, thereby having a profound effect on economic relations as well as on the exercise of military power. It made possible specialization and an international division of labor on an unprecedented global scale.

To understand why Great Britain took advantage of this strategic and technological situation so as to create an interdependent world economy, one must appreciate the revolution which took place in British economic thought, namely, the triumph of liberalism.

The essence of the teaching of Adam Smith and of later free traders was that wealth from trade was due to the exchange of goods, not to territorial possession. Smith and other liberals argued that the costs and disadvantages of empire and territorial control outweighed the benefits; that imperial self-sufficiency and exclusive economic spheres impeded the natural flow of trade and handicapped growth; and that British supremacy rested on manufacturing, not on empire. They pointed out that England, with only half the population of France, was turning out two-thirds of the world's coal and half of its iron and cloth. Technologically more advanced than her competitors, the liberals argued, Britain could capture world markets with cheaper goods. Why, then, they inquired, should Britain restrict her trade to a closed empire when the whole world lay open and desired her goods? Britain's interest lay in universal free trade and the removal of all barriers to the exchange of goods. Through concentration on industrial efficiency, Great Britain could create an empire of trade rather than one of colonies.

The objective of British foreign economic policy became the creation of complementary economic relations between the British industrial core and an overseas periphery which would supply cheap food, raw materials, and markets. Through the migration of labor and the export of capital to developing lands (the United States, Canada, Australia, and so forth) Britain could acquire cheap imports and also develop a market for her growing industrial exports. She could sell her textiles, invest her capital, and purchase necessities nearly wherever she pleased. In the words of the distinguished economist Stanley Jevons, "Unfettered commerce . . . has made the several quarters of the globe our willing tributaries" (Gilpin, 1975, pp. 79–84; text revised).

Thus the message of Adam Smith and other liberal free traders in their attacks on mercantilism was that empire was no longer cost-effective. In the industrial era, Great Britain had more to gain by exploiting her comparative industrial advantage and technological superiority in world markets than by acquiring an overseas empire. In the early nineteenth century, these doctrines of free trade and laissez-faire were accepted by Great Britain's rising middle class. In time, a primary objective of British foreign policy became the creation of a world market economy based on free trade, freedom of capital movements, and a unified international monetary system. The achievement of this objective required primarily the creation and enforcement of a set of international rules protecting private property rights rather than the more costly and less beneficial task of conquering an empire.[13] In the nineteenth century this responsibility fell mainly on Great Britain; in the middle of the twentieth century the United States assumed this task.

In the modern era, expansion by means of the world market economy and extension of political influence have largely displaced empire and territorial expansion as a means of acquiring wealth (McNeill, 1954; 1974). The principal reason for this change is that markets are much more efficient than other forms of human organization. Through specialization in the international division of labor, everyone can benefit from international exchange. The larger the market and the greater the volume of transactions, the greater the efficiency of the market and the overall maximization of wealth. Thus states have an incentive to participate in the international economy and share in the benefits of an enlarged trading system.

Although most states tend to benefit in absolute terms from the operation of the world market economy, the more efficient and more technologically advanced economies tend to benefit relatively more than other states. They enjoy higher rates of profit and more favorable terms of trade. As a consequence, a market economy tends, up to a point, to concentrate wealth in the more advanced economies. For this reason, the dominant economic (and military) powers in the modern era (Great Britain

---

[13] The major exception to this anti-imperial stance of the British until the revival of empire-building in the late nineteenth century was India. The possession of India was a critical factor in England's global political and economic position.

in the nineteenth century and the United states in the twentieth century) assumed the responsibility of organizing and defending the world market economy; they promoted free trade, provided investment capital, and supplied the international currency. In effect, they provided the public goods necessary for the functioning of efficient world markets because it was profitable for them to do so.

A distinguishing feature of the modern world has been that superior economic competitiveness and superior military power have tended to accompany one another. Great Britain and the United States have had an incentive to use their military power to create a competitive world market economy. In the past, on the other hand, economic efficiency and military efficiency did not necessarily coincide. Historically, in fact, as Montesquieu long ago observed, commercial powers in the premodern period usually became the prey of more aggressive military powers (Montesquieu, 1965, p. 47), and even today this still occurs. It should be noted that the Soviet Union has used its superior military power to organize the Eastern European economies into a rather traditional imperial-type command economy. Also, a relative decline in the economic efficiency of a dominant power stimulates moves toward economic protectionism, as is happening with the United States in the latter decades of the twentieth century. In short, although the efficiency and benefits of a world market economy were factors in its predominance over localism and imperial-type economies, it is worth noting that the dominant powers enforced the rules that made this possible, and they did so because they believed it to be in their economic interests. This may not be the case in the future.

The numerous wars and conquests of the past century and a half appear to challenge the thesis that the significance of territorial control and expansion has declined in the modern world. However, we do not intend to assert that territorial control and noneconomic forms of expansion have ceased to be important; indeed, this is obviously not correct. However, it is the case that, at least for established states (an important qualification), internal economic efficiency has become the more important source of wealth. Although Alastair Buchan overstated the point, there is a fundamental truth in his statement "that there is nothing which a country can now do to augment its prosperity, power, or status by way of territorial expansion which it cannot also do by the stimulation of technology and by capital investment within its existing boundaries" (Porter, 1972, p. 177).

Furthermore, if the importance of territorial conquest has declined, how is one to account for the late-nineteenth-century overseas imperialism in which, during three or four decades, sub-Saharan Africa and many other territories were colonized by the major powers? Again, this is a valid point. It is noteworthy, however, that these overseas conquests had become relatively inexpensive because of nineteenth-century advances in transportation and the vast military superiority of the Europeans. In effect, outside of Europe, empire building had once again become profitable. Yet, by historical standards, these late-nineteenth-century empires in themselves were of relatively little consequence. They did not weigh heavily in the global balance of power.[14] They were remarkably short-lived because the colonized people quickly learned the ways of the colonizers, and in a few decades revolting colonial peoples made empire once again no longer cost-effective. Today, these former colonial peoples are creating states of their own.

Of more significance is the fact that the purpose of these overseas empires was less to plunder and exploit (though both occurred) than to provide a stable legal and political framework for trade and investment, that is, protection of European property rights (Hawtrey, 1952, p. V–VI). What the colonial powers most frequently desired was to have exclusive commercial rights or, alternatively, to prevent other nations from excluding their traders and investors from potential markets. In the judgment of Lionel Robbins, the primary motive (certainly in the case of the biggest imperialist power of them all, Great Britain) was to keep overseas territories open for British traders and investors (Robbins, 1971, pp. 246–7). When Great Britain was no longer able

---

[14] The major exception, as stated earlier, was India, which was a major ingredient in Great Britain's world position. However, it was a holdover from the earlier preindustrial phase of colonialism. Even so, its profitability for the British is a matter of dispute among scholars.

to contain the imperialist ambitions of its continental European rivals because of its relative decline in power, it engaged in a massive effort of "preclusive" imperialism; the object of colonialism, in other words, was to minimize potential losses more than to maximize potential gains. Indeed, with the exception of minerals production in particular areas (the gold of South Africa, the copper of the Belgian Congo, the tin of Malaya, etc.), these late-nineteenth-century empires were not especially profitable (Condliffe, 1950, p. 235).

For the colonized peoples themselves, the most significant impact of these empires resulted from the unleashing of market forces. It was market forces, more than deliberate exploitation and political subjugation, that had such a devastating effect on traditional cultures (McNeill, 1954, p. 45).[15] As has already been noted, markets and a money economy are highly destructive of traditional society; they transform every aspect of life. It is precisely for this reason that they are frequently resisted by those who suffer their impact. In retrospect, the most serious charge made against the nineteenth-century imperial system is that it weakened the traditional cultures and the localized economies while putting little in their place (Condliffe, 1950, p. 316). Deprived of a government of their own, colonies lacked the opportunity to resist these forces and create an efficient internal economic organization. Whether or not they would have done so in the absence of colonial rule is, alas, a large unanswerable question.

Finally, although there were major military conflicts and territorial conquests on the continent of Europe and elsewhere during the nineteenth century, they were basically incidental aspects of state building. The obvious success of the nation-state as an economic and political entity stimulated one people after another to seek national unity and thereby gave rise to the several wars of national unification. However, a fundamental purpose of na-

[15] A major difference between ancient and modern empires is that the former transformed the religion and civilization of the conquered peoples; thus, Arab and other conquerors converted a great swath of humanity to Islam. In contrast, the primary impact of Western imperialism and the market forces associated with it was to uproot traditional peasant societies. Whereas these societies have tended to accept Western science and technology, they have generally rejected its moral and religious values, especially in those cases in which powerful religions held sway.

tional unity was to create the social and political framework for internal economic development and to resist untoward consequences of the world market system; it was seldom a revival of the imperial game of territorial conquest for the sake of exploitation – a game discovered by Napoleonic France to be costly in an age of nationalism.

Contemporary Marxists and dependency theorists would object to the preceding analysis. In particular, they would counter that capitalistic exploitation of lesser-developed peoples, rather than efficient internal organization, explains the maldistribution of wealth in the contemporary world. The rich are rich, and the poor are poor, it is argued, because the latter have been exploited and stripped of their wealth by the former.

Although plunder and exploitation have taken place, they have not been of sufficient magnitude to account for the existing distribution of wealth among countries. The external transfer of wealth from colonies to colonial powers cannot possibly explain the distribution of wealth and power in the contemporary world. Moreover, international economic relations have existed primarily among the more advanced countries themselves. Furthermore, as Marx and Lenin correctly acknowledged, trade and investment between advanced economies and less advanced economies tend to favor and develop the latter (Avineri, 1969; Lenin, 1939). A more legitimate point would be that the patterns of trade and investment created by capitalist economies distorted or bypassed certain less developed economies, thus thwarting economic growth and development.

Although capitalist economies had an incentive to colonize the world, they also have an incentive to develop it, as Marx and Lenin fully appreciated. The capitalists cannot realize even their ill-gotten profits unless they are willing to transfer capital, technology, and managerial skills to colonies and dependent economies. It was precisely for this reason that nineteenth-century Marxists regarded capitalist imperialism, despite its many crimes, as ultimately progressive and a necessary step to the emancipation of the human race from poverty and millennia of stagnation: "England has to fulfill a double mission in India: one destructive, the other regenerating – the annihilation of old Asiatic society, and the laying of the material foundations of Western society in Asia" (Marx, quoted by Avineri, 1969, pp. 132–3). On the other hand, one does not find a similar redeeming feature in socialism or communism. Such economies must be based either on strong bonds of fellowship and community or on governmental coercion. The human capacity for community and cooperation with one's fellows appears to be very limited, and socialist economies of this communal type (e.g., utopian communes, Israeli kibbutzim) have been based on strong ideological or religious ties. Although these socialist communities may not exploit others, they have little incentive to benefit others outside the narrow bounds of the religious or ideological community.

Likewise, communist systems based on coercion have no strong incentive to develop other societies, including fellow communist economies. The Soviet Union, for political reasons, has provided financial and technical assistance to several underdeveloped countries such as Cuba, Egypt, and, of course, China. As has been the case with American official foreign aid, such economic and technical transfers are motivated more by political and military considerations than by the economic and developmental needs of recipient countries. Finally, although trade involving communist countries may benefit all concerned, it is seldom of sufficient magnitude to be "the engine of growth" that one finds in capitalist trading relations.

The political significance of the world market economy created by capitalism was that it developed the world. For Marx, this was indeed the historic mission of international capitalism. Although the dominant capitalist power may gain the most (at least initially) from the capitalist international division of labor, other economies (including colonies) may benefit as well. As a consequence, the world market economy has become a principal mechanism for both concentration and diffusion of wealth and power among states.

A world market economy does develop the world; yet it does not do so evenly. Although most states may gain in absolute terms from participation in the world market, some gain relatively more than others, and some are certainly harmed by their integration into the world economy. Whether this differential growth in wealth is due to the greater economic efficiency of certain states (as most Western economists would agree) or to exploitation of the weak by the strong (as contemporary dependency theorists assert), a market economy does have a profound effect on the international distribution of wealth.[16] This development has brought into existence a profoundly divisive political issue unique to the modern world.

In the premodern world, the distribution of wealth within countries was usually wider than the distribution of wealth among countries; the poor in nearly all societies were at comparable levels of material wealth. In the modern world, wealth is more evenly distributed within societies than among societies; the "poor" in industrialized nations of the Northern Hemisphere are immensely more wealthy than the great fraction of mankind in the Southern Hemisphere. Whether one is well off or poor today has become primarily a function of one's nationality. As a consequence, the distribution of wealth has become "internationalized" and has joined security and the distribution of power as a major issue in world politics.

The succession of hegemonies

These several developments (the nation-state, economic growth, and the world economy) resulted in the nineteenth century in the displacement of the cycle of empires by a succession of hegemonies. First in the European system and then on a global scale, successive political and economic hegemonies have supplanted the pattern of successive empires as the fundamental ordering principle of international relations. Since the Industrial Revolution, the two successive hegemonic powers in the global system (Great Britain and the United States) have sought to organize political, territorial, and especially economic relations in terms of their respective security and economic interests. They have succeeded in this hegemonic role partially because they have imposed their will on lesser states and partially because other states have benefited from and accepted their leadership.

As was the case with premodern empires, the hegemonic

---

[16] For a balanced assessment of these matters, see the work of Gould (1972, pp. 218–94).

powers may be said to supply public goods (security and protection of property rights) in exchange for revenue (Hirsch, Doyle, and Morse, 1977, pp. 19–21). The Pax Britannica and Pax Americana, like the Pax Romana, ensured an international system of relative peace and security. Great Britain and the United States created and enforced the rules of a liberal international economic order.[17] British and American policies fostered free trade and freedom of capital movements. These great powers supplied the key currency and managed the international monetary system. As has already been noted, they assumed these responsibilities because it was profitable to do so. The benefits to them of a secure status quo, free trade, foreign investment, and a well-functioning international monetary system were greater than the associated costs. While bringing benefits to themselves, however, the policies of the hegemonic powers were also beneficial to those other states that desired to and could take advantage of the international political and economic status quo.

Although in this study we argue that the cycle of empires has been replaced by a succession of hegemonies in the modern world, a major qualification must be posited. Ours, of course, is not the first international system to experience a succession of hegemons – witness the classical Greek city-state system from which the concept of hegemony or leadership comes. Now, as then, the reason for this situation is a particular set of environmental circumstances rather than the eradication of the imperial impulse itself. When environmental conditions seem to make it profitable and domestic incentives are sufficiently strong, ambitious states seek to create empires and unite the international system by force. Indeed, this was the case during World War I and World War II. There are no guarantees that there will be no future attempts to forge imperial systems, and it is conceivable that the succession of hegemonies of the nineteenth and twentieth centuries (like the Greek city-state system) will be seen as merely an interlude in the more universal pattern of unifying imperialisms.

[17] In a very interesting article, George Modelski (1978) argued that a cycle of global powers characterizes the modern world: Portugal, the Netherlands, Great Britain (twice), and the United States. Although the first two certainly did dominate world trade, their political dominance over the international system never equaled that of Great Britain or the United States. For this reason, the present formulation is preferred.

LIMITATIONS ON CHANGE AND EXPANSION

Thus far it has been argued that states seek to change the international system through territorial, political, and/or economic expansion until the marginal costs of further expansion and change are equal to or greater than the marginal benefits. In the imperial era this expansion took place primarily through territorial conquest. In the modern world, domestic consolidation and economic expansion in world markets have complemented and partially supplanted territorial expansion. Furthermore, it has been pointed out that the growth of power of a state and its expansion tend to reinforce one another, as expansion increases the economic surplus and resources available to the expanding state.

In the absence of countervailing forces, the logic of this situation would culminate in a universal political empire or global economic monopoly. As was indicated earlier, however, the growth and expansion of a state and economy at some point encounter and even generate countervailing forces. As a consequence, the marginal benefits of expansion decline, and the marginal costs increase, thereby decreasing the economic surplus and placing a limit on further expansion. We shall next examine the character of these countervailing forces: First will be those forces that apply particularly, although not exclusively, to the expansion of empires and territorial expansion, followed by examination of the special case of economic expansion in the modern world.

Among the countervailing forces that limit expansion, the most important historically have been natural barriers and the loss-of-strength gradient, as described earlier. Modes of transportation, topography, climate, precipitation, fertility of the soil, disease, etc., affect the costs and benefits of expansion and conquest. Consequently, at some point as a state expands its territorial base and political influence, the net benefits and resulting economic surplus decline. Thus, "the extent of the Roman empire was limited by the desert to the South, the Germans and the forest to the North, the sea to the West, and the early Parthian 'empire' to the East" (Rader, 1971, p. 47). Although this type of natural limitation is less significant in the contemporary world, it is still a factor in world politics – witness the American debacle in the jungles of Southeast Asia.

A second countervailing force that limits the expansion of a state and international change is the generation of opposing power. In all international systems of which we have knowledge, we find the notion of the balance of power. As David Hume observed in a statement on the balance of power, the idea of allying forces to resist an expanding state has always been a universal principle of prudent politics (quoted by Seabury, 1965, pp. 32–6). Although this technique is not always effective, the tendency is for opposition to an expanding state to be generated in the form of counterbalancing political and economic alliances. What is unique about the modern world is that this technique of balancing power with power became a systematic and institutionalized feature of the European state system and a major reason that the European states retained their independence in the face of the several attempts to unify the Continent. As a result, the European state system escaped the fate of all previous systems of being unified by a universal empire.

The operation of the balance-of-power mechanism is a function of the "density" of an international system. International systems differ with respect to the room or space available for territorial or economic expansion. In the early phase of an international system there is open space or frontier for the expansionist ambitions of states. A Carthage, Rome, or Parthia may grow in power for decades and expand in relative isolation from other states. As states expand, the open frontier shrinks, and they begin to encroach on one another. They increasingly collide, and conflict intensifies among them, raising the costs of further expansion. In time, either one state becomes dominant or a balance is established among states.

A third and more speculative limit to the territorial, political, and economic expansion of a state is the notion that economic, technical, and other factors determine an optimum size for political entities in a particular historical era (Bean, 1973; Auster and Silver, 1979, Chapter 3). Below that optimum size the state cannot generate sufficient resources to protect itself and survive. Above that optimum size, diseconomies of scale, political fragmentation, and problems of centralized command begin to chip away at the power of an expanding state and arrest its further growth. A number of theorists and historians have observed this phenomenon. Mark Elvin, for example, in his brilliant study of the Chinese Empire, suggested that the costs of empire tend to increase geometrically as its size increases, whereas its resources increase only arithmetically. This situation is due to the need for a larger army to defend its borders and a larger bureaucracy to manage the society. Thus the scale and limits of an empire are determined by the trade-off between the "burdens of scale and technological capacity" (Elvin, 1973, p. 110). As a consequence, "the larger the unit the more it has to excel its neighbours if it is to survive for long" (Elvin, 1973, p. 19).

Other scholars have made similar observations regarding the limits to the scale of political organization. Kenneth Boulding speculated that the size of political organization is governed by the law of the optimum size of organization due to the increasing cost of administration (Boulding, 1953, pp. 22–5). Anthony Downs (1967, p. 143) spoke of the law of diminishing control, and Karl Wittfogel (1957, p. 110) spoke of the law of diminishing administrative returns. Another theory is William Riker's size principle: As the size of a political coalition increases, the returns to its members decrease. At some point a coalition member can increase its gains by leaving the coalition (suboptimization). This trade-off between the size of a coalition and the returns to its members is said to impose a limit on the size of coalitions (and states) (Riker, 1962).[18] Yet a third theory is that a trade-off exists between the size of a political entity and the optimal returns to individuals (Olson, 1968); although enlargement of a political unit creates economies of scale with respect to the provision of public goods, the total range of individual preferences to be satisfied becomes more diverse. As a consequence, individuals and groups begin to believe that their own interests will be better served by bringing government closer to home (Cox, Reynolds, and Rokkan, 1974, p. 129). The limiting effects of this tendency toward suboptimization will be discussed later.

[18] The theory of clubs addresses this question (Frey, 1978, p. 99; Russett, 1968, pp. 50–63).

The fact that political entities of greatly varying sizes coexist in a particular age suggests that the notion of an optimum size should be regarded with some reserve (Dahl and Tufte, 1973). Yet it must also be noted that the sizes of the principal actors within a particular international system differ from the sizes of the actors in another. Furthermore, as economic and technological conditions change, the characteristic size of the dominant powers increases or decreases. Thus the Italian city-state was eclipsed by the larger western European nation-state, just as the latter is now subordinate to the continental superpower. One must ask, therefore, if this tendency is mere chance or if economic, technological, or other environmental conditions in a particular era place a limit on the scale of political organization.

The basic principle at work was stated most succinctly by Brian Barry: "The important criterion for size . . . is that the unit of collective decision-making should be one that . . . internalizes all costs and benefits" (Barry, 1974, p. 492); see also the work of Buchanan and Tullock (1962, p. 113). Unless an actor can capture the benefits of increasing size, it will have insufficient incentive and capacity to pay the necessary costs of expansion. As has already been noted, this situation limited the sizes of feudal organizations; it was not until the economic-technical environment changed that a larger political entity, the nation-state, was possible. In the contemporary world, economic and technological developments may call for even larger units of political organization.

In addition to administrative, economic, and technical limitations, the scale of a society is limited by a tendency toward political disintegration and fragmentation as size increases. This is due to suboptimization on the part of peripheral groups.[19] The fundamental political problem of any large state or empire is how to organize power and resources over a large area while keeping the periphery loyal to central control (Elvin, 1973, pp. 20, 63–8). As the scale of a state, empire, or even a market economy increases in size, groups frequently begin to believe that they can increase their own gains by breaking off or, in the case of markets, by erecting tariff barriers in order to tax trade

[19] By "suboptimization" we mean the effort of a subgroup to increase its relative gains at the expense of the larger group.

or to protect domestic industries (Rader, 1971, p. 48). The success and endurance of many large states and empires have been possible partially because they have invented devices to counter centrifugal forces. The principal unifying devices have been a centralized bureaucracy, a universal religion (or ideology), and the sharing of material benefits (so-called side payments).[20] In the modern world, perhaps the most effective devices for creating loyalty to a large-scale state have been the institution of federalism and the ideology of nationalism. The common feature of these devices is that they give potential breakaway groups a stake in the larger system and identity with the larger system.

The tendency for suboptimization and fragmentation to take place is frequently a function of economic development. An integrated political and economic area tends to foster commerce and economic development because of the decline of trade barriers and the increased flow of resources. However, commerce and development do not take place evenly throughout the system. Trade flows through particular channels, and economic development tends to concentrate at particular nodal points in an economic system. As trade increases and economic centers develop, particular subgroups in a society or trading system develop an incentive to capture increased gains for themselves by breaking off from the center. This tendency toward suboptimization and fragmentation was the curse of successive premodern empires.[21] In the modern world, suboptimization has frequently taken the form of economic nationalism and tariff protectionism as developing states seek to industrialize and reduce their dependence on more advanced economies.

Every empire and dominant state has pursued policies to prevent the phenomenon of suboptimization from taking place. Imperial bureaucracies, for example, sought to maintain a monopoly

[20] The short-lived nature of barbarian conquest was due to the inability of tribal and nomadic peoples to manage the economies they periodically overran. The military superiority of the steppe peoples was seldom supported by an internal political organization and competence that could enable them to consolidate their advanced positions. Sustained expansion requires consolidation, centralization, and a bureaucracy.

[21] For the example of Alexander's short-lived empire that fragmented into three parts, see the work of Clough (1970, pp. 106–7).

of economic resources. The Chinese Empire pursued a deliberate policy of preventing the development of economic centers that might break off. Chinese cities were administrative centers responsive to the imperial center; they seldom became commercial centers. The stability of the Roman Empire was due largely to the fact that Rome under Augustus offered colonial elites Roman citizenship and gave them a stake in the system (Syme, 1939). Soviet Russia has populated its Islamic cities and republics with Great Russians to prevent fragmentation as these republics develop. The modern democratic welfare state pursues regional and redistributive policies that seek to counter the political destabilizing effects of uneven economic development. Dominant economies employ both positive and negative inducements to counter tendencies toward economic nationalism and protectionism.

The most important inhibition against the dangers of suboptimization is the existence of an economic core controlled by the central government or, in the case of a market economy, by the dominant economic power. This means that the central government or dominant economic power is in control of resources superior to those of potential breakaway groups or states. Although he was speaking about the political cohesion of an empire, the following observation by Trout Rader is equally relevant for large states and international markets:

In addition there is a condition for internal stability of the empire. This requires that no combination of regions could break off and obtain a higher return than the empire. If such a grouping did exist, it would be motivated to revolt and the capital would be unable to expend the resources to return the region to its control. From the stability condition and the fact that transportation costs are positive, there would be no reason for the expansion of the empire beyond the locale, were it not that the capital is in command of resources which are not available to smaller sub-units, even acting in consort. Part of the resources might be due to superior military technology, but surely this would be a short-lived advantage. Indeed, were the empire's dominance entirely dependent upon the military factor, generals would be tempted to initate the breakup of the empire and place themselves at the head of a new sub-empire. Therefore, the basis of the empire must rest upon some economic grounds such as the key location of a city *vis à vis* trade or minerals.

In particular, there are the gains of *pax Romana* which appear when wars between states are lessened. One should keep in mind that states who do not war must nonetheless be ever prepared for war since threats of retaliation require actual and not just potential resources. This itself should be regarded as an economic resource of large organization.

In general, it is by taking advantage of the diverse resources of different regions that an empire can obtain extra resources which a smaller region cannot provide. Of course, many of the advantages of conglomeration might accrue to a group of smaller regions practising free international trade. However, the smaller regions would be tempted to put up barriers to trade in hopes of collecting taxes and/or protecting home industries (Rader, 1971, p. 48).

In brief, the scale of a state, empire, or market is governed by the interaction of two sets of forces. On the one hand, there are certain benefits of large size, such as a greater resource base and economies of scale. On the other hand, increasing scale tends to stimulate centrifugal forces and fragmentation on the part of groups that believe they can maximize their own gains through breaking off. This dual set of forces helps to account for both the initial rapid expansion in the power of a state and the subsequent deceleration in growth producing the S curve that has already been noted. Thus, although a state may enhance its power by incorporating other centers of power, there is a powerful tendency over the long term for these centers to break off. This inherent tendency toward suboptimization on the part of groups limits economies of scale in political organization and constitutes an important limitation on the aggregation of political and economic power on the part of expanding states (Russett, 1968, pp. 306–7).

Finally, the expansion of a state is limited by internal transformations in society. As has been argued earlier, one set of reasons for growth in the power of a state and its expansion is to be found in its internal structure and the nature of domestic society. Factors such as the values and interests of the elite and the relationship of private and public gains from growth and expansion are of particular significance. These factors determine the efficiency of the society and influence the power and interests of the state, thus providing incentives or disincentives for economic and political expansion. During the initial growth of a state or empire, private and public gains coincide; in time, because of social and other changes attendant on the growth in power and wealth of the society, they may come into conflict. This divergence between private and public interests limits further growth in the power and wealth of the society.

The notion that the growth of a society is regulated by some type of internal feedback mechanism was common among classical writers. In the words of a distinguished classicist, the ancient historians searched for "the reason why the rise of a state turns to its downfall" (de Romilly, 1977, p. 19). They found the answer in the idea that when a society extends its control and dominion over others, increased power and wealth lead to moral decay and the corruption of the original virtues that enabled the society to grow in the first place. This theme engaged later writers as well. Montesquieu, it will be recalled, believed republics were naturally expansive because they were better able than monarchies to harness private drive and initiative for the larger glory and power of the state. Yet, as he wrote in *Considerations on the Causes of the Greatness of the Romans and Their Decline*, republics are subject to a self-regulating mechanism that limits their size and eventually leads to their destruction. Up to a certain point of physical growth, republican government can maintain its integrity; beyond this point, however, the republican principle weakens. Republican virtue and ambition that created the empire die out, and once republican virtue dies, the empire decays internally until it can no longer resist the outside forces that are always there seeking to expand and grow in their turn. In the case of Rome, Montesquieu wrote, it was the great size of the republic that led to its destruction.

As Polybius, Montesquieu, and numerous other writers have observed, the effects and experience of growth and expansion eventually weaken or destroy the conditions that initially favored expansion and rob the society of its sources of political and economic momentum. Among these societal changes, several should be noted. The growth in wealth and power of the state alters the internal political balances within the society and may bring into power certain groups whose interests are threatened by the continued expansion of the state. In the society as a whole, there is an erosion of the original élan that supported an aggressive and expansionist foreign policy. The society grows conservative, less innovative, and less willing to run risks; it becomes more interested in upholding present privileges than in risking their loss in further efforts to increase wealth and power. Finally, the society becomes less willing to pay the costs in blood, political stability, or economic dislocation that may be associated with political and economic expansion.

Polybius also had something worthwhile to say on political decay. Surveying Rome at the height of its wealth and power, he predicted that Rome would follow the course of other once-great ancient empires: "When a commonwealth, after warding off many great dangers, has arrived at a high pitch of prosperity and undisputed power, it is evident that, by the lengthened continuance of great wealth within it, the manner of life of its citizens will become more extravagant." Leaders and people become corrupt. Avarice, resentment, and anger will sweep the society as the people demand more and more. "And when that comes to pass the constitution will receive a new name, which sounds better than any other in the world, liberty or democracy; but, in fact, it will become that worst of all governments, mob-rule" (Polybius, 1962, p. 507).

In Marxist terminology, one may say that economic and political expansion by a society tends to plant the seeds of its destruction. Ibn Khaldûn had something like this in mind when he observed that great empires decline because the impoverished nomads who fight to forge them become city dwellers corrupted by the spoils of conquest (Ibn Khaldûn, 1967). The same theme appears in Joseph Schumpeter's belief (1960) that the success of capitalism destroys the risk-taking entrepreneur who is ultimately responsible for economic progress; he becomes a manager and rentier content to live off the accumulated capital of the past. Thus, as private and public interests diverge from the requirements for further growth in power and wealth, the society loses its forward thrust and thereby provides others an opportunity to catch up and eventually overtake it.

CONCLUSION

In this chapter we have analyzed the proposition that states seek to change the international system through expansion until the costs of further change and expansion exceed the benefits. We have contrasted two primary mechanisms of expansion and change that have been employed historically: territorial conquest in the imperial era and economic expansion in the modern era. Specifically, we have argued that as a consequence first of increasing returns and then of diminishing returns from expansion, the growth and contraction of a state tend to follow an S curve or logistics curve. At first, because of its initial advantages over other states, the growing state tends to expand very rapidly. In time, however, the returns to expansion diminish, and the rate of expansion slows. Finally, as the marginal costs of further expansion begin to equal or exceed the marginal benefits, expansion ceases, and an equilibrium is achieved. As will be argued in the next chapter, this equilibrium is merely a temporary phenomenon in the continuing process of international political change.

4

Equilibrium and decline

Assumption 4. Once an equilibrium between the costs and benefits of further change and expansion is reached, the tendency is for the economic costs of maintaining the status quo to rise faster than the economic capacity to support the status quo.

The governance of international systems has been provided by empires, hegemonies, and great powers that have risen and fallen over the millennia. These successive dominant states have changed the system, expanding until an equilibrium is reached between the costs and benefits of further change and expansion. Once this equilibrium position is reached, developments both internal to the dominant power and in its external environment begin to undermine it. In consequence, there is a tendency for the economic costs of maintaining the international status quo to rise faster than the financial capacity of the dominant power to support its position and the status quo. The purpose of this chapter is to account for this tendency.

The governance of an international system involves a fundamental economic problem. Although control over an international system provides economic benefits (revenues) to the dominant power or powers, domination also involves costs in manpower and material resources. In order to maintain its dominant position, a state must expend its resources on military forces, the financing of allies, foreign aid, and the costs associated with maintaining the

156

international economy. These protection and related costs are not productive investments; they constitute an economic drain on the economy of the dominant state. Domination, therefore, requires the existence of a continuing economic surplus.

This economic surplus initially tends to rise more rapidly than the costs of expansion; if it were otherwise, a state would have neither the motive nor the capacity to expand. In time, however, there will be diminishing returns and increasing costs, which will limit the further expansion of a state. At some point an equilibrium may be said to exist between the costs and benefits of further expansion and efforts to change the international system.

The thesis of this chapter is that once an equilibrium between the costs and benefits of expansion is reached, the tendency is for the costs of maintaining the status quo to rise faster than the capacity to finance the status quo. For reasons that will be spelled out later, it becomes more difficult to generate sufficient revenues to cover the protection costs, and the protection costs themselves increase over time. As a consequence of the increasing costs of protection and the decreasing benefits of empire or hegemony, the preservation of the status quo becomes even more difficult, and the international system enters a state of disequilibrium.

Disequilibrium entails a disjuncture between the basic components of the existing international system and the capacity of the dominant state or states to maintain the system, between the costs of defending the existing distribution of territory, spheres of influence, rules of the system, and international economy, on the one hand, and the revenues necessary to finance these arrangements. This divergence between costs and resources in turn produces a "fiscal crisis" for the dominant power or powers. The consequence of continuing disequilibrium and of the financial drain it entails if it is not resolved is the eventual economic and political decline of the dominant power.

In the premodern imperial era of relatively slow economic and technological change, this process of growth and eventual decline usually took many centuries; both the Byzantine Empire and the Chinese Empire lasted a millennium, and they may be said to have been in decline for several hundred years. In the modern era of rapid economic and technological change, this process has accelerated. The duration of British global hegemony was approximately a century. The Pax Americana is under severe strain after only a few decades.

In effect, of course, this discussion is considering the obverse of the law of uneven growth. Whereas in Chapter 2 we analyzed the factors affecting the growth and expansion of a state, here we are examining how these same sets of factors undermine the power of a state. Because power is a relative matter, the rise or decline of one state by definition entails the decline or rise of another, and to a degree the same types of factors are involved in both cases. In this section the emphasis will be on the ways in which these domestic and environmental factors cause the power of a dominant state to decline relative to the powers of other states in the system.

Speaking broadly, the national income of a society is distributed into three general sectors: protection; consumption (private and nonmilitary public); productive investment. Protection relates to the costs of national security and the costs of protecting the property rights of citizens. Consumption refers to private and public consumption of goods and services. Investment is that part of the national product that is returned to the productive sector of the economy to increase the efficiency and productivity of land, labor, and, in the modern world, industrial plant.

For a number of reasons that will be discussed later, the historical tendency is for the protection and consumption (private and nonmilitary public) shares of national income to increase as a society ages. This, in turn, means that the share of gross national product reinvested in the economy must of necessity decrease (unless, of course, additional resources can be obtained from other economies). As a consequence, the efficiency and productivity of the productive sector of the economy on which all else rests will decline. If the productive base of the economy erodes, it becomes more difficult to meet the rising demands of protection and consumption without further cutbacks in productive investment, thus further weakening the future economic health of the society. The society enters a downward spiral of rising consumption and declining investment that undermines the economic, military, and political foundations of the state's international position. As a consequence of these developments, the declining power begins to experience what Harold and Margaret Sprout aptly called "the dilemma of rising demands and insufficient resources" (1968).[1]

We shall now discuss this dilemma and the process of decline. First the internal changes that tend to undermine the power and wealth of a society will be discussed; then the external developments will be considered. In reality, internal and external developments are in many cases merely different aspects of the same set of operating forces; they are to be distinguished from one another for analytical purposes only.

INTERNAL FACTORS THAT AFFECT POLITICAL DECLINE

Perhaps the most significant changes that undermine the power of the dominant state are structural changes in its economy. A number of factors transform the internal economy in ways that are inimical to the long-term military and economic capabilities of the state. Military strength tends to erode; economic efficiency gives way to various diseconomies and a slackening in economic growth; the military and economic competitiveness of the society declines.

In premodern societies with relatively low rates of economic growth, the retardation of economic growth was obviously of less importance than it is in the modern world. However, the law of diminishing returns has universal applicability and causes the growth of every society to describe an S-shaped curve. When a society has ceased to expand, the limited availability of high-quality agricultural land, the depletion of resources, and the growth of population lead to a reduced (or, more likely, negative) rate of growth and a reduction in the economic surplus available for consumption, protection, and investment.

In the contemporary world, technological advance has moderated the operation of the law of diminishing returns as agricultural and industrial innovation has ushered in an era of unprecedented economic growth. Yet every innovation is subject to what Simon Kuznets called the law of industrial growth, that is, the

---

[1] For an excellent analysis of the contemporary world in terms of this dilemma, see the work of Sprout and Sprout (1972).

tendency for the growth impulse of any innovation to come to an end (Kuznets, 1930, Chapter 1). Moreover, economic and technological innovations tend to cluster in time and space, favoring this society, then that society. In the absence of new spurts of innovation or a borrowing of technology from abroad, the growth of the wealth and power of a society begins to slow, describing an S-shaped curve. The society undergoes an economic climacteric, as did Great Britain in the latter part of the nineteenth century, and many believe that the United States is experiencing the same thing in the contemporary world. Thus the modern industrial economy ultimately may not be any better at escaping the law of diminishing returns than its preindustrial predecessors (Hicks, 1974, pp. 211–25).

A valuable analysis of the causes of an S-shaped curve for the growth of an economy was presented by Harvey Leibenstein (1978, pp. 98–122). In his analysis, Leibenstein divided the growth of a typical economy into three phases (Figure 4). In phase I, an underdeveloped economy is characterized by primitive techniques of production and a low rate of investment. The rate of economic growth may be zero, very low, or negative; this was the situation for most premodern societies. In phase II, however, growth takes place very rapidly because of the incorporation of new production techniques into the economy, usually imported from more advanced economies, thereby providing the so-called advantages of backwardness. During this phase the rate of economic growth is affected by the choice of appropriate techniques, the rate of adoption of these techniques, and the amount of savings or investment. Finally, in phase III, the economy has become mainly urban and industrial. Its growth (as in phase I) takes place at a slow rate because the rate of innovation has become relatively limited. The mature society tends to be overtaken by more rapidly developing economies still in phase II (Rostow, 1980, pp. 259–301).

The idea that every society reaches a point in its development at which further growth becomes difficult or even impossible is a frequently encountered idea. In general, these limits-of-growth theories or stagnation theories emphasize the supply side or the demand side of economic activity. For some theorists, the supply

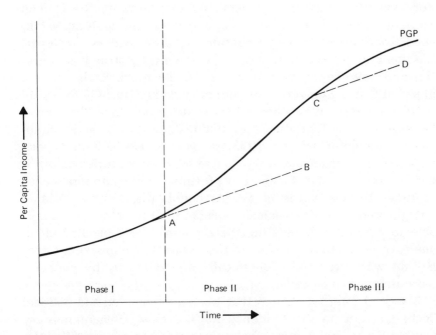

Figure 4. Growth curve of an economy. [Adapted from Leibenstein (1978, p. 99).]

of one or more of the factors of production is determinant. Thus, as Carlo Cipolla said, "historians have always felt instinctively that the main economic troubles of mature empires stemmed from the side of supply . . . real or imagined bottlenecks such as shortage of slaves, or of population, or of bullions, or . . . stagnant technology" (1970, p. 7). For other theorists, the social structure and the demands of society determine the limits of growth. Thus, in the view of Arnold Toynbee, the impulse to growth is always provided by "a creative minority," whereas in Marxist analysis it is the class structure that at first facilitates and eventually retards growth.

These and other stagnation theories contain important insights with respect to the phenomenon of political and economic decline. Because of one or another underlying cause, every society eventually declines following the erosion of its economic base.

For example, after several centuries of prosperity the Roman economy ceased to be innovative, and the resulting decay weakened Rome in the face of mounting barbarian attacks. However, this general observation should not be misconstrued; societies can and have rejuvenated themselves. As Mark Elvin argued, imperial China innovated economically and technically for many centuries before it reached what he described as a "high-level equilibrium trap," produced by diminishing returns and technological stagnation (Elvin, 1973, p. 314). Great Britain experienced several renewals in the course of three centuries before it entered on a secular decline in its fortunes in the late nineteenth century. In the words of W. Arthur Lewis, Britain became "caught in a set of ideological traps [and] all the strategies available to her [for rejuvenating the economy] were blocked off in one way or another" (1978, p. 133). Once this happened, Great Britain was surpassed economically and militarily by younger, more innovative societies.

A second internal change that leads to economic and political decline is due to the tendency for the most efficient military techniques to rise in cost, what numerous writers have called the "law of the increasing cost of war." Adam Smith was perhaps the first to observe that as a civilization ages, war expenditures tend to rise at an ever more rapid rate (Smith, 1937, pp. 653–69). Because of the increased costs of military capabilities and the diffusion of military technology from the dominant state to rising competitors, the costs to the dominant state of maintaining the system rise with time. These rising costs of protection place an increasingly heavy burden on the resources of the dominant power. The conflict over the budget priorities of consumption, investment, and protection becomes more intense, producing a severe fiscal crisis.

Further, affluence appears to have a corrosive effect on the martial spirit. As Brooks Adams (1943) and others have noted, the conquering warrior is displaced by a more pacific commercial elite. Because of competition from other sectors for scarce manpower and resources, greater monetary incentives are required to induce young men and women to forgo the pleasures of civilian life for the regimented life of the barracks. The Romans were forced to hire mercenaries to defend their frontiers; the American military has become increasingly a force composed of the less educated and the unskilled. As a consequence, the tendency is for the cost of military power in an affluent society to rise at a disproportionately rapid rate and for the quality of the military to decline.

Despite contemporary criticisms of the "warfare state," there appears today to be less of a tendency than in the past for the costs of war to rise at a faster rate than national income (Kennedy, 1975, p. 80; Milward, 1977, p. 3). At the same time that the destructiveness of war has been greatly magnified, the relative cost of military power has actually declined; in other words, the cost of protection claims a smaller share of national income. This has been due to the increased effectiveness of modern weapons and the security provided for the greater majority of states first by the Pax Britannia and then by the Pax Americana. Furthermore, the relative costs to these hegemonic states of providing this collective good have been less than the historical norm. This situation led one writer to suggest that the declining costs of protection have been at least partially responsible for the unprecedented rate of economic growth in the modern world (Lane, 1958, p. 413). This is certainly not intended to suggest that the costs of protection have become negligible nor that they no longer compete with welfare and other social goals.[2] Indeed, in an age of rapidly rising social and economic expectations, this clash becomes acute, especially if, for whatever reason, the overall rate of economic growth slows.

A third internal change that undermines the power and wealth of a state is a general tendency for both private and public consumption to grow faster than the gross national product as a society becomes more affluent. An increasing demand for consumer goods and services develops and spreads downward through the social hierarchy. A general rule of social evolution is that the masses begin to demand to share the amenities of the elite (Cipolla, 1970, p. 4). Private consumption, especially

---

[2] This argument should not be misconstrued to mean that the destructiveness of war has decreased. On the contrary, it may very well be that the increased destructiveness of modern weapons is responsible for the decreased cost of protection.

among the upper classes, increases, as does the provision of public welfare, whether in the form of bread and circuses in the
ancient world or medical care for the lower classes and social
security for the aged in the modern world (Lewis, 1970, pp. 239,
396). The apparent universality of this tendency for the public
sector to expand more rapidly than the economy as a whole has
long been known by students of public finance as Wagner's "law
of expanding state expenditures."[3]

This tendency of public expenditures for warfare, and even
more for welfare, to rise and sap the productive economy is the
important conclusion of one of the few comparative studies of the
decline of imperial powers:

We do not have reliable quantitative data that enable us to assess that
composition of public expenditures in most of the mature empires of the
past, but it is not hard to believe that the structures of public expenditure
must have shown remarkable differences. In one place the construction
of temples and pyramids may have weighed heavily on the economy; in
another place the extravagances of a dynasty of rulers may have burd-
ened the public treasury; in another place military expenditures and
administration may have absorbed an increasingly larger share of gross
national product. *The fundamental fact remains that public consumption
in mature empires shows a distinct tendency to rise sharply.*

The phenomenon is reflected in the growth of taxation. One of the
remarkably common features of empires at the later stage of their
development is the growing amount of wealth pumped by the State
from the economy. In the later Roman Empire taxation reached such
heights that land was abandoned and many peasants, after paying their
rents or taxes, had too little food left to nourish their children. In
sixteenth-century Spain the revenue from the two taxes, the alcabala
and the millones (which was introduced in 1590), increased from 1504
to 1596 by more than five times. It is true that in the meantime the
general index of prices more than trebled, but it is also true that while
the revenue from the alcabala represented in 1504 about 85 per cent of
the government revenues, in 1596 its yield represented only 25 per

---

[3] Adolph Wagner was a mid-nineteenth-century German economist who wrote a series of
articles on this subject. Recent investigations tend to support his analysis, though the
phenomenon may be cyclical rather than linear (see *Public Finance*, Vol. 26, No. 1,
1971). For the recent American experience, see the work of Samuel Huntington. (*The
Public Interest*, No. 41, Fall 1975). Ironically, the "workers' " states of the Soviet bloc
appear to have an advantage over the capitalist economies in that they can suppress the
consumption of the masses in favor of defense and military-related investments.

cent. Of sixteenth-century Italians, Fynes Moryson wrote that they lived under "cruell exactions under which they grone as under the bondage of Egypt". Figures relating to tax revenues, however, do not always tell the whole story. In the later Roman Empire, in the late Byzantine Empire, in seventeenth-century Spain, inflation was rampant. Debasing the currency is just another form of taxation. The Italian decline in the seventeenth century was exceptional in the sense that inflation was not part of the scenario (Cipolla, 1970, pp. 6–7; italics added).

A fourth internal change closely related to the preceding two changes is a structural change in the character of the economy. As Colin Clark argued in *The Conditions of Economic Progress* (1957), the evolution of an economy, in particular a modern one, tends to follow a discernible course. In the early phase of an economy the largest fraction of the labor force is in agriculture. In a more developed economy, the largest fraction is in manufacturing. Finally, in a mature economy, the largest fraction is in the so-called service sector (the professions, banking, etc.). Although a service economy continues to grow through its investment in the creation of knowledge and human capital, service industries tend to have a lower rate of productivity growth than manufactures (Rostow, 1978, p. 172). Thus a service economy, such as Great Britain in the late nineteenth century and the United States in the late twentieth century, tends to experience declining productivity and economic retardation relative to its own past and relative to less advanced industrializing economies.

A fifth, and one of the most important, internal change that weakens a state is the "corrupting" influence of affluence. As Gibbon, Montesquieu, Polybius, and other classical authors stressed, the prosperity generated by political conquest or economic growth leads to "the loss of moral virtues" and eventual decline (de Romilly, 1977, p. 82). In more contemporary parlance, economic decline and political decline are characterized by a psychological shift. Social values, attitudes, and behavior change in ways that undercut the efficiency of the economy and the dedication of individuals and groups to the commonweal. Private and public interests that formerly had converged now diverge to the detriment of the power and welfare of the society.

During such periods of decline, conservatives lament the corruption of the moral fiber of society. Their indictments of their contemporaries sound similar themes throughout history: the triumph of individual rights over social responsibility, of debilitating equality over creative liberty, of easy leisure over hard work, of governmental bureaucracies over productive enterprise, of loss of will over steadfastness, and so forth.[4] The discerning scholar should be wary of accepting at face value such moralizing. Yet the recurrence of these themes in one declining society after another suggests there is a truth embedded in what Cipolla called "the third generation effect." "In every good family there is the generation that builds up a fortune, the generation that holds on to it, and the generation that dissipates it. In this respect, societies differ little from families" (Cipolla, 1970, p. 12).

Perhaps the most pernicious aspect of this "corruption" (a term used in its classical sense to mean decay) is the generation in the minds of a dominant people of the belief that the world they (or, rather, their forebears) created is the right, natural, and God-given state of affairs. To such a people the idea that the world of their rule and privilege could be otherwise becomes inconceivable. The goodness and benefits of the status quo, as they know it, are so obvious that all reasonable men will assent to its worth and preservation. With such a state of mind, a people neither concedes to the just demands of rising challengers nor makes the necessary sacrifices to defend its threatened world. Thus, as E. H. Carr charged his fellow Englishmen in the 1930s, they neither met the just demands of the Weimar Republic (and thereby they hastened its end) nor were willing to die for king and country to stop Hitler. When the crisis finally came in 1939, the seemingly endless world of British power and privilege collapsed (Carr, 1951).

These internal changes (the decreased rate of economic growth, the rising cost of protection, the increase in private and public consumption, the structural shift to services, and the corrupting effects of affluence and preeminence) manifest themselves in an increasingly severe political conflict over the allocation of national income among protection, consumption, and investment. This, of course, is the classic conflict between guns and butter that might

---

[4] For a recent recitation of these themes, see the work of Silver (1980).

more appropriately be termed guns, butter, or productivity. As a dominant power ages, the struggle over these conflicting demands transforms a relatively benign politics of growth into a more virulent politics of distribution.

Although the growth of wealth and the advance of society produce social fissures, the fissures can be contained as long as the income of the society continues to increase. The conflict over shares is muted because of an increase in the overall amount of wealth, whether that increase comes from tribute, economic growth, or some other source. As the flow of tribute or economic growth slows, however, the conflict over relative shares of the economic surplus intensifies, despite its detrimental consequences for the overall welfare of society. As a result, periods of decline tend to be characterized by exacerbation of internal social and political conflicts, which in turn further weaken the society, as in Great Britain today and perhaps in the United States tomorrow.

This three-way struggle over priorities (protection, consumption, and investment) produces a profound dilemma for society. If it suppresses consumption, the consequence can be severe internal social tensions and class conflict; social wars have rent the social fabric and weakened many once-great powers. If the society neglects to pay the costs of defense, external weakness will inevitably lead to its defeat by rising powers. If the society fails to save and reinvest a sufficient fraction of its surplus wealth in industry and agriculture, the economic basis of the society and its capacity to sustain either consumption or protection will decline.

A classic example of a state entrapped by this resource dilemma was the Netherlands in the seventeenth century. During the middle decades of that century the Dutch Republic was the financial and industrial leader of Europe. Dutch goods outcompeted all others in world markets; Dutch ships were technically superior to others, and Amsterdam was the principal capital market of Europe. As the century wore on, however, the Dutch had to fend off increasing foreign enemies and their industrial base eroded. The cost of defense increased, and so did the land taxes to finance fleets and armies. In turn, the cost of food rose, and with it the demands of workers for higher wages. Industrial decline and wage inflation decreased the competitiveness of Dutch goods on the world market. As a consequence, although the Netherlands did not suffer an absolute decline, the loss of high profit margins and economic surplus led to the eventual eclipse of the Netherlands by her more efficient British rival (Wilson, 1969).

The capacity of a state to resolve this severe fiscal crisis profoundly influences its viability over the long term (Schumpeter, 1954a). In general, the tendency is for the rate of consumption to increase at the expense of protection or investment, because it is politically very difficult to suppress consumption and to force a society to decrease its economic expectations. Nevertheless, as the next chapter will show, certain societies have devised solutions to the dilemma of increasing demands and scarce resources that have enabled them to survive in a hostile environment for hundreds of years.

EXTERNAL FACTORS THAT AFFECT POLITICAL DECLINE

The second general set of factors that eventually undermine the position of a dominant power is external. These factors are found in the material and political environment. Changes in these military, technological, and economic factors are precisely the same as those discussed earlier in accounting for the differential growth of power among states. The purpose here, however, is to look at this process of changing power relationships from the perspective of the decline of the dominant power. This process of political decline involves two related developments: the increasing costs of political dominance and the loss of economic and technological leadership.

Increasing costs of political dominance

The principal external factor undermining the position of the dominant state is the increasing costs of dominance. It has already been mentioned that the costs of protection tend to rise because of internal economic developments and the increasing costs of the most efficient weapons. The costs of protection also tend to rise because of changes in the international environment, primarily detrimental shifts in the international distribution of power. Increases in the numbers and strengths of rival, challenging powers force the dominant state to expend more resources to maintain its superior military or political position.

Earlier it was argued that an empire or hegemonic state seeks to expand and increase its control over the international system if it is profitable to do so, providing protection in exchange for revenue. However, the theory of public goods tells us that the provider of such goods tends to overpay (Olson and Zeckhauser, 1966). Because the dominant power will defend the status quo in its own interest, lesser states have little incentive to pay their "fair" share of these protection costs (the free-rider problem). In the fifth century B.C. this was a source of contention between Athens and its "ungrateful" allies with respect to their common defense against the Persians. The American Revolution began with the effort of the British crown to get "ungrateful" colonists to pay their "fair" share in the defense against the Indians and the French. And in the contemporary world, both Americans and Russians complain about defending "ungrateful," free-riding allies.

The increasing costs of protection and the fact that empires as well as hegemonic powers tend to overpay mean that in time the costs of protection of the status quo rise faster than the economic benefits of the status quo. Eventually the revenues generated by continuing political, territorial, and economic expansion are insufficient to underwrite the costs of an imperial or hegemonic position. With increasing costs and decreasing revenues, empire and hegemony become decreasingly profitable. As in any enterprise, a decrease in the rate of profit is a sign of potential bankruptcy.

The decreasing profitability of the status quo imposes severe financial burdens on empires and hegemonic powers. The costs of armies, navies, and foreign wars are nonproductive expenditures; they constitute a balance-of-payments drain on the economy. Meeting these protection costs necessitates the generation of an economic surplus and the acquisition of what we today would call "hard currency." If this financial problem cannot be resolved, it undermines the economic and military position of the imperial or hegemonic power.

A major difference between premodern and modern international relations is the manner in which dominant powers manage this financial burden. In the premodern world the costs of empire were met by the extraction of wealth from peasant agriculture and the acquisition of precious metals (the only hard currency that then existed) through plunder or the taxation of long-distance trade. Under these circumstances, the economic resources available to an empire rested primarily on the availability of fertile lands, the possession of gold or silver mines, or control over lucrative trade routes. These sources of wealth were extremely vulnerable, and fortuitous developments frequently played a central role in the rise and decline of empires.

In the modern world the financial burdens of empire and hegemony have been managed by different techniques. The domestic economic revolution and the rise of an international market have meant greater reliance on economic growth to produce the necessary economic surplus and on international trade (as well as for foreign investment and the sale of services) to secure hard currency. Thus, modern dominant powers have financed the burdens of hegemony through rapid rates of economic growth and favorable international terms of trade or investment. They have had sufficient economic surpluses to meet the combined expenditures for consumption, protection, and investment, and they have had sufficient trade, investment, or services surpluses to meet the balance-of-payments burden of hegemony. We can best understand this change in the financial basis of hegemony through a brief review of historical developments.

The mercantilist era of the seventeenth and eighteenth centuries witnessed the transition from the premodern system to the modern system. The first overseas empires created by the European nation-states were the empires of Spain and Portugal, and they were hardly more than tribute-gathering and plundering empires; this was also the case for the initial British and French acquisitions in India. In time, however, the Dutch, the British, and others created a new type of empire, one founded on trade. These exclusive mercantile empires composed of a metropolitan mother country and overseas colonies were based on the exchange of European manufactured goods for the food and minerals of the colonies. The merchants of the colonial power also reaped profits from the lucrative carrying trade, a commerce encouraged and protected by the European state because it stimulated growth at home, fostered naval power, and poured bullion into the national coffers.

The several varieties of mercantilist thought and practice all at least partially subordinated the economy to the perceived security and welfare needs of the state and society. Measures and practices advocated by mercantilist writers and statesmen were intended to lead to the creation and maintenance of a strong nation-state and strong national economy. In effect, mercantilism can be described as a striving for security through economic means. Under the conditions of the times, this meant encouragement of trade and manufactures through protectionism.

Mercantilism reflected and was a response to the political, economic, and military developments of the early modern period: the emergence of strong national states in constant competition, the rise of a middle class devoted at first to commerce and then increasingly to manufacturing, and the quickening of economic activities because of internal changes within Europe and the discovery of the New World. However, the evolution of a monetarized market economy and the wide range of changes in the nature of warfare that have been characterized as the "military revolution" (Roberts, 1956) were also of critical importance.

The mercantilists identified a favorable balance of trade with national power. This was necessary because of the rise of standing armies; military forces were becoming increasingly expensive and required new bureaucracies to support them. Thus, in this new environment of warfare, nation-states needed large quantities of bullion to finance both the new professional armies and the balance-of-payments drain caused by foreign campaigns. Money or bullion became the sine qua non of national power. The primary task of foreign economic policy was to finance the expanding demands of foreign policy.

A major and paradoxical consequence of the military revolution was that the great European powers became less self-sufficient and more dependent on the world economy. The rise of professional armies and the new technology of warfare required supplies of vital war materiel such as naval stores and saltpeter for gunpowder that frequently could be acquired only through foreign trade or export of bullion. Mercantilists appreciated that the international economy had become an important source of both the financial and material sinews of national power. The frequent and seemingly petty commercial wars of the mercantilist era were really conflicts over access to and control over markets, sources of treasure, and supplies of raw materials on which national security increasingly depended. This loss of self-sufficiency and the new vulnerability contributed greatly to the insecurity of states.

The mercantile empires established by the northern European powers characteristic of this age reflected this new insecurity and the new dependence on trade and markets to acquire treasure and the materiel of war. They were primarily trading empires rather than tribute empires like the mobilization empires of the Assyrians or the Romans. The European states regarded their colonial possessions as secure sources of raw materials (gold, furs, timber, sugar, tobacco, etc.) and as consumers of their expanding output of manufactured goods. The purpose of the Navigation Acts and other acts governing trade was to "regulate colonial trade so that raw materials were produced for the mother country and manufactured goods were purchased from her" (Morgan, 1956, pp. 8–9).

While the several mercantile empires dominated the world economy, trade among the European states also increased. In truth, prior to the Industrial Revolution, international economic integration was proceeding at a more rapid pace than national economic integration. Only in the nineteenth century, with improvements in land communications (particularly the railroad), an increased pace of industrial development, and the advent of stronger nation-states, did national economic integration catch up with international economic integration. When this occurred in the nineteenth century, domestic economic efficiency and favorable terms of trade and investment became the primary means of financing the burdens of hegemony.

Following the Industrial Revolution and the emergence of an industrial center in Great Britain, the British created an essentially new type of international economy based on specialization, multilateral free trade, and an international division of labor. Initially this international division of labor was composed of the British industrial center and the nonindustrial periphery, the former exporting manufactured goods in exchange for the food and raw materials of the latter. Subsequently, as other industrial centers arose in western Europe, North America, and elsewhere, there evolved among the industrial countries themselves a division of labor based on industrial specialization. These essential features of interdependence have continued to characterize the world economy in the twentieth century.

The British were able to finance their world position initially through high profits on this trade. After 1870, despite a declining trade balance (and, finally, a negative trade balance), the British continued to enjoy a balance-of-payments surplus because of high returns on overseas investments, the sale of services, and the benefits conferred by the international role of sterling. Unfortunately, for reasons that cannot be explored here, the industrial base on which British power ultimately depended deteriorated during these decades, and the British were decreasingly able to sustain their dominant global position when faced with rising challengers. In the next chapter we shall discuss the British response to this disequilibrium between their resources and commitments.

The displacement of Great Britain by the United States as the global hegemonic power did not initially pose for the United States the usual problem of finding ways to finance its dominant position. At the close of World War II the economic and military supremacy of the United States over other countries was of such magnitude that economists and officials regarded the problem to be exactly the opposite: how to insure a sufficient flow of financial resources from the United States to other countries to keep the international economy in balance (the so-called dollar-shortage problem). Within a few decades the revival of the European and Japanese economies and the unanticipated growth of Soviet military capabilities dramatically reversed this situation that had been so favorable for the United States.

History affords no more remarkable reversal of fortunes in a relatively short period of time than the reversal the United States experienced in the decades following World War II. The reestablished competitiveness of Europe and Japan cut into the American balance-of-payments surplus at the same time that the Soviet military challenge increased the costs of maintaining the international status quo. The contrast with the financial burden of the Pax Britannica is especially noteworthy, as the following quotation from Harold and Margaret Sprout indicates:

At the peak of British power and influence, the decade of the 1860's total expenditures for military purposes averaged less than £30 million per year. Adjusting for inflation and changes in the dollar price of sterling, this works out to something in the range of 1 to 2 percent of average U.S. military expenditures in the 1950's and early 1960's. In short, mid-nineteenth century British governments policed a worldwide empire . . . and exerted on other nations an influence as great as, if not considerably greater than, the United States can achieve today at a real cost fifty to one hundred times larger (Sprout and Sprout, 1972, pp. 311–12).

During the first decade or so of the cold war, the United States financed the cost of reviving the world economy and the cost of the struggle with the Soviet Union by drawing down America's international financial reserves and depressing American domestic consumption. At the end of World War II the United States had held a substantial fraction of the world's supply of gold and enjoyed a massive trade surplus. Until 1959, therefore, the United States was able to finance the reconstruction of its allies' economies and the containment of the Soviet Union through its overall trade surplus and gold reserves. But by 1959 this trade surplus was insufficient to finance America's balance of payments alone, and within three decades the United States had heavily depleted the gold and monetary reserves that it had acquired over the better part of a century.

During the second decade of the cold war, 1961 to 1971, the United States financed its global military and political position by its trade surplus (which peaked in 1967 and declined thereafter) and by printing money. The dollar had become the basis of the world monetary system, and the United States had become the world's banker. The United States controlled the printing press and printed dollars to meet its international needs: foreign investment by American corporations, the importation of goods, the supply of foreign aid, the maintenance of troops abroad, and the fighting of the Vietnam war. Under the system of fixed exchange rates, others were obligated (and in most cases desired) to accept and honor these dollars. In effect, America's allies extended credit to the United States to finance its world position because it was in their economic and security interests to do so. The crisis of the world economy in the 1980s (a topic beyond the scope of this study) is due in part to the fact that this mechanism of financing the global position of the United States resulted in costly inflation that has helped undermine the stability of the world economy (Cohen, 1977, pp. 90–107).

Loss of economic and technological leadership

The experiences of both Great Britain and the United States also illustrate a second external development that undermines the position of the dominant state. Earlier it was argued that the growth in power of a state was due to some comparative advantage over its neighbors. The nature of this relative advantage may be organizational, economic, technological, etc. In the premodern world, this advantage was most frequently in the form of military techniques or political organization. In the modern period, economic factors in particular have become an important source of national power and advantage. In both the premodern world and the modern world a principal advantage of an expanding state has been its military and/or productive capabilities, especially its technology. In time, however, this technological advantage disappears. As this superiority decreases, the costs of domination increase.

The positions of dominant states and empires have differed greatly with respect to the magnitude of the costs of protection and the time it has taken for these positions of dominance to erode. These differences may be due to geopolitical, technological, or systemic factors. The longevity of the Byzantine Empire, for example, was due in part to its possession of low-cost internal lines of communication. The greater longevity of the Pax Britannica relative to the Pax Americana is explained in part by the rapidity with which America's technological advantages were diffused to its economic and military competitors.

As many observers have noted, there is a historical tendency for the military and economic techniques of the dominant state or empire to be diffused to other states in the system or, more especially, to states on the periphery of the international system in question (Clough, 1970; Cipolla, 1970; McNeill, 1974). That is to say, through a process of diffusion to other states, the dominant power loses the advantage on which its political, military, or economic success has been based. Thus, by example, and frequently in more direct fashion, the dominant power helps to create challenging powers. Ironically, as Marx himself appreciated, one of the greatest forces for diffusion has been imperialism (Avineri, 1969). The imperial power has stimulated the colonized peoples to learn its ways and frequently has taught them advanced military, political, and economic techniques (Fairbank, Reischauer, and Craig, 1965, p. 487).

This process by which the techniques of power radiate from the more advanced society and transform the international distribution of power was well summarized in *The Economic Decline of Empires:*

One of the major items of public expenditure for mature empires is, of course, defense. A number of interrelated factors contribute to the expansion of military expenditures. Empires do not exist in a vacuum. They are surrounded by countries that in one way or another gain some advantage from the very existence of the empire itself. The prosperous economy and the progressive technology of a growing empire are bound to radiate beneficient effects beyond its boundaries and contribute to the development of its neighbours. In the course of time these neighbours become a threat and force the empire into greater military expenditure. The story of what Greece did to Egypt, the Germanic tribes did to Rome, early sixteenth-century France did to Italy, and England did to Spain and to Holland are significant in this regard. On the other hand, the growth of living standards within an empire pushes up the cost of an army. In the modern world the economic problems are less that of paying manpower than that of possessing very expensive equipment that becomes very rapidly obsolete. But whatever the specific elements involved, the problem remains essentially the same: military expenditure powerfully contributes to the growth of total public consumption (Cipolla, 1970, pp. 5–6).

The diffusion of military and economic technology from more advanced societies to less advanced societies is a key element in the international redistribution of power. Although technology is expensive and not easily created, once it is created it usually diffuses relatively easily. Efforts to prevent the diffusion of technology to military opponents or economic competitors fail over the long term; it makes no difference whether one is concerned with military technologies such as Greek fire and nuclear energy or productive technologies such as the spinning jenny and electronic computers.[5] At best, states can only slow the diffusion of the technology underlying their military or economic power; they cannot prevent it, especially today in a world in which technology rests on easily accessible scientific knowledge.

In the premodern world, the diffusion of military techniques from advanced societies to more primitive societies was a principal factor in the rise of new powers. In an age characterized by a slow rate of economic and technological advance, the adoption of new weapons, tactics, and organization seldom necessitated a sophisticated economic or technical infrastructure. Thus the diffusion of Roman military skills to the barbarian German tribes was a major factor in the collapse of ancient Mediterranean civilization (Oman, 1924, p. 12). The acquisition of Chinese metallurgy techniques by the Mongol horsemen of the Siberian steppes enabled them to subdue the superior Chinese and other civilizations (Elvin, 1973, p. 18). In the modern world, on the other hand, an advanced economic and scientific base on which to build is a much more important precondition for the adoption of advanced military techniques. The operation of the world economy has become an important factor in the diffusion of advanced techniques to less advanced societies.

In the preceding chapter it was pointed out that a world market economy tends to favor and to concentrate wealth in the more advanced and more efficient economy. At least in the short

---

[5] Greek fire was a secret incendiary weapon of the Byzantine Empire that was used against ships.

run this is true. In the long run, however, a world market economy fosters the spread of economic growth throughout the international system. Through trade, foreign investment, and the
transfer of technology, wealth and economic activities tend to
diffuse from the old centers to new centers of economic growth.
Enjoying the "advantages of backwardness," which will be described later, these new centers frequently overtake and surpass
the original center.[6]

Whether or not diffusion takes place depends on the recipient
society's capacity and willingness to learn. For reasons beyond
our present understanding, societies differ greatly in terms of
capacity to learn from others. As was noted earlier, the medieval
Muslim empires never adopted artillery to any significant extent. In other cases (notably, the late Chinese Empire, premodern Japan, and early modern Europe), societies have
pursued deliberate policies of preventing the adoption of advanced military techniques, fearing that the arming of the lower
social orders would upset their stratified social structures. On the
other hand, some societies, such as the Romans in the ancient
world and the Europeans, the Americans, and the Japanese in
the modern era, have displayed unique capacities to learn from
the mistakes and experiences of others. Such an enhanced capacity to learn from others is frequently associated with the growth
and expansion of great states and empires.

Although societies differ in regard to capacity to learn and to
absorb military and productive technologies, less advanced societies frequently enjoy what Alexander Gerschenkron (1962)
called the advantages of backwardness.[7] As Thorstein Veblen
observed in his classic work *Imperial Germany and the Industrial Revolution* (1939), one reason for this advantage is that the
imitators, who have lower standards of living and less wasteful
habits, can use the imported technology more efficiently. Moreover, they can adopt the most advanced and most thoroughly
proven techniques, whereas prior research-and-development

---

[6] This process of "polarization and spread" and its implications for the world economy
have been spelled out in greater detail elsewhere (Gilpin, 1975, pp. 47–59).

[7] Obviously, backwardness is not always an advantage; for an analysis of this issue, see
the work of Ames and Rosenberg (1971).

costs and vested interests deter the more advanced economy from substituting the very latest techniques for obsolescent techniques. Thus, with lower costs, untapped resources, and equivalent technology, backward societies frequently can outcompete the more affluent advanced society economically or militarily.

In contemporary economic discourse, the diffusion of industry and economic activities from advanced economies to less advanced economies is explained by "product cycle theory" (Vernon, 1971). This tendency and its historical significance was recognized by Leon Trotsky, who must be credited as an early theorist of economic development. Unevenness of development, Trotsky argued, characterizes the progress of all backward countries. "From the universal law of unevenness thus derives another law which for the lack of a better name, we may call the law of *combined development* – by which we mean a drawing together of the different stages of the journey, a combining of separate steps, an amalgam of archaic with more contemporary forms" (quoted by Knei-Paz, 1978, p. 89). Although it is primarily relevant to the contemporary era, Trotsky's law of combined development is relevant to earlier societies as well.

Trotsky rejected the orthodox Marxist view that every society must pass through the same stages that were followed by European capitalist development. Although the impact of capitalism may provoke a backward country to modernize, the backward country modernizes by combining backward forms and more advanced forms in a unique amalgam. In adopting new forms, the backward society is able to skip historical stages, exploit the experience of the more advanced society, and thereby outstrip its predecessors:

Although compelled to follow after the advanced countries, a backward country does not take things in the same order. The privilege of historic backwardness – and such privilege exists – permits, or rather compels, the adoption of whatever is ready in advance of any specified date, skipping a whole series of intermediate stages. Savages throw away their bows and arrows for rifles all at once, without travelling the road which lay between those two weapons in the past. The European colonists in America did not begin history all over again from the beginning. The fact that Germany and the United States have now economically outstripped England was made possible by the very backwardness of their capitalist development (Trotsky quoted by Knei-Paz, 1978, pp. 91–2).

The transfer of advanced techniques from advanced societies to less advanced societies is undoubtedly one of the most significant causes of the redistribution of power in an international system. This process also accounts for the critical role of open and exploited frontiers in international political change. The migration of skilled people to the open frontier and the resultant combining of existing techniques with the frontier's vast untapped resources have led to massive advances in wealth and power from Greek colonialization of the Mediterranean to the European conquest of the New World. The significance of open frontiers for wealth and power has made them a constant prize of interstate conflict.

The importance of the frontier phenomenon for state power was illustrated by Mark Elvin in *The Pattern of the Chinese Past* (1973). Elvin argued that the endurance of the Chinese Empire, as compared with that of the Romans, was due to a continuing moderate rate of economic innovation and an open frontier of exploitable resources. The exploitation of this southern frontier enabled the Chinese to escape the restraint of diminishing returns and to generate the economic surplus required to finance protection against foreign invaders (Elvin, 1973, p. 313). By moving the great Han people into the frontier and extending its bureaucratic control over the acquired territory, the Chinese Empire was able to capture for itself the gains associated with the advantages of backwardness. Similarly, the unprecedented power of the United States and Russia has resulted from their exploitation of their western and eastern frontiers, respectively. The future of the international balance of power will in large measure rest on the ability of the Soviet Union to apply modern techniques in the exploitation of Siberia's riches (McNeill, 1974, pp.170–172).

The Chinese, American, and Soviet exploitations of internal frontiers have been exceptions. The more common phenomenon has been the existence of a frontier beyond the control of the advanced society. It is for this reason that the diffusion of technology from the dominant power tends to favor states on the frontier or periphery of the international system. In contrast to states at the core of the system, these peripheral societies (e.g., Macedonia and Rome in the ancient world, Great Britain in early modern Europe, the United States in the nineteenth century) share several favorable characteristics. In the first place, usually they are at an optimum distance from the core of the system: close enough to absorb the technology of the dominant power, but sufficiently far away to be protected by the loss-of-strength gradient. Second, frequently their social institutions are less well developed and more receptive of new ideas. Third, they exist in a zone of relative peace and therefore do not dissipate their energies in continual warfare.

In addition to the tendency for techniques and technology to diffuse from the dominant power to lesser but rising powers within the system or on its periphery, the locus of innovation and economic activity may shift to another part of the system or to its periphery. As William McNeill demonstrated in *The Shape of European History* (1974), political, economic, and technological innovations produce fundamental shifts in the locus of power and wealth over time. A state strategically placed and advantaged with respect to trade, technology, and geography may in time find itself bypassed by more innovative societies because of fundamental changes in the political and economic environment. Thus the closing off of the Eastern trade routes by the Turks and the rise of an innovative Atlantic economy brought to a close Venice's thousand-year domination of Mediterranean trade.

In the modern world the centers of technological innovation have experienced several significant mutations. Although innovation, on the whole, is a continuous and incremental process, key innovations in industrial methods and technological products "tend to cluster in time and space" (McNeill, 1974, p. 37). The points of origin for various distinct phases in the evolution of modern industry have shifted over time from one economy to another, bringing in their train significant changes in the international distribution of power:

The first phase of the Industrial Revolution and the rise of Great Britain as the core of the world economy were dependent upon a cluster of technical breakthroughs in steam power, iron metallurgy, and textiles. Subsequently, the railroad and the opening of new lands were the great stimuli to investment at home and abroad. In the latter part of the nineteenth century, new methods of industrial organization, the advent of new industries (electrical, steel, and chemical), and the application of scientific theory to industry led to the industrial and political rise of Germany on the European continent. In the twentieth century, the industrial and economic hegemony of the United States has rested in large measure on the cluster of innovations in managerial know-how and advanced technologies (automobile, electronics, petrochemicals) that have constituted the fundamental factors in economic and industrial growth over the past half century (Gilpin, 1975, p. 67).

The tendency for the loci of technological innovations to cluster and shift from one economy to another is an important concern of contemporary scholarship, a concern stimulated by the current relative decline in American innovation and the implications of this development for the American economy and the slowing of world economic growth. For some, the answer lies in general economic phenomena that have temporarily reduced the demand for new technologies; for others, the contemporary situation seems to be due to a more fundamental inadequate supply of relevant theoretical knowledge.[8] Whatever the answer, the economy that breaks through the apparent technological stagnation of the present will undoubtedly become the technological innovator and global power of the future.

The tendency for technology and inventiveness to diffuse from dominant powers to peripheral states (which in turn become the dominant powers of an enlarged international system) and the occurrence of fundamental shifts in the locus of political and economic power led Arnold Toynbee to formulate in *A Study of History* and elsewhere a set of generalizations regarding the dynamics of international politics.[9] Whether or not Toynbee's "laws" of politics and history are accepted wholeheartedly, they

---

[8] For interesting studies of this question, see the work of Mensch (1979), OECD (1980), and Rostow (1980).

[9] In particular, Toynbee's views are set forth in the annual *Survey of International Affairs,* which he edited for many years.

do provide penetrating insights into the dynamics of international politics.

Writing on the sad fate of Europe in 1930, Toynbee noted that "the dwarfing of the European states by the states of the outer world was the most conspicuous feature of the post-war map" (1931, p. 131). In contrast to Europe, these peripheral states were of immense size. The United States was the most powerful, but it "was simply the first to develop strength out of a whole family of giants" (1931, p. 132). He foresaw that other giants would one day also emerge: the Soviet Union, Brazil, Canada, China, India, etc. Yet the sizes of European states had actually decreased in the twentieth century. In 1910 there had been only 21 sovereignties in Europe; in 1930 there were 30 European states.

Toynbee reasoned that this development was a consequence of a universal law: the tendency for the locus of power to shift from the center to the periphery of an international system. Throughout history, Toynbee observed, the powers at the centers of international systems (what he called civilizations) have tended to decrease in size and eventually to be dominated by great powers arising on the peripheries of the systems. Thus, four centuries earlier, the European nation-states of Spain, France, England, and Austria had risen to a position of dominance over the previously flourishing city-states of Italy and the Netherlands. And despite the call of Machiavelli for a unified Italy and the call of Count Coudenhove-Kalergi for pan-Europa to match the strength of the rising peripheral powers, the center of the system at that time was (as is usually the case) too beset by warring rivalries to unite its fragmented strength:

Thus the tableau of the world in 1930, in which the states of Europe were encircled and overshadowed by a ring of vaster states that had been called into existence by the radiation of European civilization into Asia and overseas, could be matched by the tableau of Europe itself four centuries earlier, in which the states of Italy were encircled and overshadowed by the greater states in the transalpine and transmarine quarters of Europe that had been awaked to new life by the magic touch of the Italian Renaissance. And the same tableau can be discerned in other epochs of history, in other geographical settings. When

we turn the pages of our historical atlas backwards till we come to the
Mediterranean in the third century B.C., we see the city-states of
Greece – an Athens, a Sparta, a Sicyon, a Megalopolis, a Rhodes –
encircled and dwarfed by a ring of outer Powers which owed their own
vitality to the elixir of Hellenism – Macedon, a Syria, and Egypt, a
Carthage, a Rome – and, in this Greece at bay, the project of a Pan-
Hellenic Union was seeking realization in the rival Aetolian and Ach-
aean Leagues. If we then mark time in the same century while we turn
our eyes from the Mediterranean to the Far Eastern extremity of the
Old World, we shall similarly perceive the little states in the centre – a
Song, a Chou, a Lu – which had been the seedbeds of Chinese culture,
on the point of succumbing to the contending Great Powers on the
periphery: a Ts'i, a Ch'u, a Ts'in (Toynbee, 1931, p. 133).

In answer to the question why "the peoples at the heart of the
civilized world [were] proving conspicuously less successful than
the peoples on the outskirts in the task of political construction
on the grand scale," even though their very destinies were at
issue, Toynbee postulated a twofold process at work (1931, p.
133). First, the expansion of the center against the periphery
arouses the peripheral peoples; they become aware of the superiority of the "advanced" civilization and seek to adopt its ways.
The diffusion of ideas and techniques from the center to the
periphery narrows the gap in military and other capabilities between the advanced civilization and the barbarians. This diffusion of advanced techniques from the center into the backward
periphery leads to consolidation of power on a scale that eventually dwarfs the center states. As a consequence, the difficulty
and costs of dominating the periphery increase.

The second aspect of this process of ebbing strength in the
center relative to the rising periphery is the operation of the
power struggle in the center. The balance of power in the center
"operates in a general way to keep the average calibre of states
low in terms of every criterion for the measurement of political
power: in extent of territory and in head of population and in
aggregate of wealth" (Toynbee, 1951, Vol. 3, p. 302). The
struggle both weakens them and blinds them to the threat of a
Macedonia or Rome gathering strength and consolidating the
land mass over the horizon. Failing to unite against the rising

peripheral power, they become its victims. History is replete with examples of power struggles that exhausted states at the center of the system and made them vulnerable to external conquest and domination. The fate of Europe in the first half of the twentieth century, Toynbee reasoned, was merely the most recent example of this universal phenomenon.

One need not accept Toynbee's formulation to appreciate the critical role in the redistribution of power in an international system played by the diffusion of techniques from advanced states to less advanced states. In the premodern era, these diffusing techniques were essentially those relating to political organization and military capabilities. In the modern world, the diffusion of techniques relating to economic organization and industrial production has become an increasingly important factor in the undermining of the position of the dominant power.

CONCLUSION

The process of disequilibrium described in this chapter may be summarized in the following fashion: Once a society reaches the limits of its expansion, it has great difficulty in maintaining its position and arresting its eventual decline. Further, it begins to encounter marginal returns in agricultural or industrial production. Both internal and external changes increase consumption and the costs of protection and production; it begins to experience a severe fiscal crisis. The diffusion of its economic, technological, or organizational skills undercuts its comparative advantage over other societies, especially those on the periphery of the system. These rising states, on the other hand, enjoy lower costs, rising rates of return on their resources, and the advantages of backwardness. In time, the differential rates of growth of declining and rising states in the system produce a decisive redistribution of power and result in disequilibrium in the system.

5

Hegemonic war and international change

Assumption 5. If the disequilibrium in the international system is not resolved, then the system will be changed, and a new equilibrium reflecting the redistribution of power will be established.

The disequilibrium in the international system is due to increasing disjuncture between the existing governance of the system and the redistribution of power in the system. Although the hierarchy of prestige, the distribution of territory, the rules of the system, and the international division of labor continue to favor the traditional dominant power or powers, the power base on which the governance of the system ultimately rests has eroded because of differential growth and development among states. This disjuncture among the components of the international system creates challenges for the dominant states and opportunities for the rising states in the system.

This disequilibrium may be expressed by different formulations, depending on the perspective taken. From the perspective of the system, it involves disjuncture among the components of the system. As noted in the preceding paragraph, although the international distribution of power has undergone a significant change, the other components of the system have remained relatively constant. From the perspective of dominant powers, the costs of maintaining the international status quo have increased, producing a serious discrepancy between one's power and one's commitments. From the perspective of rising powers, the perceived costs of changing the international system have declined relative to the potential benefits of doing so. However the disequilibrium is viewed, what has changed is the distribution of power among the states in the system.

Because of the redistribution of power, the costs to the traditional dominant state of maintaining the international system increase relative to its capacity to pay; this, in turn, produces the severe fiscal crisis of which we have already taken note.[1] By the same token, the costs to the rising state of changing the system decrease; it begins to appreciate that it can increase its own gains by forcing changes in the nature of the system. Its enhanced power position means that the relative costs of changing the system and securing its interests have decreased. Thus, in accordance with the law of demand, the rising state, as its power increases, will seek to change the status quo as the perceived potential benefits begin to exceed the perceived costs of undertaking a change in the system.

As its relative power increases, a rising state attempts to change the rules governing the international system, the division of the spheres of influence, and, most important of all, the international distribution of territory. In response, the dominant power counters this challenge through changes in its policies that attempt to restore equilibrium in the system. The historical record reveals that if it fails in this attempt, the disequilibrium will be resolved by war. Shepard Clough, in his book *The Rise and Fall of Civilization,* drew on a distinguished career in historical scholarship to make the point: "At least in all the cases which we have passed . . . , in review in these pages, cultures with inferior civilization but with growing economic power have always attacked the most civilized cultures during the latters' economic decline" (1970, p. 263). The fundamental task of the challenged dominant state is to solve what Walter Lippmann once characterized as the fundamental problem of foreign policy – the balancing of commitments and resources (Lippmann, 1943, p. 7). An imperial, hegemonic, or great power has essentially two

---

[1] The singular form is used here, although it is possible that two or more states may be seeking to maintain or change the system.

courses of action open to it as it attempts to restore equilibrium in the system. The first and preferred solution is that the challenged power can seek to increase the resources devoted to maintaining its commitments and position in the international system. The second is that it can attempt to reduce its existing commitments (and associated costs) in a way that does not ultimately jeopardize its international position. Although neither response will be followed to the exclusion of the other, they may be considered analytically as separate policies. The logic and the pitfalls of each policy will be considered in turn.

Historically, the most frequently employed devices to generate new resources to meet the increasing costs of dominance and to forestall decline have been to increase domestic taxation and to exact tribute from other states. Both of these courses of action have inherent dangers in that they can provoke resistance and rebellion. The French Revolution was triggered in part by the effort of the monarchy to levy the higher taxes required to meet the British challenge (von Ranke, 1950, p. 211). Athens's "allies" revolted against Athenian demands for increased tribute. Because higher taxes (or tribute) mean decreased productive investment and a lowered standard of living, in most instances such expedients can be employed for only relatively short periods of time, such as during a war.

The powerful resistance within a society to higher taxes or tribute encourages the government to employ more indirect methods of generating additional resources to meet a fiscal crisis. Most frequently, a government will resort to inflationary policies or seek to manipulate the terms of trade with other countries. As Carlo Cipolla observed (1970, p. 13), the invariable symptoms of a society's decline are excessive taxation, inflation, and balance-of-payments difficulties as government and society spend beyond their means. But these indirect devices also bring hardship and encounter strong resistance over the long run.

The most satisfactory solution to the problem of increasing costs is increased efficiency in the use of existing resources. Through organizational, technological, and other types of innovations, a state can either economize with respect to the resources at its disposal or increase the total amount of disposable resources. Thus, as Mark Elvin explained, the fundamental reason that imperial China survived intact for so long was its unusually high rate of economic and technological innovation; over long periods China was able to generate sufficient resources to finance the costs of protection against successive invaders (Elvin, 1973). Conversely, the Roman economy stagnated and failed to innovate. Among the reasons for the decline and destruction of Rome was its inability to generate resources sufficient to stave off barbarian invaders.[2] More recently, the calls for greater industrial productivity in contemporary America derive from the realization that technological innovation and more efficient use of existing resources are needed to meet the increasing demands of consumption, investment, and protection.

This innovative solution involves rejuvenation of the society's military, economic, and political institutions. In the case of declining Rome, for example, a recasting of its increasingly inefficient system of agricultural production and a revised system of taxation were required. Unfortunately, social reform and institutional rejuvenation become increasingly difficult as a society ages, because this implies more general changes in customs, attitudes, motivation, and sets of values that constitute a cultural heritage (Cipolla, 1970, p. 11). Vested interests resist the loss of their privileges. Institutional rigidities frustrate abandonment of "tried and true" methods (Downs, 1967, pp. 158–66). One could hardly expect it to be otherwise: "Innovations are important not for their immediate, actual results but for their potential for future development, and potential is very difficult to assess" (Cipolla, 1970, pp. 9–10).

A declining society experiences a vicious cycle of decay and immobility, much as a rising society enjoys a virtuous cycle of growth and expansion. On the one hand, decline is accompanied by lack of social cooperation, by emphasis on rights rather than emphasis on duty, and by decreasing productivity. On the other hand, the frustration and pessimism generated by this gloomy atmosphere inhibit renewal and innovation. The failure to innovate accentuates the decline and its psychologically debilitating

---

[2] The explanation for the decline of Rome obviously is not simple, but this was a critical factor (Walbank, 1969).

consequences. Once caught up in this cycle, it is difficult for the society to break out (Cipolla, 1970, p. 11). For this reason, a more rational and more efficient use of existing resources to meet increasing military and productive needs is seldom achieved.

There have been societies that have managed their resources with great skill for hundreds of years and have rejuvenated themselves in response to external challenges, and this resilience has enabled them to survive for centuries in a hostile environment. In fact, those states that have been notable for their longevity have been the ones most successful in allocating their scarce resources in an optimal fashion in order to balance, over a period of centuries, the conflicting demands of consumption, protection, and investment. An outstanding example was the Venetian city-state. Within this aristocratic republic the governing elite moderated consumption and shifted resources back and forth between protection and investment as need required over the centuries (Lane, 1973). The Chinese Empire was even more significant. Its longevity and unity were due to the fact that the Chinese were able to increase their production more rapidly than the rise in the costs of protection (Elvin, 1973, pp. 92–3, 317). The progressive nature of the imperial Chinese economy meant that sufficient resources were in most cases available to meet external threats and preserve the integrity of the empire for centuries. In contrast to the Romans, who were eventually inundated and destroyed by the barbarians, the Chinese "on the whole . . . managed to keep one step ahead of their neighbours in the relevant technical skills, military, economic and organizational" (Elvin, 1973, p. 20).

An example of social rejuvenation intended to meet an external challenge was that of revolutionary France. The point has already been made that European aristocracies were reluctant to place firearms in the hands of the lower social orders, preferring to rely on small professional armies. The French Revolution and the innovation of nationalism made it possible for the French state to tap the energies of the masses of French citizens. The so-called *levée en masse* greatly increased the human resources available to the republic and, later, to Napoleon. Although this imperial venture was ultimately unsuccessful, it does illustrate the potentiality for domestic rejuvenation of a society in response to decline.

The second type of response to declining fortunes is to bring costs and resources into balance by reducing costs. This can be attempted in three general ways. The first is to eliminate the reason for the increasing costs (i.e., to weaken or destroy the rising challenger). The second is to expand to a more secure and less costly defensive perimeter. The third is to reduce international commitments. Each of these alternative strategies has its attractions and its dangers.

The first and most attractive response to a society's decline is to eliminate the source of the problem. By launching a preventive war the declining power destroys or weakens the rising challenger while the military advantage is still with the declining power. Thus, as Thucydides explained, the Spartans initiated the Peloponnesian War in an attempt to crush the rising Athenian challenger while Sparta still had the power to do so. When the choice ahead has appeared to be to decline or to fight, statesmen have most generally fought. However, besides causing unnecessary loss of life, the greatest danger inherent in preventive war is that it sets in motion a course of events over which statesmen soon lose control (see the subsequent discussion of hegemonic war).

Second, a state may seek to reduce the costs of maintaining its position by means of further expansion.[3] In effect, the state hopes to reduce its long-term costs by acquiring less costly defensive positions. As Edward Luttwak (1976) demonstrated in his brilliant study of Roman grand strategy, Roman expansion in its later phases was an attempt to find more secure and less costly defensive positions and to eliminate potential challengers. Although this response to declining fortunes can be effective, it can also lead to further overextension of commitments, to increasing costs, and thereby to acceleration of the decline. It is

---

[3] This cause of expansion is frequently explained by the "turbulent-frontier" thesis. A classic example was Britain's steady and incremental conquest of India in order to eliminate threatening political disturbances on the frontier of the empire. Two recent examples are the American invasion of Cambodia during the Vietnam War and the Soviet invasion of Afghanistan.

difficult for a successful and expanding state to break the habit of expansion, and it is all too easy to believe that "expand or die" is the imperative of international survival. Perhaps the greatest danger for every imperial or hegemonic power, as it proved eventually to be for Rome, is overextension of commitments that gradually begin to sap its strength (Grant, 1968, p. 246).[4]

The third means of bringing costs and resources into balance is, of course, to reduce foreign-policy commitments. Through political, territorial, or economic retrenchment, a society can reduce the costs of maintaining its international position. However, this strategy is politically difficult, and carrying it out is a delicate matter. Its success is highly uncertain and strongly dependent on timing and circumstances. The problem of retrenchment will be considered first in general terms; then a case of relatively successful retrenchment by a great power will be discussed.

The most direct method of retrenchment is unilateral abandonment of certain of a state's economic, political, or military commitments. For example, a state may withdraw from exposed and costly strategic positions. Venice, as was pointed out, pursued for centuries a conscious policy of alternating advance and retreat. The longevity of the later Roman Empire or Byzantine Empire may be partially explained by its withdrawal from its exposed and difficult-to-defend western provinces and consolidation of its position on a less costly basis in its eastern provinces; its survival for a thousand years was due to the fact that it brought the scale of empire and resources into balance (Cipolla, 1970, p. 82; Rader, 1971, p. 54). In our own time, the so-called Nixon doctrine may be interpreted as an effort on the part of the United States to disengage from vulnerable commitments and to shift part of the burden of defending the international status quo to other powers (Hoffmann, 1978, pp. 46–7).

A second standard technique of retrenchment is to enter into alliances with or seek rapprochement with less threatening powers. In effect, the dominant but declining power makes concessions to another state and agrees to share the benefits of the

---

[4] As Raymond Aron argued (1974), defeat in Vietnam may, in the long run, save the United States from the corrupting and ultimately weakening vice of overexpansion of commitments.

status quo with that other state in exchange for sharing the costs of preserving the status quo. Thus the Romans brought the Goths into the empire (much to their later regret) in exchange for their assistance in defending the frontiers of the empire. As will be pointed out in a moment, the policy of entente or rapprochement was pursued by the British prior to World War I as they sought to meet the rising German challenge. The American rapprochement with Communist China is a late-twentieth-century example. In exchange for weakening the American commitment to Taiwan, the Americans seek Chinese assistance in containing the expanding power of the Soviet Union.

Unfortunately, there are several dangers associated with this response to decline. First, in an alliance between a great power and a lesser power there is a tendency for the former to overpay in the long run, as has occurred with the United States and the North Atlantic Treaty Organization (NATO); the great power increases its commitments without a commensurate increase in the resources devoted by its allies to finance those commitments. Further, the ally is benefited materially by the alliance, and as its capabilities increase, it may turn against the declining power. Thus the Romans educated the Goths in their military techniques only to have the latter turn these techniques against them. Second, the utility of alliances is limited by Riker's theory of coalitions: An increase in the number of allies decreases the benefits to each. Therefore, as an alliance increases in number, the probability of defection increases (Riker, 1962). Third, the minor ally may involve the major ally in disputes of its own from which the latter cannot disengage itself without heavy costs to its prestige. For these reasons, the utility of an alliance as a response to decline and a means to decrease costs is severely restricted.

The third and most difficult method of retrenchment is to make concessions to the rising power and thereby seek to appease its ambitions. Since the Munich conference in 1938, "appeasement" as a policy has been in disrepute and has been regarded as inappropriate under every conceivable set of circumstances. This is unfortunate, because there are historical examples in which appeasement has succeeded. Contending states have not only avoided conflict but also achieved a relationship satisfactory to both. A notable example was British appeasement of the rising United States in the decades prior to World War I (Perkins, 1968). The two countries ended a century-long hosility and laid the basis for what has come to be known as the "special relationship" of the two Anglo-Saxon powers.

The fundamental problem with a policy of appeasement and accommodation is to find a way to pursue it that does not lead to continuing deterioration in a state's prestige and international position. Retrenchment by its very nature is an indication of relative weakness and declining power, and thus retrenchment can have a deteriorating effect on relations with allies and rivals. Sensing the decline of their protector, allies try to obtain the best deal they can from the rising master of the system. Rivals are stimulated to "close in," and frequently they precipitate a conflict in the process. Thus World War I began as a conflict between Russia and Austria over the disposition of the remnants of the retreating Ottoman Empire (Hawtrey, 1952, pp. 75–81).

Because retrenchment signals waning power, a state seldom retrenches or makes concessions on its own initiative. Yet, not to retrench voluntarily and then to retrench in response to threats or military defeat means an even more severe loss of prestige and weakening of one's diplomatic standing. As a consequence of such defeats, allies defect to the victorious party, opponents press their advantage, and the retrenching society itself becomes demoralized. Moreover, if the forced retrenchment involves the loss of a "vital interest," then the security and integrity of the state are placed in jeopardy. For these reasons, retrenchment is a hazardous course for a state; it is a course seldom pursued by a declining power. However, there have been cases of a retrenchment policy being carried out rather successfully.

An excellent example of a declining hegemon that successfully brought its resources and commitments into balance is provided by Great Britain in the decades just prior to World War I. Following its victory over France in the Napoleonic wars, Great Britain had become the world's most powerful and most prestigious state. It gave its name to a century of relative peace, the Pax Britannica. British naval power was supreme on the high seas, and British industry and commerce were unchallengeable in world markets. An equilibrium had been established on the European continent by the Congress of Vienna (1814), and no military or industrial rivals then existed outside of Europe. By the last decades of the century, however, a profound transformation had taken place. Naval and industrial rivals had risen to challenge British supremacy both on the Continent and overseas. France, Germany, the United States, Japan, and Russia, to various degrees, had become expanding imperial powers. The unification of Germany by Prussia had destroyed the protective Continental equilibrium, and Germany's growing naval might threatened Britain's command of the seas.

As a consequence of these commercial, naval, and imperial challenges, Great Britain began to encounter the problems that face every mature or declining power. On the one hand, external demands were placing steadily increasing strains on the economy; on the other hand, the capacity of the economy to meet these demands had deteriorated. Thus, at the same time that the costs of protection were escalating, both private consumption and public consumption were also increasing because of greater affluence. Superficially the economy appeared strong, but the rates of industrial expansion, technological innovation, and domestic investment had slowed. Thus the rise of foreign challenges and the climacteric of the economy had brought on disequilibrium between British global commitments and British resources.

As the disequilibrium between its global hegemony and its limited resources intensified, Britain faced the dilemma of increasing its resources or reducing its commitments or both. In the national debate on this critical issue the proponents of increasing the available resources proposed two general courses of action. First, they proposed a drawing together of the empire and drawing on these combined resources, as well as the creation of what John Seeley (1905) called Greater Britain, especially the white dominions. This idea, however, did not have sufficient appeal at home or abroad. Second, reformers advocated measures to rejuvenate the declining British economy and to achieve greater efficiency. Unfortunately, as W. Arthur Lewis argued, all the roads that would have led to industrial innovation and a higher rate of economic growth were closed to the British for social, political, or ideological reasons (Lewis, 1978, p. 133). The primary solution to the problem of decline and disequilibrium, therefore, necessarily lay in the reduction of overseas diplomatic and strategic commitments.

The specific diplomatic and strategic issue that faced British leadership was whether to maintain the global position identified with the Pax Britannica or to bring about a retrenchment of its global commitments. By the last decade of the century, Great Britain was confronted by rival land and sea powers on every continent and every sea. European rivals were everywhere: Russia in the Far East, south Asia, and the Middle East; France in Asia, the Middle East, and north Africa; Germany in the Far East, the Middle East, and Africa. Furthermore, in the Far East, Japan had suddenly emerged as a great power; the United States also was becoming a naval power of consequence and was challenging Great Britain in the Western Hemisphere and the Pacific Ocean.

At the turn of the century, however, the predominant problem was perceived to be the challenge of German naval expansionism. Whereas all the other challenges posed limited and long-term threats, the danger embodied in Germany's decision to build a battle fleet was immediate and portentous. Despite intense negotiations, no compromise of this naval armaments race could be reached. The only course open to the British was retrenchment of their power and commitments around the globe in order to concentrate their total efforts on the German challenge.

Great Britain settled its differences with its other foreign rivals one after another. In the 1890s came the settlement of the Venezuela–British Guiana border dispute in accordance with American desires; in effect, Britain acquiesced in America's primacy in the Caribbean Sea. A century of American–British uneasiness came to an end, and the foundation was laid for the Anglo-American alliance that would prevail in two world wars. Next, in the Anglo-Japanese alliance of 1902, Great Britain gave up its policy of going it alone and took Japan as its partner in the Far East. Accepting Japanese supremacy in the northwestern Pacific as a counterweight to Russia, Great Britain withdrew to the south. This was immediately followed in 1904 by the *entente cordiale,* which settled the Mediterranean and colonial confrontation between France and Great Britain and ended centuries of conflict. In 1907 the Anglo-Russian agreement resolved the British–Russian confrontation in the Far East, turned Russia's interest toward the Balkans, and eventually aligned Russia, Great Britain, and France against Germany and Austria. Thus, by the eve of World War I, British commitments had been retrenched to a point that Britain could employ whatever power it possessed to arrest further decline in the face of expanding German power.[5]

Thus far we have described two alternative sets of strategies that a great power may pursue in order to arrest its decline: to increase resources or to decrease costs. Each of these policies has succeeded to some degree at one time or another. Most frequently, however, the dominant state is unable to generate sufficient additional resources to defend its vital commitments; alternatively, it may be unable to reduce its cost and commitments to some manageable size. In these situations, the disequilibrium in the system becomes increasingly acute as the declining power tries to maintain its position and the rising power attempts to transform the system in ways that will advance its interests. As a consequence of this persisting disequilibrium, the international system is beset by tensions, uncertainties, and crises. However, such a stalemate in the system seldom persists for a long period of time.

Throughout history the primary means of resolving the disequilibrium between the structure of the international system and the redistribution of power has been war, more particularly, what we shall call a hegemonic war. In the words of Raymond Aron, describing World War I, a hegemonic war "is characterized less by its immediate causes or its explicit purposes than by its extent and the stakes involved. It affected all the political units inside one system of relations between sovereign states. Let

---

[5] There is a school of thought whose members argue that Great Britain did not go far enough: Britain should have retreated from India and "east of Suez" and become fully a European power. Failure to do so only continued the drain on resources and weakened Britain in the face of first the Hitlerite challenge and subsequently the American challenge (Barnett, 1972). Others will no doubt criticize this analysis for suggesting that Great Britain was following a conscious policy of retrenchment in response to the German threat. Conscious or not, response to disequilibrium describes British policy.

us call it, for want of a better term, a war of hegemony,[6] hegemony being, if not conscious motive, at any rate the inevitable consequence of the victory of at least one of the states or groups" (Aron, 1964, p. 359). Thus, a hegemonic war is the ultimate test of change in the relative standings of the powers in the existing system.

Every international system that the world has known has been a consequence of the territorial, economic, and diplomatic realignments that have followed such hegemonic struggles. The most important consequence of a hegemonic war is that it changes the system in accordance with the new international distribution of power; it brings about a reordering of the basic components of the system. Victory and defeat reestablish an unambiguous hierarchy of prestige congruent with the new distribution of power in the system. The war determines who will govern the international system and whose interests will be primarily served by the new international order. The war leads to a redistribution of territory among the states in the system, a new set of rules of the system, a revised international division of labor, etc. As a consequence of these changes, a relatively more stable international order and effective governance of the international system are created based on the new realities of the international distribution of power. In short, hegemonic wars have (unfortunately) been functional and integral parts of the evolution and dynamics of international systems.

It is not inevitable, of course, that a hegemonic struggle will give rise immediately to a new hegemonic power and a renovated international order. As has frequently occurred, the combatants may exhaust themselves, and the "victorious" power may be unable to reorder the international system. The destruction of Rome by barbarian hordes led to the chaos of the Dark Ages. The Pax Britannica was not immediately replaced by the Pax Americana; there was a twenty year interregnum, what E. H. Carr called the "twenty years' crisis." Eventually, however, a new power or set of powers emerges to give governance to the international system.

[6] Aron's footnote: "Such wars could also be called wars of equilibrium if they were defined with reference to the side which is on the defensive."

What, then, are the defining characteristics of a hegemonic war? How does it differ from more limited conflicts among states? In the first place, such a war involves a direct contest between the dominant power or powers in an international system and the rising challenger or challengers. The conflict becomes total and in time is characterized by participation of all the major states and most of the minor states in the system. The tendency, in fact, is for every state in the system to be drawn into one or another of the opposing camps. Inflexible bipolar configurations of power (the Delian League versus the Peloponnesian League, the Triple Alliance versus the Triple Entente) frequently presage the outbreak of hegemonic conflict.

Second, the fundamental issue at stake is the nature and governance of the system. The legitimacy of the system may be said to be challenged. For this reason, hegemonic wars are unlimited conflicts; they are at once political, economic, and ideological in terms of significance and consequences. They become directed at the destruction of the offending social, political, or economic system and are usually followed by religious, political, or social transformation of the defeated society. The leveling of Carthage by Rome, the conversion of the Middle East to Islam by the Arabs, and the democratization of contemporary Japan and West Germany by the United States are salient examples.

As Thucydides told us, the issue in the great war between Sparta and Athens was hegemony over Hellas, not the more limited matters in contention between the opposing states. Although politicians on both sides regarded the conflict as limited and hence negotiable, Pericles went to the heart of the issue in response to those Athenian politicians willing to accept Sparta's seemingly limited demands:

They order us to raise the siege of Potidæa, to let Ægina be independent, to revoke the Megara decree; and they conclude with an ultimatum warning us to leave the Hellenes independent. I hope that you will none of you think that we shall be going to war for a trifle if we refuse to revoke the Megara decree, which appears in front of their complaints, and the revocation of which is to save us from war, or let any feeling of self-reproach linger in your minds, as if you went to war for slight cause. Why, this trifle contains the whole seal and trial of your resolution. If you give way, you will instantly have to meet some greater demand, as having been frightened into obedience in the first instance; while a firm refusal will make them clearly understand that they must treat you more as equals. Make your decision therefore at once, either to submit before you are harmed, or if we are to go to war, as I for one think we ought, to do so without caring whether the ostensible cause be great or small, resolved against making concessions or consenting to a precarious tenure of our possessions. For all claims from an equal, urged upon a neighbour as commands, before any attempt at legal settlement, be they great or be they small, have only one meaning, and that is slavery (Thucydides, 1951, pp. 79–80).

Third, a hegemonic war is characterized by the unlimited means employed and by the general scope of the warfare. Because all parties are drawn into the war and the stakes involved are high, few limitations, if any, are observed with respect to the means employed; the limitations on violence and treachery tend to be only those necessarily imposed by the state of technology, the available resources, and the fear of retaliation. Similarly, the geographic scope of the war tends to expand to encompass the entire international system; these are "world" wars. Thus, hegemonic wars are characterized by their intensity, scope, and duration.

From the premodern world, the Peloponnesian War between Athens and Sparta and the Second Punic War between Carthage and Rome meet these criteria of hegemonic war. In the modern era, several wars have been hegemonic struggles: the Thirty Years' War (1618–48); the wars of Louis XIV (1667–1713); the wars of the French Revolution and Napoleon (1792–1814); World Wars I and II (1914–18, 1939–45) (Mowat, 1928, pp. 1–2). At issue in each of these great conflicts was the governance of the international system.

In addition to the preceding criteria that define hegemonic war, three preconditions generally appear to be associated with the outbreak of hegemonic war. In the first place, the intensification of conflicts among states is a consequence of the "closing in" of space and opportunities. With the aging of an international system and the expansion of states, the distance between states decreases, thereby causing them increasingly to come into conflict

with one another. The once-empty space around the centers of
power in the system is appropriated. The exploitable resources
begin to be used up, and opportunities for economic growth decline. The system begins to encounter limits to the growth and
expansion of member states; states increasingly come into conflict
with one another. Interstate relations become more and more a
zero-sum game in which one state's gain is another's loss.

Marxists and realists share a sense of the importance of con-
tracting frontiers and their significance for the stability and peace
of the system. As long as expansion is possible, the law of uneven
growth (or development) can operate with little disturbing effect
on the overall stability of the system. In time, however, limits are
reached, and the international system enters a period of crisis.
The clashes among states for territory, resources, and markets
increase in frequency and magnitude and eventually culminate in
hegemonic war. Thus, as E. H Carr told us, the relative peace of
nineteenth-century Europe and the belief that a harmony of interest was providing a basis for increasing economic interdependence
were due to the existence of "continuously expanding territories
and markets" (1951, p. 224). The closing in of political and economic space led to the intensification of conflict and the final
collapse of the system in the two world wars.

The second condition preceding hegemonic war is temporal
and psychological rather than spatial; it is the perception that a
fundamental historical change is taking place and the gnawing
fear of one or more of the great powers that time is somehow
beginning to work against it and that one should settle matters
through preemptive war while the advantage is still on one's
side. It was anxiety of this nature that Thucydides had in mind
when he wrote that the growth of Athenian power inspired fear
on the part of the Lacedaemonians and was the unseen cause of
the war. The alternatives open to a state whose relative power is
being eclipsed are seldom those of waging war versus promoting
peace, but rather waging war while the balance is still in that
state's favor or waging war later when the tide may have turned
against it.[7] Thus the motive for hegemonic war, at least from the

---

[7] For the case of World War I, see the work of Hawtrey (1952, p. 81).

perspective of the dominant power, is to minimize one's losses rather than to maximize one's gains. In effect, a precondition for hegemonic war is the realization that the law of uneven growth has begun to operate to one's disadvantage.

The third precondition of hegemonic war is that the course of events begins to escape human control. Thus far, the argument of this study has proceeded as if mankind controlled its own destiny. The propositions presented and explored in an attempt to understand international political change have been phrased in terms of rational cost/benefit calculations. Up to a point, rationality does appear to apply; statesmen do explicitly or implicitly make rational calculations and then attempt to set the course of the ship of state accordingly. But it is equally true that events, especially those associated with the passions of war, can easily escape from human control.

"What is the force that moves nations?" Tolstoy inquires in the concluding part of War and Peace, and he answers that ultimately it is the masses in motion (1961, Vol. II, p. 1404). Leadership, calculation, control over events—these are merely the illusions of statesmen and scholars. The passions of men and the momentum of events take over and propel societies in novel and unanticipated directions. This is especially true during times of war. As the Athenians counseled the Peloponnesians in seeking to forestall war, "consider the vast influence of accident in war, before you engage in it. As it continues, it generally becomes an affair of chances, chances from which neither of us is exempt, and whose event we must risk in the dark. It is a common mistake in going to war to begin at the wrong end, to act first, and wait for disaster to discuss the matter" (Thucydides, 1951, p. 45).

Indeed, men seldom determine or even anticipate the consequences of hegemonic war. Although in going to war they desire to increase their gains or minimize their losses, they do not get the war they want or expect; they fail to recognize the pent-up forces they are unleashing or the larger historical significance of the decisions they are taking. They underestimate the eventual scope and intensity of the conflict on which they are embarking and its implications for their civilization. Hegemonic war arises from the structural conditions and disequilibrium of an international system, but its consequences are seldom predicted by statesmen. As Toynbee suggested, the law governing such conflicts would appear to favor rising states on the periphery of an international system rather than the contending states in the system itself. States directly engaged in hegemonic conflict, by weakening themselves, frequently actually eliminate obstacles to conquest by a peripheral power.

The great turning points in world history have been provided by these hegemonic struggles among political rivals; these periodic conflicts have reordered the international system and propelled history in new and uncharted directions. They resolve the question of which state will govern the system, as well as what ideas and values will predominate, thereby determining the ethos of succeeding ages. The outcomes of these wars affect the economic, social, and ideological structures of individual societies as well as the structure of the larger international system.

In contrast to the emphasis placed here on the role of hegemonic war in changing the international system, it might be argued that domestic revolution can change the international system. This is partially correct. It would be foolish to suggest, for example, that the great revolutions of the twentieth century (the Russian, Chinese, and perhaps Iranian) have not had a profound impact on world politics. However, the primary consequence of these social and political upheavals (at least of the first two) has been to facilitate the mobilization of the society's resources for purposes of national power. In other words, the significance of these revolutions for world politics is that they have served to strengthen (or weaken) their respective states and thereby cause a redistribution of power in the system.

As the distinguished French historian Elie Halévy put it, "all great convulsions in the history of the world, and more particularly in modern Europe, have been at the same time wars and revolutions" (1965, p. 212).[8] Thus the Thirty Years' War was both an international war among Sweden, France, and the Haps-

[8] Halévy's essay "The World Crises of 1914–1918: An Interpretation," first published in 1930, is a brilliant analysis of the roles of social forces and political ideas in the outbreak of war.

burg Empire and a series of domestic conflicts among Protestant and Catholic parties. The wars of the French Revolution and the Napoleonic period that pitted France against the rest of Europe triggered political upheavals of class and national revolutions throughout Europe. World Wars I and II represented not only the decay of the European international political order but also an onslaught against political liberalism and economic laissez-faire. The triumph of American power in these wars meant not only American governance of the system but also reestablishment of a liberal world order.

The importance of hegemonic wars in diverting history into new channels has stimulated numerous scholars to inquire if their occurrences are governed by a historical law and if they display a discernible pattern (Toynbee, 1961; Wright, 1942; Beer, 1981). It is suggested that there exists, at least in modern history, a recurring cycle of war and peace. In the words of the eminent historian George Clark, "in all its different forms [this idea] asserts that during a state of peace there are conditions which necessarily lead to an outbreak of war, that during the ensuing war there are others which bring peace back again, and that the process, having returned to a point where it was before is, and presumably will be, repeated indefinitely" (1958, p. 131). Thus, this deterministic idea holds that periodic hegemonic wars are caused by the systematic expansion and contraction of social, psychological, and economic forces.

In recent scholarship, the idea of cycles of war and peace has been explored by such writers as Gerhard Mensch (1979), Walter Rostow (1980), and George Modelski (1978). Among these writers, the most interesting theory is perhaps that of Modelski, who argued that modern history is characterized by "long cycles of global politics" (1978, pp. 214–35). These hundred-year-long cycles, inaugurated by and concluded by what he called "global wars," correspond to the dominance over international relations of five successive world powers: Portugal, the Netherlands, Great Britain (twice), and the United States. During their reigns, these world powers provided order for the international system.

Modelski's stress on world powers and global wars in ordering and changing the international system is similar to the position advanced in this study. However, the difference between Modelski's formulation regarding global hegemonic war and the formulation presented here is fundamental.[9] Although Modelski's idea of cycles of war and peace is intellectually attractive, the difficulties of long-wave theories in politics as in economics is that no mechanism is known to exist that can explain them. Thus, Modelski's positing "of a Buddenbrooks syndrome . . . one generation builds, the next consolidates and the third loses control" (1978, p. 232) is no more convincing than the more elaborate sixteenth-century formulation of the idea: "I have always heard it said that peace bring riches; riches bring pride; pride brings anger; anger brings war; war brings poverty; poverty brings humanity; humanity brings peace; peace, as I have said, brings riches, and so the world's affairs go round" (quoted by Clark, 1958, p. 134). Although a hundred-year cycle of war and peace may exist, until the mechanism that determines and generates the cycles is defined, the idea must remain speculative, albeit interesting.

In truth it must be said that uncertainty rules the world, and all political theory from Thucydides and Machiavelli to contemporary scholarship addresses one fundamental question: How can the human race, whether for selfish or more cosmopolitan ends, understand and control the seemingly blind forces of history? In the contemporary world this issue has become especially acute because of the development of nuclear and other weapons of mass destruction. In the context of this study, we must ask whether or not in the nuclear age hegemonic war will continue to be the fundamental mechanism of adjusting relations among states. Is it possible for statesmen to gain better control over the seemingly blind forces of political change?

During the prelude to World War II, a number of scholars of international relations sought to find an answer to this question (Dunn, 1937; Carr, 1951; Manning 1937). Great wars, these

---

[9] There are other important differences as well. For example, we would not classify Portugal and the Netherlands as world powers on a par with Great Britain and the United States. Although Modelski foreswore determinism, his scheme tended in that direction more than does our scheme.

scholars argued, could hardly be justified in terms of what we today would call cost/benefit calculations; all participants, to various degrees, are losers. There was a need, these reformers reasoned, to substitute methods of peaceful change for the historical recourse to war as the principal means of making the fundamental adjustments in the system necessitated by the differential growth of power among states.

The classic analysis and defense of peaceful change as the solution to the problem of hegemonic war was E. H. Carr's *The Twenty Years' Crisis, 1919–1939*, written on the eve of World War II.[10] For peaceful change to be successful, Carr argued, two things are necessary. First, the state challenging the international status quo must be able to bring threats and pressures to bear on the dominant states in the system. Unless this is the case, the latter will have no incentive to make changes in the international status quo. Second, because the dominant states benefit most from the status quo, they have a moral obligation to make the greater concessions in order to achieve successful compromise. Policies of appeasement, Carr reasoned, will bring the components of the international system (the distribution of territory, the rules of the system, economic relations, etc.) into conformity once again with the realities of power. Then it will be unnecessary to resort to war (or, at least, hegemonic war) to bring about international political change and resolve the disequilibrium in the system.

The policy of appeasement failed in the 1930s, Carr believed, because Germany (previously disarmed by the Versailles Treaty) was unable, at least initially, to make its demands for change effective; thus the British and the French had no incentive to make the necessary concessions to appease Germany's legitimate demands. By the time Germany could enforce its demands, the concessions offered by the status quo powers were no longer sufficient and were regarded as a sign of weakness rather than as an act of generosity. Instead of appeasing Germany, they stimulated demands for even greater concessions beyond those that might have satisfied Germany but a few years earlier. As a

---

[10] The book was first published in 1939; in this study we shall refer to the 1951 edition.

consequence, the policy of appeasement led not to peaceful change but to major conflict.

The inherent difficulty in achieving peaceful change was appreciated by Thucydides in the speech of the Athenian ambassadors responding to Spartan demands that Athens make a number of concessions, including partial dismemberment of the Athenian empire, in order to prevent war:

The nature of the case first compelled us to advance our empire to its present height; fear being our principal motive, though honor and interest afterwards came in. And at last, when almost all hated us, when some had already revolted and had been subdued, when you had ceased to be the friends that you once were, and had become objects of suspicion and dislike, it appeared no longer safe to give up our empire; especially as all who left us would fall to you. And no one can quarrel with a people for making, in matters of tremendous risk, the best provision that it can for its interest (Thucydides, 1951, pp. 43–4).

The Athenian speech poses well the dilemma of peaceful change. Until a state is pressed by others, it has little incentive to make concessions for the sake of peace; it gives highest priority to its own security and economic interests. However, once the challenging state is in a position to make its demands effective, it demands greater concessions than would have been deemed acceptable earlier; for its part, the challenged state now dares not meet these demands. Appeasement, it is feared, will only whet the appetite for still greater concessions. Perhaps the greatest task of the prudent and responsible statesman is to be able to judge when appeasement will and will not lead to peaceful resolution of disputes.

Nevertheless, resolution of disputes frequently has taken place through the process of peaceful change. Through mutual concessions, agreement on spheres of influence, and such measures, antagonistic states have accommodated one another and achieved a condition of peaceful detente. We have already considered the example of Great Britain, who reached accommodation with almost all of its major rivals in the years prior to World War I. This case also illustrates the inherent difficulties of peaceful change and its yet-to-be-proven capacity to resolve the more fundamental problems posed by the differential growth of power among states.

Great Britain was able to reach accommodation with every other major state, but not with Germany. For British and German leaders alike, the British–German naval rivalry held the key to their fundamental security and ultimately to the fate of the European state system. Neither could compromise for fear of placing itself and its security in the hands of the other. This basic distrust was a major factor in the transformation of a minor dispute in the Balkans into a hegemonic struggle involving all the European powers, a struggle that would profoundly affect the government and structure of the European political system.

A more recent and more dramatic example of peaceful change occurred when the oil-producing and -exporting countries (OPEC) wrested control of the world petroleum market from American and other multinational corporations. This action was undoubtedly the greatest forced redistribution of wealth in the history of the world, but its significance with respect to the capacity of economic power to effect political change should not be exaggerated or overemphasized. Two factors were important in moderating the American response: Two of the leading members of OPEC (Iran and Saudia Arabia) were political allies of the United States, and their action did not appear to be a direct threat to the security interests of the United States. They did not challenge the international position of the United States and in some ways appeared actually to strengthen it. If these and certain other conditions had not existed, it is questionable that this change in property rights would have taken place peacefully.

The point of this discussion is that peaceful international change appears to be most feasible when it involves changes *in* an international system and to be most difficult when it involves change *of* an international system. Whereas Great Britain might be willing to make concessions and the United States might be willing to suffer a serious economic defeat in order to preserve the existing international system, there do not appear to be any examples of a dominant power willingly conceding dominance over an international system to a rising power in order to avoid war. Nor are there examples of rising powers that have failed to press their advantage and have refrained from attempts to re-structure the system to accommodate their security and economic interests. A close reading of Carr's work will reveal that not even he was willing to see German or Japanese leadership substituted for that of Great Britain. If British leadership were indeed doomed, then he believed the mantle of world leadership should pass to the Americans. He foresaw either a Pax Americana or, better still, a Pax Anglo-Saxonica, an Anglo-American condominium, as the best available alternative to the decaying Pax Britannica. This was desirable, Carr reasoned, because these two "tolerant and unoppressive [powers were] . . . preferable to any practicable alternative" (Carr, 1951, p. 236).

Carr's preference for a humane and democratic governance of the international system betrays a fundamental truth. Although men desire peace, it is not their highest value. If it were, peace and peaceful change could easily be achieved; a people need only refuse to defend itself. Throughout history, however, societies have placed other values and interests above their desire for peace. From this perspective the basic task of peaceful change is not merely to secure peace; it is to foster change and achieve a peace that secures one's basic values. Determining how this goal is to be achieved in specific historical circumstances is the ultimate task of wise and prudent statesmanship.

In the absence of shared values and interests, the mechanism of peaceful change has little chance of success. Indeed, if it were otherwise, one would no longer be in the realm of international politics but rather in that of domestic politics, and even in domestic society there are limits on the range of feasible peaceful changes. When these limits are transgressed, the result is civil strife. Despite some recent writings to the contrary, there is little evidence to suggest that the values and interests that unite the human race have displaced those that divide it into a world of competing groups and sovereign states.

CONCLUSION

Hegemonic war historically has been the basic mechanism of systemic change in world politics. Hegemonic conflict, arising from an increasing disequilibrium between the burden of maintaining an empire or hegemonic position and the resources available to the dominant power to carry out this task, leads to the creation of a new international system. The distribution of territory, the pattern of economic relations, and the hierarchy of prestige reflect the new distribution of power in the system, as they did in the previous system. The emergent dominant states in the system attempt to extend their dominion to the limits of their economic, military, and other capabilities. In time, these powers will also mature, and new challengers will arise on the periphery of their power and influence. Then the process of decline, disequilibrium, and hegemonic struggle will resume once again.

The conclusion of one hegemonic war is the beginning of another cycle of growth, expansion, and eventual decline. The law of uneven growth continues to redistribute power, thus undermining the status quo established by the last hegemonic struggle. Disequilibrium replaces equilibrium, and the world moves toward a new round of hegemonic conflict. It has always been thus and always will be, until men either destroy themselves or learn to develop an effective mechanism of peaceful change.

6

Change and continuity in world politics

The basic assumption of this study has been that the nature of international relations has not changed fundamentally over the millennia. Believing that the past is not merely prologue and that the present does not have a monopoly on the truth, we have drawn on historical experience and the insights of numerous earlier writers. Although the purpose of this study has been to understand international political change, it also has assumed that an underlying continuity characterizes world politics: The history of Thucydides provides insights today as it did when it was written in the fifth century B.C. One must suspect that if somehow Thucydides were placed in our midst, he would (following an appropriate short course in geography, economics, and modern technology) have little trouble in understanding the power struggle of our age.

This assumption of continuity in the affairs of states has been challenged by much recent scholarship in the field of international relations. Contemporary changes in technology, economics, and human consciousness are said to have transformed the very nature of international relations. International actors, foreign-policy goals, and the means to achieve goals are said to have experienced decisive and benign changes; it is said that the nation-state has receded in importance, that welfare goals have displaced security goals as the highest priority of societies, and that force has declined as an effective instrument of foreign policy. One witnesses, in fact, a curious tension between the prevail-

211

ing mood of public pessimism and current scholarship on international relations. The emphasis of much recent scholarship in the field of international relations has been on developments that are judged to have changed the anarchic competitive nature of international relations.

The distinguished sociologist Alex Inkeles best captured the spirit of much contemporary scholarship and its assertion that a discontinuity has appeared in international relations:

> In the second half of the twentieth century, laymen and professional intellectuals alike have frequently expressed the sense that the relationship of all of us, all humankind, to each other and to our world has been undergoing a series of profound changes. We seem to be living in one of those rare historical eras in which a progressive quantitative process becomes a qualitative transformation. Even when, in more sober moments, we recognize that we are yet far from being there, we have the unmistakable sense that we are definitely set off on some new trajectory, and that we are not merely launched but are already well along toward an only vaguely identified destination. The widespread diffusion of this sense of a new, emergent global interrelatedness is expressed in numerous ideas, slogans, and catchphrases which have wide currency, such as "world government," "the global village," "spaceship earth," "the biosphere," and the ubiquitous cartoon of a crowded globe with a lighted fuse protruding from one end, the whole labelled "the world population bomb." Although the pervasiveness of the response to this emergent situation certainly tells us that *something* is happening, its diversity highlights our confusion as to exactly *what* it is that is happening (Inkeles, 1975, p. 467).

If a qualitative transformation has taken place in world politics, then this historic discontinuity obviously will invalidate the conception of international political change set forth in this study, transcending our model of change and the propositions drawn from the model, as well as the historical evidence to support them. Feeble guide that this model is, it (and, of course, all other efforts to learn from the past) will have to be cast aside. If the world has changed as much as many contemporary scholars suggest, then historical experience has little to say regarding the meaning of contemporary events. We will be intellectually cast adrift. For this reason, the purpose of this chapter is to evaluate the argument that contemporary developments have qualitatively transformed the nature of international relations.

To many contemporary scholars of international relations, three profound developments suggest a fundamental transformation in the nature of international relations. The first is the technological revolution in warfare due to the advent of nuclear weapons and other weapons of mass destruction. The second is the high level of economic interdependence among national economies. The third is the advent of global society, accompanied by a change in human consciousness and a set of planetary problems. These developments have suggested to scholarly observers major shifts in the costs of war, the benefits of peace, and the necessity of international cooperation. Taken together, these three developments are believed to have transformed international relations and to have made peaceful change the new reality.

Although this vision that technological, economic, and other developments have transformed the nature of international relations is appealing, it is not convincing. The world has indeed changed, and profoundly so, because of these factors. Both the risks of conflict and the benefits of cooperation have increased. However, although modern science, technology, and economics have changed the world, there is little evidence to suggest that the human race has solved the problems associated with international political change, especially the problem of war.

THE NUCLEAR REVOLUTION IN CONTEMPORARY WARFARE

The belief that military power is no longer a rational instrument of statecraft and a mechanism for international political change has been set forth by numerous scholars of international relations. Ironically, no one has made the argument more forcefully than Hans Morgenthau, the leading modern spokesman for political realism: "I think a revolution has occurred, perhaps the first true revolution in foreign policy since the beginning of history, through the introduction of nuclear weapons into the arsenal of warfare. [In the past] . . . there existed a rational relationship between violence as a means of foreign policy, and the ends of foreign policy. That is to say, a statesman could ask himself—

and always did ask himself—whether he could achieve what he sought for his nation by peaceful diplomatic means or whether he had to resort to war. . . . The statesman in the pre-nuclear age was very much in the position of a gambler—a reasonable gambler, that is—who is willing to risk a certain fraction of his material and human resources. If he wins, his risk is justified by victory; if he loses, he has not lost everything. His losses, in other words, are bearable. *This rational relationship between violence as a means of foreign policy and the ends of foreign policy has been destroyed by the possibility of all-out nuclear war"* (Morgenthau et al., 1961, p. 280; italics added).

Although nuclear weapons have indeed made total war (what we have called hegemonic war) extremely costly, they have by no means eliminated the problems of war. The categories of war expanded during the decades following World War II: proxy wars involving the nuclear powers; conventional limited wars; guerrilla wars; civil wars; terrorism; etc.[1] Such wars can and do function to force political change, despite the dangers of escalation. These so-called limited wars have taken their toll in tens of thousands of lives (indirectly, hundreds of thousands of lives) since the end of World War II. It is very difficult to reconcile this carnage with the thesis that modern weapons have transformed the nature of international relations.

A major and disturbing consequence of the advent of weapons of mass destruction is that they have enhanced the threat of war as an instrument of policy. In part, this threat does serve to deter war between the superpowers and their allies. On the other hand, however, there is the ever-present danger that statesmen, in utilizing and/or responding to nuclear blackmail, will permit events to get out of control and escalate into a nuclear war sought by no one.

The exercise of power is still the central feature of international relations. The fact that it has been ineptly used by one or both of the two superpowers does not make it less relevant. However, it would be foolish to argue that the advent of nuclear weapons and other weapons of mass destruction have not altered

---

[1] One of the best discussions of this subject was provided by Osgood and Tucker (1967).

the role and the use of force in the contemporary world. Indeed, these weapons have had a profound effect on the conduct of statecraft. Although their ultimate consequences have yet to be determined, weapons of mass destruction appear to have had three general effects on international relations (Smart, 1975, pp. 544–53).

First, the primary purpose of military power (at least for the moment) has become the deterrence of another great war. Mutual deterrence among antagonistic nuclear states places a limitation on violence and in turn protects international society as a whole from total war. The achievement of successful deterrence has resulted from the use of power to balance power, not from any obsolescence of power itself. As Kenneth Waltz pointed out, the nuclear revolution has had the effect that "force is more useful than ever for upholding the status quo, though not for changing it, and maintaining the status quo is the minimum goal of any great power" (1979, p. 191). If this system of mutual deterrence were to break down, modern instruments of national power would undoubtedly be unleashed in their full ferocity.

Second, nuclear weapons provide the nuclear state "with an infrangible guarantee of its independence and physical integrity" (Smart, 1975, p. 548). Although nuclear weapons have proved thus far to have little "compellance" capability (i.e., to compel one state to do the will of another state), they do constitute an insurance policy against ultimate disaster. Like the six-shooter of the American frontier, to some extent they make everyone equal. The most powerful state will think twice before attacking the smallest state armed with nuclear weapons. As a consequence, the spread of nuclear weapons, some believe, could create a system of universal deterrence and ultimate peace. Although there is some merit in this idea, gradations of power and capabilities obviously do continue in a nuclear-armed world.

Third, and more troubling, is the fact that the possession of nuclear weapons largely determines a nation's rank in the hierarchy of international prestige. Because even a relatively backward society may be economically capable of acquiring nuclear weapons, the modern identification of industrial capability with military power and prestige has been weakened. Nuclear weap-

ons in themselves confer an enhanced status and have become
status symbols coveted by more and more states. Thus the acquisition of nuclear weapons has become an important objective for
increasing numbers of contemporary states. The implications of
this situation for the proliferation of nuclear arsenals and international stability are, to say the least, not conducive to a san-
guine view of the future (see Waltz for a contrasting view).

The threat of war and the use of force and war have historically been governed by a fundamental relationship between the
destructiveness and probability of war: The more potentially destructive a war seemed to be, the less the probability of its
occurring, and vice versa.[2] The pacifist Leo Tolstoy appreciated
this relationship and prayed that wars would become sufficiently
destructive that men would refuse to fight them. The Hobson's
choice of modern man is that insofar as he makes the world safe
from total nuclear war through arms control and an effective
system of deterrence, he also makes the world that much safer
for limited wars and the calculated exploitation of nuclear
threats.

Under conditions of mutual deterrence and a stable system of
arms control, a series of limited wars could serve to change the
international system (Kissinger, 1961, p. 90). If a threat to resort
to nuclear war should lack credibility, then local superiority
would prevail, and a rising state could use limited force to
change the territorial status quo. The subsequent loss of access to
critical resources or strategic territory could, in turn, reduce the
dominant power to an inferior position and transform the governance of the international system. In the past, nations have precipitated total war to protect vital interests threatened by such a
piecemeal strategy (known colloquially as bologna tactics). It is
possible, despite much current speculation to the contrary, that
mutual deterrence may serve ultimately to inhibit the dominant
power from defending the status quo rather than preventing the
rising power from seeking to change it.[3]

As Ronald L. Tammen stated the basic issue, "the great unre-

---

[2] I am indebted to Hedley Bull for this observation. See Bull (1963).
[3] The dominant state obviously could follow the same strategy and thereby reinforce its
control over the system.

solved dilemma of nuclear weapons is how to use them aside from deterring an all-out war" (quoted by Smart, 1975, p. 551). The history of war and weaponry indicates that the great changes in international systems have been due not to weapons innovations by themselves but to the use of these weapons by political and military geniuses who have learned how to apply new weapons to gain advantages over other states. Thus the Romans were able to capture an empire because of their organizational, tactical, and strategic innovations, not because of the novelty of their weapons.[4] We are but a few decades into the nuclear age, and it is far too early to conclude that there will not be a Gaius Marius, Alexander,[5] or Napoleon who will develop tactics and strategy to make nuclear weapons and the nuclear threat effective instruments of national policy. Although such an effort to translate nuclear weapons into political gains might very well turn out to be irrational, can one with assurance deny that a future statesman might be daring enough or desperate enough to exploit mankind's fear of nuclear war in order to advance his political goals, especially if success promises mastery of the planet itself? Unfortunately, the history of international politics provides no reassurance that nuclear weapons will forever serve only a deterrent function.

Finally, the advent of nuclear weapons may make the task of diplomacy and the goal of instituting a mechanism of peaceful change more difficult rather than less difficult. In the prenuclear age, as Kissinger observed, diplomats were able to resolve interstate disputes and to find acceptable compromises because of the high probability that deadlock at the negotiating table would lead to decision on the battlefield (Kissinger, 1961, p. 170). Today, the destructiveness of war has decreased the probability that war will result from diplomatic impasse, and as a conse-

---

[4] A more recent example was the German innovation of blitzkreig warfare, which accounted for their rapid successes in the early days of World War II. Although the technologies involved in this novel form of warfare (the tank and the airplane) had been introduced during World War I, only later did the Germans develop the tactics, doctrine, and organization required to integrate them into powerful instruments of aggression.

[5] Actually, the military techniques used by Alexander the Great were developed by his father, Philip II of Macedon.

quence statesmen feel less pressured to make or accept the compromises required for peaceful resolution of disputes. Thus, the
hope of many current writers that the nuclear revolution in warfare will lead to an issue-by-issue resolution of disputes through
bargaining and mutual concession may be a vain hope.

The thesis that nuclear weapons have made hegemonic war or
a system-changing series of limited wars an impossibility must
remain inconclusive. That the superpowers have avoided war
and exercised restraint over several decades of conflict is cause
for optimism. However, one must recognize that the thesis has
yet to be seriously tested. In their many confrontations, the vital
interests of the two states have not been directly at issue.
Whereas the existence of nuclear weapons must be credited for
this restraint, the real test will come if a vital interest of one or
the other superpowers becomes involved and events threaten to
get out of control. The avoidance of such a situation must be a
major responsibility of contemporary statesmanship. A further
argument is that under contemporary conditions economic power
has displaced military power. The use of economic power by
OPEC to transform the world economy is certainly unprecedented. It was due, however, to a peculiar set of circumstances,
and there is little reason to believe this type of action could be
repeated in other areas. More generally, economic power defined as "the power to interrupt commercial or financial relations" for political purposes is nothing new in international relations [Hirschman, 1969, p. 16]. Thucydides tells us that an act of
economic warfare, the Megara Decree, was a precipitator of the
Peloponnesian War.[6] In the modern world, the great expansion
of world market relations has obviously enhanced the role of
economic power as an instrument of statecraft. However, as the
recent American experience with economic sanctions against
Iran and the Soviet Union indicates, the use of economic power
(like military power for that matter) remains highly limited.[7]
Whether economic power or some other form of power will be

---

[6] The decree sought to bring economic ruin to the Megarans by barring the ports of the
Athenian empire.

[7] A thorough evaluation of economic power is provided by Knorr, 1975, especially
Chapter 6.

cost effective to achieve an objective in a particular situation is an empirical question today as it was in the past.

THE INTERDEPENDENCE OF NATIONAL ECONOMIES

At the same time that war is said to have declined as a rational means of securing the objectives of states, the objectives themselves are said to have been transformed. In the modern world, economic welfare (as well as development, in the case of developing economies), rather than narrow national security, is said to have become the principal objective of all societies. This objective can best be achieved, it is argued, through economic growth, international cooperation, and rational use of the world's scarce resources, rather than through war and competitive struggle. The inherent logic of these welfare and development objectives leads to an increasingly interdependent world economy and to a global society in which economic cooperation displaces the traditional conflict over territory, relative gain, and the international balance of power.

The argument that the current level of economic interdependence has transformed world politics must also be viewed with skepticism. In evaluating this idea, one should note that the modern era of international relations has been characterized by a paradox. Since the advent and spread of industrialism (today so closely associated with the concept of modernization), groups and states have been able to maximize their mutual gains through international cooperation and the establishment of an efficient economic organization both domestically and internationally. The gradual creation of the world market economy over the past century and a half has reflected this global commitment to efficiency and growth. In fact, this changed economic reality has been the hallmark of modern world politics.

Since the very beginnings of the industrial era, successive generations of thinkers have speculated (and hoped) that the benefits of economic growth and cooperation would tame the power struggle among groups and states (Hirschman, 1977).[8] As this

[8] Marxists and political realists, of course, have a less benign view of the impact of industrialism on international relations.

study has suggested, the advent of sustained economic growth and a world market economy has moderated international relations. In the modern era, nations have most frequently had more to gain through economic efficiency, cooperation, and an international division of labor than through war, imperialism, and exclusive economic spheres. Yet economic interdependence and the promise of mutual gain have not eliminated the efforts of nations to advance their own interests at the expense of others and at the expense of the overall economic efficiency of the global economy. The historical struggle among groups and states for individual advantage and domination has continued, although not always in the same form as in the premodern era. The major change has been the displacement of the cycle of empires and imperial-command economics by the cycle of hegemony and a world market economy.

Unfortunately, the growth of economic interdependence and the prospect of mutual gain have not eliminated competition and mutual distrust among nations. Trade has not always proved to be a force for peace. On the contrary, with increasing interdependence, nations have become more apprehensive over the loss of autonomy and such matters as access to foreign markets, security for sources of raw materials, and the associated costs of interdependence. Economic nationalism has never been far below the surface, and in this century the breakdown of the international economy in response to nationalism has been a contributing factor to conflict (Gilpin, 1977).

The growth of economic interdependence, it must be readily conceded, is one of the remarkable achievements of the modern world. It has made possible unprecedented affluence for a sizable fraction of the human race. Economic interdependence today, however, is less extensive geographically than such interdependence in the late nineteenth century. In reality, it encompasses only the industrial democracies and part of the so-called Third World. The Soviet Union and its satellites have withdrawn, and they regard this economic interdependence as hostile economic encirclement.

Of equal importance, the affluence of some nations and the poverty of the majority of the human race have produced a vast fissure in the world. The universal awareness of the gap between rich and poor and the intense desire of poor peoples everywhere to catch up has become a novel and divisive force in the world. Few peoples today complacently accept their abject poverty as the will of God; they see it as the result of human decision: The rich are rich and they are poor, most peoples believe, because they are powerless and in consequence have been exploited. The desire to overturn this seemingly unjust state of human affairs is one of the most powerful political forces of our age, and it is not one that is apt to make the conduct of states more benign today than in the past (Sprout and Sprout, 1971, pp. 364–5).

One may hope that the intermeshing of national economies and the mutual absolute gains derived from interdependence, along with a global division of labor, may moderate still further the struggle over relative power and gain among competitive nation-states. But as societies have become more interdependent and have become more concerned with economic welfare, citizens have also become increasingly aware of the costs to their individual welfare and group welfare of the policies of other societies. As Henri Hauser (1937) observed decades ago, this spreading consciousness of mutual interdependence has become an increasingly disruptive factor in international relations since its beginnings in the latter part of the nineteenth century. What will be the political consequences of a rapidly urbanizing and economically conscious world with great and increasing inequalities between rich and poor within and between nations? And what will be the effects on political stability and cooperation of the seemingly intractable problems of reduced economic growth, high levels of unemployment, and global inflation? Such novel economic factors in contemporary society may have a powerful and malevolent impact on international relations.

The vision that the goal of efficiency might displace that of redistribution and that the process of international political change might become benign was set forth early in this century by a realist writer, Halford Mackinder. Writing in 1904 at the conclusion of the last and greatest phase of European expansion, Mackinder observed that the "Columbian epoch" had ended. For four hundred years, he noted, the European peoples had grown in wealth, population, and power; they had expanded their dominion over the entire globe and had fought numerous wars of territorial division and redivision. Explorers had completed the outline of the map of the world, and the European peoples had politically appropriated all but the most remote territories: the empires of China and Japan. Most significant of all, it had been a conquest against negligible resistance and involving relatively little cost to the Europeans. But now, he argued, it was finished and a new epoch was beginning. This new age would be different in that there was no longer the great "empty" space to absorb the energies and surplus populations of the European peoples. The world was now a closed system, and the explosion of social forces accompanying growth could no longer be dissipated outward against weak and pliable peoples. Instead, national ambitions and expansion would rebound back on the European nations themselves and throughout the globe. In the post-Columbian age, he predicted, the cost of territorial expansion and conflict would far outweigh any conceivable benefit. "Probably," Mackinder wrote, "some half-consciousness of this fact is at last diverting much of the attention of statesmen in all parts of the world from territorial expansion to the struggle for relative efficiency" (Mackinder, 1962, p. 242).

Since 1904, when Mackinder wrote these lines, the world has experienced two costly and devastating world wars of territorial conquest. Although this fact is cause for caution, Mackinder's prophecy that the struggle for economic efficiency rather than territorial aggrandizement would become the central feature of international relations continues to be an appealing one. The advent of nuclear weapons and the technological revolution in warfare may yet prove to have decreased the utility of the military instrument at the same time that present-day economic concerns and world economic interdependence have enhanced the importance of economic relations among nation-states; then the dream of substituting a mechanism of peaceful change for the traditional reliance on war may become a reality. Making this dream a reality should be a major objective of contemporary statecraft.

Groups and states attempt to change the international system for one of two sets of fundamental reasons: (1) to increase economic efficiency and maximize mutual gain; (2) to redistribute wealth and power in their own favor at the expense of efficiency and overall gains. Modern history has witnessed the displacement of the second motive by the first, at least to an impressive degree. But there is no guarantee that this will continue, and the eventual effects of contemporary political, economic, and technological developments are uncertain. It is as yet unclear whether cooperation to achieve efficiency or conflict over redistribution will be the predominant motivating force behind international political change in the last decades of this century.

THE ADVENT OF GLOBAL SOCIETY

Finally, contemporary developments have suggested to many observers the transcendence of the traditional mentality and character of international statecraft: Advances in communications and transportation have unified the planet physically. New types of transnational and international actors more responsive to modern science, technology, and economics have broken the monopoly of the state in the management and governance of the international system. Global ecological problems, as well as resource constraints and limits to growth, have placed on the world's agenda a set of pressing issues whose solutions are beyond the means of self-serving nation-states. Modern science, advances in knowledge, and social technologies permit a more rational approach to the solution of international problems than do strife and conflict. The universal commitment to modernization and a better life for all gives diverse peoples a common set of concerns and aspirations. In short, those values and interests that unite the human race are said to be displacing those factors that historically have divided it and have been the underlying causes of wars and violent change. Or, as Inkeles (1975, p. 495) put it, "the emergence of a uniform world culture" is a reality, and a transformation in human consciousness is occurring that will provide escape from the irrational struggle for national advantage.

This thesis that a transformation in human consciousness has taken place in concert with the advent of a global society must also be highly qualified. This position is founded on the belief that modern science and its offspring, technology, are making the world one, both mentally and physically. Advances in scientific knowledge are believed to be leading toward a more rational approach to the solution of human problems at the same time that modern technological advances have given all mankind a common destiny and the tools necessary to solve the fundamental problems of the planet. It is argued that science and technology imply a morality of international cooperation and make possible a world order that is more nearly just. Through the use of reason and the exploitation of technology, the human race can transcend the irrational struggle over relative gains in order to pursue gains for all mankind and especially to solve the global problems of ecological degradation and resource depletion.

Unfortunately, past expressions of neo-Malthusian ideas similar to the current limits-to-growth thesis have not led to the transcendence of narrow circumscribed loyalties; on the contrary, national fears concerning overpopulation and insufficiency of raw materials have led to the most destructive and irrational of human impulses. Eras of arrested growth, diminishing returns, and market constriction have historically been associated with conflict and war. Social Darwinism, imperialism, and the struggle for *Lebensraum* were the intellectual progeny of neo-Malthusian fears in the late nineteenth century and in the 1930s, and there is little evidence to suggest that mankind has advanced much beyond this level of jungle morality. The horrendous political implications of drastically reduced economic growth and scarcities of energy (particularly oil) for developed societies accustomed to ever-increasing levels of consumption and for the greater part of mankind in underdeveloped countries condemned to ever-worsening poverty become increasingly obvious to all. To the extent that the limits-to-growth thesis is correct, its influence on the behavior of nation-states may not be as benign and conducive to cooperation as many of its proponents would like to believe. Instead, intense competition may easily develop among economies for the world's dwindling supplies of petroleum, the markets required to finance energy imports, and the carving up of the last great commons (the oceans) for the resources they contain.

Even if modern science and technology have given mankind a new consciousness of shared values and common problems, this situation is no guarantee of common interest or of a willingness to subordinate selfish concerns to the larger good. On the contrary, modern science and technology may intensify the conflict over the globe's scarce resources. But it is more important to inquire whether or not a unified humanity really exists. Unfortunately, it does not. The modern "unified world" has been a creation of the West, which has sought to impose its values and way of life on a recalcitrant set of diverse cultures. This unity was shattered economically and ideologically by the Bolshevik Revolution in Russia and by the triumph there (and, after World War II, elsewhere) of a radically different mode of political and economic organization. The modern revival of Islam and the revolt of other non-Western cultures against Western values may point to an even greater schism ahead. Emergent power centers with cultural and diplomatic traditions vastly different from those of the once-dominant West may presage a return to the civilizational conflicts reminiscent of the premodern era. In short, one should not confuse the physical unity of the globe with moral unity; the human species remains deeply divided by race, religion, and wealth.

In actuality, the political fragmentation of the world has increased in recent decades. The world now encompasses approximately one hundred and fifty separate sovereignties; nationalism, with its roots in seventeenth-century Europe, has become the predominant religion of modern man. As has been the case in Europe, the continuing formation of nation-states and the spread of nationalism have unleashed powerful and dangerous forces of destruction. The present era is witnessing the proliferation of the nation-state, not its transcendence. In the late 1970s and early 1980s, the new nationalisms were pitted against one another in six wars, several of which were devastating.[9] If the history of European state formation and nationalism is any guide, a true global society and a new consciousness may be far in the future.

[9] These wars among Third-World states and Marxist (except the Islamic republic of Iran) states include the following: Vietnam–Cambodia; Ethiopia–Somalia; Tanzania–Uganda; China–Vietnam; Iraq–Iran.

Embedded in most social sciences and in the study of international relations is the belief that through science and reason the human race can gain control over its destiny. Through the advancement of knowledge, humanity can learn to master the blind forces of change and to construct a science of peace. Through an understanding of the sources of our actions and the consequences of our acts, human rationality should be able to guide statesmen through the crisis of a decaying world order to a renovated and stable world order. The fundamental problem faced, this argument continues, is not uncontrollable passions but ignorance.

Political realism is, of course, the very embodiment of this faith in reason and science. An offspring of modern science and the Enlightenment, realism holds that through calculations of power and national interest statesmen can create order out of anarchy and thereby moderate the inevitable conflicts of autonomous, self-centered, and competitive states. If states would pursue only their own security interests (forsaking religious goals and ideology) and respect equally the vital interests of other states, a basis of compromise and orderly change would be possible (Morgenthau, 1973, pp. 540–4). Although the content of international-relations theory has changed dramatically over the centuries, this faith that a "science of international relations" will ultimately save mankind still lies at the heart of its studies.

The major difference between political realism and much contemporary theorizing about international relations is that realism assumes the continuity of statecraft. Realism is based on practices of states, and it seeks to understand how states have always behaved and presumably will always behave. It does not believe that the condition of anarchy can be transcended except through a universal imperium, and thus it contrasts with a powerful strain in contemporary thinking. The advance of technology may open up opportunities for mutual benefit, but it also increases the power available for political struggle. The advance of human reason and understanding will not end this power struggle, but it does make possible a more enlightened understanding and pursuit of national self-interest.

A scholar of international relations has a responsibility to be true to this faith that the advance of knowledge will enable us to create a more just and more peaceful world. But, in honesty, one must inquire whether or not twentieth-century students of international relations know anything that Thucydides and his fifth-century compatriots did not know about the behavior of states. What advice could today's students give that would have enabled the Greeks to have prevented the great war that destroyed their civilization? Until scholars possess a better understanding of international political change, these questions cannot be answered, nor can the consequences of the actions of men be controlled. Yet it would be irresponsible for scholars to abandon their efforts to further their limited understanding of international relations.

This emphasis on the continuity of statecraft is open to the criticism that it must assume that societies do not learn and are not able to modify behavior that leads to wars they do not seek. If by "learning" one means a transcendence of the nature of the state as self-regarding and of the international system as competitive, the criticism is apt. This study does assume that the acquisition of knowledge will not make states less selfish or the system noncompetitive. But it would be incorrect to suggest that this study assumes that political leaders do not learn from historical experience or, the scholar hopes, from the outpourings of his craft. States can learn to be more enlightened in their definitions of their interests and can learn to be more cooperative in their behavior. Also, it appears that in all eras there have been "mature states" that have been chastened by the costs of conquest or have been moved by considerations of justice toward other societies (Wight, 1979, p. 155). Sweden today would be an example. Perhaps contemporary Japan and West Germany are as well.

Although states (or rather the individuals who compose them and lead them) do learn lessons from their experiences, they do not always learn the same lessons, or what some might regard as the correct lessons. History can teach the risk of misplaced trust, as in the case of Neville Chamberlain at Munich, as well as the benefits of cooperation, as in the case of West Germany and the European community today. A given experience can also teach different lessons to different people. For some, America's defeat in Vietnam taught that military intervention in the internal af-

fairs of other states is immoral and too costly; for others, failure
was the product of halfhearted measures and timid leadership.
And even though some states occasionally come to appreciate
the mutual benefits of international cooperation, unfortunately
all states have yet to learn the lesson simultaneously.

Ultimately, international politics still can be characterized as it
was by Thucydides: the interplay of impersonal forces and great
leaders. Technological, economic, and demographic factors push
states toward both war and peaceful cooperation. The prudent
and enlightened leader can guide the ship of state in one direction or the other. Though always constrained, choices always
exist. Historical experience helps teach us what these choices are
and what their probable consequences are. In this sense, one can
say that learning can take place and can influence the course of
international relations.

CONCLUSION

In the final decades of the twentieth century, technological, economic, and other developments have suggested to many individuals that the nation-state has finally ceased to be the most
efficient unit of economic and political organization. It is argued
that a larger regional or even global organization of economic
and political affairs is necessary, that new types of economic and
political entities would be more efficient than the nation-state. In
the interest of world peace and global welfare, some have proposed that more modern forms of international and transnational
organization should supplant the increasingly anachronistic nation-state.

It may very well be correct that a systems change is called for
in the contemporary world. Certainly the development and proliferation of weapons of mass destruction necessitate a more
stable and more peaceful system or world order; also, the forces
that threaten global economic welfare cannot easily be contained
by highly competitive and nationalistic nation-states. Yet, even
though such a change in economic and political arrangements
might be highly desirable, it would undoubtedly be a very costly
matter, as was the prior shift from feudalism to the nation-state.

Unfortunately (or, perhaps, fortunately), no contemporary political entrepreneur appears to regard forcing the transition from the nation-state to some other basis of world economic and political order as a profitable proposition.

Some writers would argue that a systems change has already taken place and that the traditional nation-state has been supplanted by states of continental dimensions resulting from the increased scale of economic and military power (McNeill, 1954, pp. 72–3). The American–Soviet bipolar system is viewed as the first stage of a global system dominated by superpowers of continent scale. This theory considers that World Wars I and II were responsible for this systems change. Observers see other superpowers emerging that may eventually take their places beside the United States and the Soviet Union, such as China, Brazil, India, and a united western Europe.

It is not clear, however, what the ultimate effect of contemporary military and economic developments will be on the scale of political organization. The scope of nuclear warfare and the immense cost of a retaliatory force would appear to favor an enlargement of political entities. At the same time, however, an attempt to conquer a small state possessing even a very modest nuclear capability may be prohibitively expensive. Increasing economic interdependence certainly has decreased national economic autonomy. However, it has also meant that states can have access to large markets without the necessity of integrating politically and that states have increased their intervention in the economy in order to protect national values against potentially harmful external economic forces. Although the emergence of global ecological and related problems necessitates a comparable organization of human affairs, the hold of the nation-state concept on the minds of men grows ever more tenacious. The ambiguous effects of these contemporary developments may be noted in three seemingly contradictory aspects of present-day international politics: (1) the emergence of the superpower; (2) the movement toward regional integration; (3) the proliferation of new nation-states and secession movements in older nation-states. These contradictory developments suggest that the sizes and distributions of political entities in our era have yet to be determined.

Although there are important elements of truth in all the theses discussed in this chapter, none of them leads to the conclusion that mankind has transcended the fundamental nature of international relations. World politics is still characterized by the struggle of political entities for power, prestige, and wealth in a condition of global anarchy. Nuclear weapons have not made the resort to force irrelevant; economic interdependence does not guarantee that cooperation will triumph over conflict; a global community of common values and outlook has yet to displace international anarchy. The fundamental problem of international relations in the contemporary world is the problem of peaceful adjustment to the consequences of the uneven growth of power among states, just as it was in the past. International society cannot and does not stand still. War and violence remain serious possibilities as the world moves from the decay of one international system toward the creation of another.

Epilogue:
Change and war in the contemporary world

At the end of the last hegemonic struggle in 1945, the United States stood at the apex of the international hierarchy of power and prestige. American economic and military power was supreme, and it provided the basis for an American-centered world economic and political order. By the 1980s this Pax Americana was in a state of disarray because of the differential growth of power among states over the previous few decades. The proliferation of nuclear weapons, the rise or reemergence of other centers of economic power, and especially the massive growth in Soviet military strength had weakened the political foundations of the international system established at the end of World War II. Events in Iran, Afghanistan, and elsewhere signaled that world politics were entering on a new and uncertain phase.

Sensing the ominous portents of this changed situation, numerous commentators and statesmen have reflected and written on its meaning. Parallels have been drawn between our own age and the periods preceding other great wars, particularly World War I. Contrasting unhappily with the seemingly halcyon days of the early 1960s, an uneasiness has settled over world affairs. The Middle East in 1980 has been compared to the pre-1914 Balkans, and a former secretary of state, Henry Kissinger, spoke of a period of maximum danger ahead when Soviet military power reaches its zenith. A book entitled *The Third World War – August 1985* (Hackett et al., 1978) became a best seller, and evidence mounted that the general public had begun to take seriously the possibility of a war between the superpowers.

The purpose of this epilogue is to assess the world situation at the beginning of the decade of the 1980s in terms of the ideas on international political change advanced in this study and to consider whether or not events and the fundamental forces at work suggest a world once again out of control and on the verge of another global hegemonic struggle. Although no one can predict the future, the fact is that both statesmen and the public act on assessments of the trend of events, and prognostications frequently become self-fulfilling prophecies. It is therefore prudent to turn to the past and to seek an understanding of the dynamics of world politics for guidance. It is important to appreciate the real dangers as well as the possible unappreciated opportunities of the present moment. Dispassionate analysis in an era of rapid change is needed to help avoid cataclysmic war.

Using the terminology of the model of international political change set forth in this study, we may say that a disequilibrium has developed between the existing governance of the international system and the underlying distribution of power in the system. Although the United States continues to be the dominant and most prestigious state in the system, it no longer has the power to "govern" the system as it did in the past. It is decreasingly able to maintain the existing distribution of territory, the spheres of influence, and the rules of the world economy. The redistribution of economic and military power in the system to the disadvantage of the United States has meant that the costs to the United States of governing the system have increased relative to the economic capacity of the United States to support the international status quo. The classic symptoms of a declining power characterize the United States in the early 1980s: rampant inflation, chronic balance-of-payments difficulties, and high taxation.

Responding to this disequilibrium and a severe fiscal crisis, the United States has employed the traditional techniques for reestablishing equilibrium between the costs and the benefits of the existing international system. The United States has retrenched its forces and withdrawn from exposed positions in Southeast

Asia, the Far East, Latin America, and the Middle East, frequently leaving a vacuum for the Soviet Union or other powers to occupy. It has formally recognized the Soviet sphere of influence in eastern Europe and negotiated a rapprochement with China, and it is reluctantly acceding to the wishes and ambitions of growing regional powers: India, Brazil, Nigeria, etc. It has accepted strategic nuclear parity with the Soviet Union, as well as loss of control over the world petroleum industry, and it finds itself unable to prevent the continued proliferation of nuclear weapons. It no longer unilaterally sets the rules regarding international trade, money, and investment. In brief, the United States, through political and military retrenchment, has sought to reduce its international commitments much as Great Britain did in the decades immediately preceding the outbreak of World War I.

At the same time, the United States also has attempted to generate new resources to support its reduced but still-dominant international position. It has urged its European and Japanese allies to increase their contributions to the common defense. It has increased its own defense expenditures and has moved toward a quasi-alliance with China to resist Soviet "hegemonism." Perhaps most significant of all, the United States, on August 15, 1971, announced a new foreign economic policy and forced changes in the rules governing international trading and monetary affairs that would benefit the American economy, especially to improve America's declining trade position. In addition, decreasing the public-sector consumption and increasing domestic investment in order to increase productivity and the reindustrialization of the American economy have become major preoccupations of political and economic leadership. President Ronald Reagan, in his inaugural address, called for "a national renewal." Finally, the United States has told "client" states around the globe that they will have to increase their contributions to their own defense (Nixon doctrine). Thus, through traditional techniques the United States is also attempting to increase its resources in order to maintain its dominant international position.

It is obviously too early to determine if the United States can or will retrench to a more modest but secure position, if it can generate additional resources to maintain its global hegemony, and if, through some combination of both responses, it can restore a favorable equilibrium between its power and commitments. This will depend not only on specific policy initiatives of the United States but also on those of other governments in the years ahead. The thrust of political, economic, and technological forces creates challenges and opportunities; domestic politics and political leadership create the responses of states to these challenges and opportunities. The course of history is indeterminant; only in retrospect does it appear otherwise.

In the meantime, the contemporary era has been aptly described as one of "eroding hegemony" (Keohane and Nye, 1977, pp. 42–6). Such a condition in world politics has, of course, existed in the past. The interregnum between British dominance and American dominance of international economics and politics, what E. H. Carr called the "twenty years' crisis" (1919–39), was such a period; the former hegemonic power could no longer set the rules, and the rising hegemonic power had neither the will nor the power to assume this responsibility (Carr, 1951). In the absence of rejuvenation by the old hegemony or the triumph of its successor or the establishment of some other basis of governance, the pressing issues of world order (rules governing trade, the future of the international monetary system, a new regime for the oceans, etc.) remain unresolved. Progress toward the formulation of new rules and regimes for an international system to follow the Pax Americana has been slow or nonexistent.

Yet, on the basis of the analysis of political change advanced in this study, there are reasons for believing that the present disequilibrium in the international system can be resolved without resort to hegemonic war. Although the danger of hegemonic war is very real, what is known about such wars provides grounds for guarded optimism. Whereas the contemporary world displays some of the preconditions for hegemonic conflict, other preconditions appear to be totally or partially lacking. An evaluation of the current international situation reinforces the hope that a gradual process of peaceful change, rather than war, may characterize the present era of world politics.

An extremely important reason for guarded optimism is the relative stability of the existing bipolar structure. As Waltz (1979) argued, the present bipolar system appears to be relatively stable. Historically, however, as this study has shown, five types of developments tend to destabilize bipolar systems and trigger hegemonic conflict. Fortunately, none of these destabilizing developments appears imminent in the contemporary world (1980), at least for the immediate future.

The first potentially destabilizing factor is the danger that one of the pair (like Sparta prior to the outbreak of the Peloponnesian War) will fail to play its balancing role. Through neglect, it permits a dangerous shift in the balance of power to take place. As long as the United States and the Soviet Union maintain a system of mutual nuclear deterence, this is unlikely to happen. Although many Americans and others fear that the United States has permitted a dangerous shift in the military balance to take place in favor of the Soviet Union, the strategic nuclear relationship continues to be one based firmly on the presumption of "mutually assured destruction" in the event of hegemonic war; each superpower has the capability to devastate the other. Yet, it must be added that a continuing deterioration in the American military position could remove this constraint on the system of mutual deterrence; at the least it could encourage Soviet leadership to exploit politically the belief that the Soviet Union has become the reigning hegemon.

The second potentially destabilizing factor is the danger of the rise of a third party to upset the bipolar balance. Although students of international relations disagree on the relative stability of bipolar systems versus multipolar systems, almost all agree that a tripolar system is the most unstable configuration. As long as western Europe lacks political unity, Japan remains weak militarily, and China continues in a backward state, this danger is minimized, though by no means eliminated. Certainly the Soviet Union has a genuine fear of an encircling alliance composed of these neighboring powers and the United States. The United States, for its part, would regard the loss of one of these powers or the loss of the oil fields of the Middle East as a major setback. Thus, although the contemporary bipolar distribution of power is basically stable, it does contain the potential for dangerous tripolar structures of power.

The third potentially destabilizing factor is the danger of polarization of the international system as a whole into two hostile camps. In such a situation, international relations become a zero-sum game in which a gain to one camp or bloc is a loss to the other. This was the case prior to the outbreak of World War I, when minor tensions in the Balkans flared up into a major conflagration. Such a polarization has not yet developed (1980). To repeat an earlier metaphor, political space is not closing in. On the contrary, the world is becoming more pluralistic, with the emergence of a number of regional actors and issues. The outcomes of political conflicts in Asia, Africa, and elsewhere do not necessarily advantage one or another of the two superpowers so as to force the other to take decisive counteraction. Yet the emergence of frequently unstable new powers in the so-called Third World, the proliferation of nuclear weapons to these states, and the conflicts among them could involve the superpowers in highly volatile situations.

The fourth potentially destabilizing factor is the danger of entanglement of the major powers in the ambitions and difficulties of minor allies. It was the ambitions of Sparta's ally, Corinth, and its provocations of Athens that precipitated the great war between the Peloponnesian and Delian leagues. The difficulties of Germany's ally, Austria, beset with a decaying multiethnic empire, escalated into World War I. In neither of these cases could the major power tolerate the defeat or disintegration of its minor ally. Fortunately, these dangers do not appear imminent today. Even though particular allies of both superpowers have unfulfilled ambitions and/or serious political problems of their own, it is unlikely that they could or would set in motion a series of untoward events that would precipitate conflict among the two superpowers; this is because these allies are insufficiently independent and the superpowers are sufficiently self-reliant (Waltz, 1979). Again, however, one must not too quickly dismiss this potential danger. A Sino–Soviet confrontation, workers' revolts in eastern Europe, or political instability among America's allies in western Europe and the Middle East could pose dangers for the international system.

The fifth potentially destabilizing factor is the danger of loss of control over economic, political, and social developments. Eras of rapid and revolutionary change within and among nations create dangerous uncertainties and anxieties that lead political elites in great powers to miscalculate. Hegemonic wars signal not merely changes in political relations among states but frequently social and economic upheavals as well; World War I, as Halévy showed (1965, p. 212), represented a collapse of the decaying European social and economic order. The crisis of world capitalism in the 1980s (high rate of inflation, rising level of unemployment, and low rate of economic growth) and the equally severe crisis of world communism (as represented by the workers' revolt in Poland) signal major strains in both systems.

Although the decades following World War II frequently have been called an age of political turbulence, the international system in that period has actually been characterized by remarkable resilience. It has accommodated a number of major developments: an unprecedented process of decolonization, rapid technological changes, the emergence of new powers (India, Brazil, China), sociopolitical revolutions in developing countries, massive shocks to the world economy, and the resurgence of non-Western civilizations. Yet the basic framework of an international system composed of two central blocs and a large nonaligned periphery has remained essentially intact.

This relative stability of the system has been strengthened by the domestic stability of the two dominant powers themselves. In contrast to the situations prevailing before World Wars I and II, neither power has been torn by powerful class or national conflicts. Although racial strife in the United States and ethnic problems in Russia are causing tensions in both societies, these internal difficulties pale in comparison with the nationalistic struggles of the Austro-Hungarian Empire in 1914 and the intense class conflicts of the European powers in the 1930s. The basic domestic stability of the United States and the Soviet Union today helps to ensure that revolutionary upheavals in these societies will not disrupt the international system.

Yet it would be foolish to be complacent regarding the underlying social stability of the system. A prolonged period of restricted economic growth could erode the political stability of the
United States and the Soviet Union. A more probable threat to
world stability would be untoward developments in important
peripheral areas, in particular eastern Europe and the Middle
East. The dependence of Soviet security on the subservient eastern European bloc and the dependence of the West on Middle
Eastern petroleum constitute worrisome factors in contemporary
world politics. The maintenance of stable conditions in these
areas over the long term is a formidable challenge. Another continuing danger is that one or both of the superpowers might
engage in foreign adventures in order to dampen internal dissent
and promote political unity.

Another reason for guarded optimism regarding the avoidance
of hegemonic war is that in the closing decades of the twentieth
century, economic, political, and ideological cleavages are not
coalescing but instead are running counter to one another. In the
past, a precondition for hegemonic war in many cases has been
the coalescence of political, economic, and ideological issues. In
periods prior to the outbreak of hegemonic war, conflict has
intensified because the contending parties have been at odds
with one another on all fronts and have had few interests in
common to moderate the antagonism. In such situations, compromise in one issue area becomes increasingly difficult because of
its linkage to other issue areas. As a consequence, disputes in one
area easily spill over into other areas, and the joining of issues
leads to escalation of the conflict. The great wars of world history
have tended to be at once political, economic, and ideological
struggles.

In the 1980s, however, although the United States and the
Soviet Union find themselves in political and ideological conflict,
they share a powerful interest in avoiding nuclear war and stop-
ping the proliferation of nuclear weapons. Moreover, they also
share certain economic interests, and both countries have numerous economic conflicts with their political and economic allies.
This intermingling of interests and conflicts is thus a source of
stability. Ironically, a less autarkic Soviet Union challenging the

United States in world markets and competing for scarce resources would be, and might very well become, a destabilizing
factor. A decline in Soviet production of petroleum or Soviet
entry into world markets may change this situation and increase
the level of economic tensions.

The contemporary situation is somewhat anomalous in the
multiple nature of the challenge to the dominant power in the
system. On the one hand, the position of the United States is
challenged economically by Japan, western Europe, and the
members of OPEC. On the other hand, the military and political
challenge comes principally from the Soviet Union.[1] Although
there are those writers who believe that the economic confrontation between the United States and its allies is threatening to
world peace,[2] the position of this book is that the worst danger to
international stability is the Soviet–American confrontation.
From this perspective, the primary consequence of the economic
competition between the United States and its allies has been to
undermine the capacity of the United States to meet the Soviet
challenge; however, if Japan and West Germany were to convert
their military potential into actual capability, then the balance of
military and political power could be changed dramatically, probably with important unforeseen consequences. At best, therefore,
one can say that the long-term significance of contemporary developments for the future of the system is ambiguous.

Finally, and most important of all, hegemonic wars are preceded by an important psychological change in the temporal
outlook of peoples. The outbreaks of hegemonic struggles have
most frequently been triggered by the fear of ultimate decline
and the perceived erosion of power. The desire to preserve what
one has while the advantage is still on one's side has caused
insecure and declining powers to precipitate great wars. The
purpose of such war frequently has been to minimize potential
losses rather than to maximize any particular set of gains.

Here, perhaps, is the greatest cause for anxiety in the years

---

[1] Similar, but not identical, situations have occurred in the past. For example, Dutch
preeminence in the seventeenth century was threatened militarily by the French and
economically by the British.
[2] This is the thesis of Kaldor (1978).

immediately ahead. What would be the reaction of the United States if the balance of power is seen to be shifting irrevocably to the Soviet advantage? What would be the Soviet response to a perceived threat of encirclement by a resurgent United States, an industrialized China, a dynamic Japan, a hostile Islam, an unstable eastern Europe, and a modernized NATO? How might one or another of these powers (the United States today, Russia tomorrow) respond to the continuing redistribution of world power?

A generally unappreciated factor in the preservation of world peace over the past few decades has involved the ideological perspectives of the United States and the Soviet Union. Each rival power subscribes to an ideology that promises inevitable victory to its own system of values and assures it that history is on its side. For the United States, freedom, democracy, and national independence are the most powerful forces in the world; for the Soviet Union, communism is the "wave of the future." These rival belief systems have been sources of conflict but also of reassurance for both nations. Despite their clashes and struggles, neither side has experienced the panic that has preceded the great wars of history, a panic that arises from fear that time has begun to run against one. Neither nation has felt the need to risk everything in the present in order to prevent inevitable defeat in the future. Fortunately for world peace, both the United States and the Soviet Union have believed the logic of historical development to be working for them. Each power has believed the twentieth century to be its century. But the foundations of both of these faiths are experiencing strain.

At the end of World War II, the United States held a position of unparalleled preeminence in the international system. During the first decades of the postwar period, its power and influence expanded until it was finally checked in the jungles of Southeast Asia and by more fundamental changes in the international distribution of economic and military power. The administration of Richard Nixon constituted a watershed in that it was the first to deal with the challenge posed by the increasing disequilibrium between America's international position and America's capacity to finance it. The United States has worked to meet this challenge through political retrenchment, efforts toward detente with the Soviet Union, rapprochement with China, and the generation of additional resources through changes in its domestic and foreign economic policies.

The fundamental task of the United States in the realm of foreign affairs has become one of responding to its changed position in the world as new powers arise on the world scene. It must bring its power and commitments into balance, either through increasing the former or reducing the latter or by some combination of both strategies. Although this is a serious challenge, it need not be a source of alarm. Other great powers have succeeded in this task and have survived, maintaining their vital interests and values intact. There is danger, however, that the military challenge of the Soviet Union and the changing economic fortunes of the United States might generate severe anxiety in the American public. Although there is certainly cause for concern in these matters, exaggerated rhetoric over the relative decline of American power and wealth can itself give rise to panic and irrational actions.

Despite its relative decline, the American economy remains the most powerful in the world and dwarfs that of the Soviet Union. However, American society has placed on its economy consumption demands (both public and private) and protection demands beyond its capabilities at the same time that productive investment and economic productivity have slackened. Although the Reagan Administration can greatly increase defense expenditures to meet the Soviet challenge in an era of restricted economic growth, it could do so only at high cost to consumption or investment or both. The inherent danger in a massive expansion of defense expenditures is that it will be inflationary and will further undermine the productivity of the economy.[3] The long-term well-being and security of the United States necessitate judicious allocation of national resources among the areas of consumption, protection, and investment.

The Soviet Union is, of course, the rising challenger, and it appears to be the one power that in the years to come could supplant the American dominance over the inter-national system. Although the growth and expansion of Russian power have

[3] Proposals of the Administration to extend American commitments in the Middle East and elsewhere could have the same consequence.

deep historical roots, the acceleration in the development of Soviet industrial and military might in recent decades has been formidable. The Soviet Union has fashioned a powerful military machine from a state that was near defeat and collapse during World War II. Further, it occupies a central position on the Eurasian land mass and enjoys conventional military superiority over the United States in important areas. A major question for the future is whether or not the Soviets can translate and are willing to translate these expanding military capabilities into decisive political gains in Europe, Asia, and elsewhere in the world.

Meanwhile, the relative decline in American power and the continuing restraint on the use of military force has given rise to an era of uneasy coexistence between the superpowers. The erratic process of detente, if ultimately successful, may turn out to be an unprecedented example of peaceful change.[3] What it could well signify is a change from an America-centered global system to a more nearly equal bipolar system, and, perhaps eventually, a multipolar global system. The apparent settlement of the German and central European questions has stabilized, at least for the moment, the outstanding territorial issue dividing the two superpowers. The fundamental issue in the strategic-arms-limitation talks has been the stabilization of the nuclear arms race on the basis of strategic parity. Both powers favor steps to discourage further proliferation of nuclear weapons. There remain, however, many other issues about which the two superpowers continue to have antagonistic interests that could destabilize their relations. The Soviet aggression in Afghanistan is a case in point, and, of course, the rise of other powers could undermine this emergent bipolar structure over the longer term.

At the present juncture, it is the United States whose position is threatened by the rise of Soviet power. In the decades ahead, however, the Soviet Union also must adjust to the differential growth of power among states. For the Soviet Union, the burden

---

[3] It must be acknowledged that the Soviet Union and the United States have quite different conceptions of the meaning of detente. For the Soviets, detente does not mean an end to the class struggle or the historic movement toward the victory of communism. For the United States, detente is indivisible; the Soviet Union must not use detente to advance its political control over other nations.

of adjusting to the transformation of the international system from a bipolar system to a tripolar or even multipolar system could be even more severe than it would prove to be for the United States. In the wake of the collapse of Communist ideological unity and the rise of a rival ideological center in Peking, the Soviet Union finds itself surrounded by potentially threatening and growing centers of industrial power. Although it possesses unprecedented military strength, it could lose the reassurance of its ideology, and it is sluggish with respect to economic growth and technological development. If its neighboring powers (Japan, western Europe, and China) continue to grow in economic power and military potential, Russia's logistical advantage of occupying a central position on the Eurasian continent is also a political liability. On all sides, centrifugal forces could pull at this last of the great multiethnic empires as neighbors make demands for revision of the territorial status quo and as subordinate non-Russian peoples seek greater equality and autonomy. Such external and internal challenges could give rise to powerful defensive reactions on the part of the Soviet governing elite.

Several years ago, Ernest Mandel, a leading European Marxist, ascribed the changing fortunes of the Unites States to the law of uneven development: "After having benefited from the law of unequal development for a century, the United States is now becoming its victim" (1970, p. 7). Similarly, one may make the same observation regarding the future of the Soviet Union; this law plays no favorites between capitalists and communists. Observing the growing challenge of a unified and developing Communist China, an Indian political scientist writes that the uneven development of socialism is creating contradictions in the system today. Chatterjee, 1975, p. 8, put it best: "In the long run, the law of uneven socialist development may pose a greater threat to the Soviet Union than does the law of uneven capitalist development to the United States. In the years ahead, both nations may need to adjust to a world in which power is diffusing at an unprecedented rate to a plurality of powers.

We conclude this epilogue on a cautiously optimistic note. Although there are powerful forces that could lead to hegemonic war between the superpowers, the historic conditions for such a war are only partially present. The redistribution of military power in favor of Russia as the rising state in the international system and the possibility of further redistributions of power to other states pose serious threats to the stability of the system; in response the superpowers might precipitate a course of events over which they could lose control. However, these potentially destabilizing developments are balanced by the restraint imposed by the existence of nuclear weapons, the plurality of the system, and the mutual benefits of economic cooperation. The supreme task for statesmen in the final decades of the twentieth century is to build on the positive forces of our age in the creation of a new and more stable international order.

Bibliography

Adams, Brooks. *The Law of Civilization and Decay: An Essay on History*. New York: Alfred A. Knopf, 1943.

Ames, Edward, and Rosenberg, Nathan. "Changing Technological Leadership and Industrial Growth." In *The Economics of Technological Change – Selected Readings,* edited by Nathan Rosenberg, p. 413 – 39. Middlesex, England: Penguin, 1971.

Amin, Samir. *Unequal Development – An Essay on the Social Formations of Peripheral Capitalism*. New York: Monthly Review Press, 1976.

Anderson, Perry. *Lineages of the Absolute State*. London: NLB, 1974.

Andreadēs, Andreas Michaēl. *A History of Greek Public Finance*, Vol. 1. Cambridge, Mass.: Harvard University Press, 1933.

Andreski, Stanislav. *Military Organization and Society*. Berkeley: University of California Press, 1971.

Aron, Raymond. *Peace and War – A Theory of International Relations*. Garden City, N.Y.: Doubleday, 1966.

"War and Industrial Society." In *War – Studies from Psychology, Sociology, Anthropology,* edited by Leon Bramson and George W. Goethals, pp. 351 – 394. New York: Basic Books, 1964.

The Imperial Republic. Englewood Cliffs, N.J.: Prentice-Hall, 1974.

Arrow, Kenneth J. *Social Choice and Individual Values*. 2nd ed. New Haven: Yale University Press, 1970.

Auster, Richard D., and Silver, Morris. *The State as a Firm: Economic Forces in Political Development*. Boston: Martinus Nijhoff, 1979.

Avineri, Shlomo. *Karl Marx on Colonialism and Modernization*. Garden City, N.Y.: Anchor Books, 1969.

245

Baechler, Jean. *Les Origines du capitalisme*. Paris: Editions Gallimard, 1971; English translation Oxford: Basil Blackwell, 1975.

Barnett, Correlli. *The Collapse of British Power*. New York: Morrow, 1972.

Barry, Brian. *Sociologists, Economists and Democracy*. London: Macmillan, 1970.

"Review of Robert A. Dahl and Edward R. Tufte, *Size and Democracy*." In *Government and Opposition* 9 (1974):492–503.

ed. *Power and Political Theory – Some European Perspectives*. London: John Wiley & Sons, 1976.

Baumol, William J. *Welfare Economics and the Theory of the State*. Cambridge, Mass.: Harvard University Press, 1965.

Bean, Richard. "War and the Birth of the Nation State." *Journal of Economic History* 33 (1973):203–21.

Becker, Gary. *The Economic Approach to Human Behavior*. Chicago: University of Chicago Press, 1976.

Beer, Francis A. *Peace Against War – The Ecology of International Violence*. San Francisco: W. H. Freeman, 1981.

Beitz, Charles. *Political Theory and International Relations*. Princeton: Princeton University Press, 1979.

Bendix, Reinhard, ed. *State and Society*. Berkeley: University of California Press, 1973.

Blaug, Mark. *Economic Theory in Retrospect*. 3rd ed. Cambridge University Press, 1978.

Boulding, Kenneth E. *The Organizational Revolution – A Study in the Ethics of Economic Organization*. New York: Harper & Row, 1953.

Conflict and Defense. New York: Harper & Row, 1963.

Bozeman, Adda. *Politics and Culture in International History*. Princeton: Princeton University Press, 1960.

Brodie, Bernard, ed. *The Absolute Weapon*. New York: Harcourt, Brace, Jovanovich, 1946.

Buchanan, James M. "An Individualistic Theory of Political Process." In *Varieties of Political Theory*, edited by David Easton, pp. 25–37. Englewood Cliffs, N. J.:Prentice-Hall, 1966.

Cost and Choice. Chicago: Markham Publishing, 1969.

and Tullock, Gordon. *The Calculus of Consent – Logical Foundations of Constitutional Democracy*. Ann Arbor: University of Michigan Press, 1962.

Bull, Hedley. "Limitations in Strategic Nuclear War." *The Listener* 69 (1963):147–9.

The Anarchical Society – A Study of Order in World Politics. New York: Columbia University Press, 1977.

Burns, Arthur Lee. *Of Powers and Their Politics – A Critique of Theoretical Approaches.* Englewood Cliffs, N. J.: Prentice-Hall, 1968.

Burton, John. *International Relations – A General Theory.* Cambridge University Press, 1965.

Carney, T. F. *The Economies of Antiquity – Controls, Gifts and Trade.* Lawrence, Kans.: Coronado Press, 1973.

Carr, Edward Hallett, *The Twenty Years' Crisis, 1919 – 1939. An Introduction to the Study of International Relations.* London: Macmillan, 1951.

Chatterjee, Partha. *Arms, Alliances and Stability: The Development of the Structure of International Politics.* New York: Halsted Press, 1975.

Choucri, Nazli, and North, Robert C. *Nations in Conflict – National Growth and International Violence.* San Francisco: W. H. Freeman, 1975.

Cipolla, Carlo M. *Guns, Sails and Empires – Technological Innovation and the Early Phases of European Expansion 1400 – 1700.* New York: Minerva Press, 1965.

ed. *The Economic Decline of Empires.* London: Methuen, 1970.

Clark, Colin. *The Conditions of Economic Progress.* London: Macmillan, 1957.

Clark, George. *War and Society in the Seventeenth Century.* Cambridge University Press, 1958.

Clough, Shepard B. *The Rise and Fall of Civilization.* New York: Columbia University Press, 1970.

Cohen, Benjamin J. *The Question of Imperialism, The Political Economy of Dominance and Dependence.* New York: Basic Books, 1973.

Organizing the World's Money. New York: Basic Books, 1977.

Cohen, Percey S. *Modern Social Theory.* New York: Basic Books, 1968.

Condliffe, J. B. *The Commerce of Nations.* New York: W. W. Norton, 1950.

Cox, Kevin R., Reynolds, David R., and Rokkan, Stein, eds. *Locational Approaches to Power and Conflict.* New York: John Wiley & Sons, 1974.

Curry, R. L., Jr., and Wade, L. L. *A Theory of Political Exchange – Economic Reasoning in Political Analysis.* Englewood Cliffs, N. J.: Prentice-Hall, 1968.

Cyert, Richard, and March, James G. *A Behavioral Theory of the Firm.* Englewood Cliffs, N. J.: Prentice-Hall, 1963.

Dahl, Robert, and Tufte, Edward. *Size and Democracy*. Stanford: Stanford University Press, 1973.

Dahrendorf, Ralf. *Class and Class Conflict in Industrial Society*. Stanford: Stanford University Press, 1959.

David, Paul H. and Melvin W. Reder, eds., *Nations and Households in Economic Growth – Essays in Honor of Moses Abramouitz*. New York: Academic Press, 1974.

Davis, Lance E., North, Douglass C., with the assistance of Smorodin, Calla. *Institutional Change and American Economic Growth*. Cambridge University Press, 1971.

Deane, Phyllis. *The Evolution of Economic Ideas*. Cambridge University Press, 1978.

Demsetz, Harold. "Toward a Theory of Property Rights." *American Economic Review, Papers and Proceedings* 57 (1967):347 – 59.

de Romilly, Jacqueline. *The Rise and Fall of States According to Greek Authors*. Ann Arbor: University of Michigan Press, 1977.

Dolan, Michael B., and Tomlin, Brian W. "First World – Third World Linkages: External Relations and Economic Development." *International Organization* 34 (1980):41 – 63.

Doran, Charles F. *The Politics of Assimilation – Hegemony and Its Aftermath*. Baltimore: Johns Hopkins Press, 1971.

and Wes Parsons, "War and the Cycle of Relative Power." *The American Political Science Review* 74 (1980):947–65.

Dore, Ronald. "The Prestige Factor in International Affairs" *International Affairs* 51 (1975):190 – 207.

Downs, Anthony. *An Economic Theory of Democracy*. New York: Harper & Row, 1957.

Inside Bureaucracy. Boston: Little, Brown, 1967.

Dunn, Frederick Sherwood. *Peaceful Change: A Study of International Procedures*. New York: Council on Foreign Relations, 1937.

Dupré, Louis. "Idealism and Materialism in Marx's Dialectic." *Review of Metaphysics* 30 (1977):649 – 85.

Easton, David. *The Political System: An Inquiry into the State of Political Science*. New York: Alfred A. Knopf, 1953.

Eisenstadt, S. N., ed. *The Decline of Empires*. Englewood Cliffs, N. J.: Prentice-Hall, 1967.

Elvin, Mark. *The Pattern of the Chinese Past*. Stanford: Stanford University Press, 1973.

Fairbank, John K., Reischauer, Edwin O., and Craig, Albert M. *East Asia – The Modern Transformation*. Boston: Houghton Mifflin, 1965.

Falk, Richard A. *This Endangered Planet: Prospects and Proposals for Human Survival*. New York: Random House, 1971.

Feuer, Lewis S., *Marx and the Intellectuals – A Set of Post-Ideological Essays* Garden City, N. Y.: Doubleday, 1969.

Field, Alexander James. "What is wrong with Neoclassical Institutional Economics." Unpublished. October, 1979.

Fischer, Eric. *The Passing of the European Age – A Study of the Transfer of Western Civilization and Its Renewal in Other Continents*. Cambridge, Mass.: Harvard University Press, 1948.

Frey, Bruno S. *Modern Political Economy*. New York: John Wiley & Sons, 1978.

Frohlich, Norman, Oppenheimer, Joe A., and Young, Oran R. *Political Leadership and Collective Goods*. Princeton: Princeton University Press, 1971.

Galtung, Johan. "A Structural Theory of Aggression." *Journal of Peace Research* 1 (1964):95 – 119.

Gerschenkron, Alexander. *Economic Backwardness in Historical Perspective, A Book of Essays*. Cambridge, Mass.: Belknap, Harvard University Press, 1962.

Gilbert, Felix. *To the Farewell Address – Ideas of Early American Foreign Policy*. Princeton: Princeton University Press, 1961.

Gilbert, Felix, ed. *The Historical Essays of Otto Hintze*. New York: Oxford University Press, 1975.

Gilpin, Robert. *France in the Age of the Scientific State*. Princeton: Princeton University Press, 1968.

"Economic Interdependence and National Security in Historical Perspectives." In *Economic Issues and National Security,* edited by Klaus Knorr and Frank N. Trager, pp. 19 – 66. Lawrence, Kans.: Regents Press of Kansas, 1977.

U.S. Power and the Multinational Corporation. New York: Basic Books, 1975.

Gould, J. D. *Economic Growth in History – Survey and Analysis*. London: Methuen, 1972.

Grant, Michael. *The Climax of Rome, the Final Achievements of the Ancient World*. London: Weidenfeld and Nicolson, 1968.

Greenstein, Fred I., and Polsby, Nelson W. *Handbook of Political Science*. 8 vols. Reading, Mass.: Addison-Wesley, 1975.

Haas, Ernst. *Beyond the Nation-State – Functionalism and International Organization*. Stanford: Stanford University Press, 1964.

Haas, Michael. *International Conflict*. Indianapolis: Bobbs-Merrill, 1974.

Hackett, John, et al. *The Third World War – August 1985*. New York: Macmillan, 1978.

Halévy, Elie. *The Era of Tyrannies*. New York: Doubleday, 1965.

Harsanyi, John. "Explanation and Comparative Dynamics in Social Science." *Behavioral Science* 5 (1960):136 – 45.

"Rational-Choice Models of Political Behavior vs. Functionalist and Conformist Theories." *World Politics* 21 (1969):513 – 38.

Hart, Hornell. "Technology and the Growth of Political Areas." In *Technology and International Relations,* edited by William Ogburn, pp.28 – 57. Chicago: University of Chicago Press, 1949.

Hart, Jeffrey A. "Power and Polarity in the International System." Unpublished. August, 1979.

and Cowhey, Peter F. "Theories of Collective Goods Reexamined." *Western Political Quarterly* 30 (1977):351 – 62.

Haskel, Barbara G. *The Scandinavian Option*. Oslo: Universitetforlaget, 1976.

Hauser, Henri. *Economie et diplomatie – les conditions nouvelles de la politique étrangère*. Paris: Librairie du Recueil Sirey, 1937.

Hawtrey, Ralph G. *Economic Aspects of Sovereignty*. London: Longmans, Green, 1952.

Heilbroner, Robert L., and Thurow, Lester C. *The Economic Problem*. Englewood Cliffs, N. J.: Prentice-Hall, 1978.

Herskovits, Melville. *Economic Anthropology – A Study in Comparative Economics*. New York: Alfred A. Knopf, 1952.

Herz, John H. *Political Realism and Political Idealism*. Chicago: University of Chicago Press, 1951.

Hicks, John. *A Theory of Economic History*. London: Oxford University Press, 1969.

"The Future of Industrialism." *International Affairs* 50 (1974):211 – 28.

Hinsley, F. H. *Power and the Pursuit of Peace – Theory and Practice in the History of Relations Between States*. Cambridge University Press, 1963.

Hirsch, Fred, Doyle, Michael, and Morse, Edward. *Alternatives to Monetary Disorder*. New York: McGraw-Hill, 1977.

Hirschman, Albert O. *Exit, Voice, and Loyalty – Responses to Decline in Firms, Organizations, and States*. Cambridge, Mass.: Harvard University Press, 1970a.

"The Search for Paradigms as a Hindrance to Understanding." *World Politics* 22 (1970b):329 – 43.

National Power and the Structure of Foreign Trade. Berkeley: University of California Press, 1969.

A Bias for Hope – Essays on Development and Latin America. New Haven: Yale University Press, 1971.

The Passions and the Interests – Political Arguments for Capitalism before Its Triumph. Princeton, N. J.: Princeton University Press, 1977.

Hoffmann, Stanley, ed. *Contemporary Theory in International Relations.* Englewood Cliffs, N. J.: Prentice-Hall, 1960.

"International Systems and International Law." In *The State of War – Essays on the Theory and Practice of International Politics,* edited by Stanley Hoffmann, pp. 88 – 122. New York: Praeger, 1965.

"Choices." *Foreign Policy* 12 (1973):3 – 42.

"An American Social Science: International Relations." *Daedalus* 1 (1977):41 – 60.

Primacy or World Order – American Foreign Policy since the Cold War. New York: McGraw-Hill, 1978.

Holsti, K. J. "Retreat from Utopia: International Relations Theory, 1945 – 70." *Canadian Journal of Political Science* 4 (1971): 165 – 77.

Holsti, Ole R., Siverson, Randolph M., and Alexander, George, eds. *Change in the International System.* Boulder, Colo.: Westview Press, 1980.

Huntington, Samuel P. *Political Order in Changing Societies.* New Haven: Yale University Press, 1968.

"The Change to Change." *Comparative Politics* 3 (1971):283 – 322.

"The Democratic Distemper." *The Public Interest* 41 (1975):9 – 38.

Ibn Khaldûn, *The Muqaddimah – An Introduction to History.* Princeton University Press, 1967.

Inkeles, Alex. "The Emerging Social Structure of the World." *World Politics* 27 (1975):467 – 95.

Jones, E. L. *The European Miracle: Environments, Economics, and Geopolitics in the History of Europe and Asia.* Cambridge University Press, 1981.

Kahler, Miles. "Rumors of War: The 1914 Analogy." *Foreign Affairs* 58 (1979 – 80):374 – 96.

Kaldor, Mary. *The Disintegrating West.* New York: Hill and Wang, 1978.

Kennedy, Gavin. *The Economics of Defence.* London: Faber and Faber, 1975.

Keohane, Robert O., and Nye, Joseph S. *Power and Interdependence – World Politics in Transition.* Boston: Little, Brown, 1977.

Keynes, John Maynard. *The Economic Consequences of the Peace.* New York: Harcourt, Brace, Javanovich, 1920.

Kindleberger, Charles. "International Political Theory from Outside."
    In *Theoretical Aspects of International Relations,* edited by Wil-
    liam T. R. Fox, pp. 69–82. Notre Dame: University of Notre
    Dame Press, 1959.

Kissinger, Henry A. *A World Restored–Metternich, Castlereagh and
    the Problems of Peace 1812–22.* Boston: Hougton Mifflin, 1957.
    The Necessity for Choice–Prospects of American Foreign Policy.
    New York: Harper & Row, 1961.

Knei-Paz, Baruch. *The Social and Political Thought of Leon Trotsky.*
    Oxford: Clarendon Press, 1978.

Knorr, Klaus. *The Power of Nations–The Political Economy of Inter-
    national Relations.* New York: Basic Books, 1975.

Kratochwil, Friedrich V. *International Order and Foreign Policy–A
    Theoretical Sketch of Post-war International Politics.* Boulder,
    Colo.: Westview Press, 1978.

Kroeber, A. L. *Configurations of Culture Growth.* Berkeley: University
    of California Press, 1944.

Kuznets, Simon S. *Secular Movements in Production and Prices–
    Their Nature and Their Bearing upon Cyclical Fluctuations.* Bos-
    ton: Houghton Mifflin, 1930.
    *Economic Change–Selected Essays in Business Cycles, National In-
    come, and Economic Growth.* New York: W. W. Norton, 1953.

Lane, Frederic C. "The Economic Meaning of War and Protection."
    Journal of Social Philosophy and Jurisprudence 7 (1942):254–70.
    "Economic Consequences of Organized Violence." *The Journal of
    Economic History* 18 (1958):401–17.
    Venice and History: The Collected Papers of Frederic C. Lane.
    Baltimore: Johns Hopkins University Press, 1966.
    Venice–A Maritime Republic. Baltimore: Johns Hopkins University
    Press, 1973.

Lasswell, Harold D., and Kaplan, Abraham. *Power and Society–A
    Framework for Political Inquiry.* New Haven: Yale University
    Press, 1950.

Leibenstein, Harvey. *Economic Theory and Organizational Analysis.*
    New York: Harper & Row, 1960.
    General X-Efficiency Theory and Economic Development. New
    York: Oxford University Press, 1978.

Lenin, V. I. *Imperialism–The Highest Stage of Capitalism.* New York:
    International Publishers, 1939.

Lewis, Bernard. *The Arabs in History.* New York: Harper & Row,
    1966.

Lewis, W. Arthur. *The Theory of Economic Growth*. New York: Harper & Row, 1970.

   Growth and Fluctuations 1870–1913. London: George Allen and Unwin, 1978.

Lippmann, Walter. *U.S. Foreign Policy: Shield of the Republic*. Boston: Little, Brown, 1943.

List, Friedrich. *National System of Political Economy*. Philadelphia: J. B. Lippincott, 1856.

Luard, Evan. *Types of International Society*. New York: Free Press, 1976.

Luttwak, Edward. *The Grand Strategy of the Roman Empire – From the First Century A.D. to the Third*. Baltimore: Johns Hopkins University Press, 1976.

Mackinder, Halford J. *Democratic Ideals and Reality*. New York: W. W. Norton, 1962.

Mandel, Ernest. *Europe vs. America – Contradictions of Imperialism*. New York: Monthly Review Press, 1970.

Mansfield, Edwin. *Microeconomics – Theory and Applications*. New York: W. W. Norton, 1979.

McKenzie, Richard B., and Tullock, Gordon. *The New World of Economics*. Homewood, Ill.: Richard D. Irwin, 1975.

McNeill, William H., *Past and Future*. Chicago: University of Chicago Press, 1954.

   The Rise of the West. Chicago: University of Chicago Press, 1963.

   A World History. London: Oxford University Press, 1967.

   The Shape of European History. New York: Oxford University Press, 1974.

Manning, C.A.W., ed. *Peaceful Change—An International Problem*. New York: Macmillan, 1937.

Mansbach, Richard W., and Vasquez, John A. *In Search of Theory – A New Paradigm for Global Politics*. New York: Columbia University Press, 1981.

Mensch, Gerhard. *Stalemate in Technology – Innovations Overcome the Depression*. Cambridge, Mass.: Ballinger Publishing, 1979.

Mill, John Stuart. *A System of Logic*. 2 vols. London: Longmans, Green, Reader, and Dyer, 1875.

Milward, Alan S. *War, Economy, and Society, 1939–1945*. Berkeley: University of California Press, 1977.

Modelski, George. "Agraria and Industria: Two Models of the International System." *World Politics* 14 (1961):118–43.

Principles of World Politics. New York: Free Press, 1972.

"The Long Cycle of Global Politics and the Nation-State." *Comparative Studies in Society and History* 20 (1978):214 – 35.

Montesquieu. *Considerations on the Causes of the Greatness of the Romans and Their Decline.* New York: Free Press, 1965.

Moore, Barrington, Jr. *Political Power and Social Theory.* New York: Harper & Row, 1965.

Moore, Wilbert E. "Social Change." In *International Encyclopedia of the Social Sciences,* edited by David Sills, Vol. 14, pp. 365 – 75. New York: Crowell Collier and Macmillan, 1968.

Morgan, Edmund S. *The Birth of the Republic 1763 – 1789.* Chicago: University of Chicago Press, 1956.

Morgenthau, Hans J. *Politics among Nations.* New York: Alfred A. Knopf, 1973.

and Hook, Sidney, Hughes, H. Stuart, and Snow, C. P. "Western Values and Total War." *Commentary* 32 (1961):277 – 304.

Morse, Edwad L. *Modernization of International Relations.* New York: Free Press, 1976.

Mowat, R. B. *A History of European Diplomacy 1451 – 1789.* New York: Longmans, Green, 1928.

Mundell, Robert A., and Swoboda, Alexander K., eds. *Monetary Problems of the International Economy.* Chicago: University of Chicago Press, 1969.

Nisbet, Robert, ed. *Social Change.* New York: Harper & Row, 1972.

North, Douglass C. "Markets and Other Allocation Systems in History." *Journal of European Economic History* 6 (1977): 703–16.

and Thomas, Robert Paul. *The Rise of the Western World – A New Economic History.* Cambridge University Press, 1973.

Northrop, F. S. C. *The Logic of the Sciences and the Humanities.* New York: Macmillan, 1947.

Ogburn, William F., ed. *Technology and International Relations.* Chicago: University of Chicago Press, 1949.

Olson, Mancur, Jr. *The Logic of Collective Action.* New York: Schocken Books, 1968.

and Zeckhauser, Richard. "An Economic Theory of Alliances." *The Review of Economics and Statistics* 48 (1966):266 – 79.

Oman, Charles. *A History of the Art of War in the Middle Ages.* 2 vols. New York: Burt Franklin, 1924.

Organization for Economic Co-operation and Development (OECD). *Technical Change and Economic Policy.* Paris: OECD, 1980.

Organski, A. F. K. *World Politics.* New York: Alfred A. Knopf, 1968.

and Kugler, Jacek. *The War Ledger*. Chicago: University of Chicago Press, 1980.

Osgood, Robert E., and Tucker, Robert W. *Force, Order and Justice*. Baltimore: Johns Hopkins University Press, 1967.

Pareto, Vilfredo. *The Rise and Fall of the Elites*. Totowa, N. J.: Bedminster Press, 1968.

Perkins, Bradford. *The Great Rapprochement – England and the United States, 1895 – 1914*. New York: Atheneum, 1968.

Pettman, Ralph. *State and Class – A Sociology of International Affairs*. London: Croom Helm, 1979.

Plato. *The Republic of Plato*. New York: Oxford University Press, 1945.

Podhoretz, Norman. *The Present Danger*. New York: Simon and Schuster, 1980.

Polanyi, Karl. *The Great Transformation – The Political and Economic Origins of our Time*. Boston: Beacon Press, 1957.

Polybius. *The Histories of Polybius*. Vol. 1. Bloomington: Indiana University Press, 1962.

Porter, Brian, ed. *International Politics 1919–1969 – The Aberystwyth Papers*. London: Oxford University Press, 1972.

Posner, Richard A. *Economic Analysis of Law*. Boston: Little, Brown, 1977.

Public Finance 26 (1971):1 – 105.

Quester, George. *Offense and Defense in the International System*. New York: John Wiley & Sons, 1977.

Rader, Trout. *The Economics of Feudalism*. New York: Gordon & Breach, 1971.

Randle, Robert. *The Origins of Peace – A Study of Peacemaking and the Structure of Peace Settlements*. New York: Free Press, 1973.

Reynolds, Charles. *Theory and Explanation in International Politics*. London: Martin Robertson, 1973.

Riker, William H. *The Theory of Political Coalitions*. New Haven: Yale University Press, 1962.

Robbins, Lionel. *Money, Trade and International Relations*. New York: St. Martin's Press, 1971.

Roberts, Michael. *The Military Revolution 1560 – 1660*. Belfast: Boyd, 1956.

Rogowski, Ronald. "Rationalist Theories of Politics: A Midterm Report." *World Politics* 30 (1978):296 – 323.

Rosecrance, Richard. *Action and Reaction in World Politics – International Systems in Perspective*. Boston: Little, Brown, 1963.

Rostow, W. W. *Politics and the Stages of Growth*. Cambridge University Press, 1971.

   Getting from Here to There. New York: McGraw-Hill, 1978.

   Why the Poor Get Richer and the Rich Slow Down: Essays in the Marshallian Long Period. Austin: University of Texas Press, 1980.

Roumasset, James A. "Induced Institutional Change, Welfare Economics, and the Science of Public Policy." Working paper series No. 46, Department of Economics, University of California, Davis, October 1974.

Russett, Bruce M., ed. *Economic Theories of International Politics*. Chicago: Markham Publishing, 1968.

Samuelson, Paul A. "The Pure Theory of Public Expenditure." *Review of Economics and Statistics* 36 (1954):387 – 9.

   Economics – An Introductory Analysis. 7th ed. New York: McGraw-Hill, 1967.

Schlesinger, James R. *The Political Economy of National Security – A Study of the Economic Aspects of the Contemporary Power Struggle*. New York: Praeger, 1960.

   Capitalism, Socialism and Democracy. New York: Harper & Row, 1962.

   "The Crisis of the Tax State." In *International Economic Papers*. No. 4, pp. 5 – 38. London: Macmillan, 1954a.

   History of Economic Analysis. New York: Oxford University Press, 1954b.

Schurman, Herbert Franz. *Ideology and Organization in Communist China*. 2nd ed. Berkeley: University of California Press, 1968.

Seabury, Paul, ed. *Balance of Power*. San Francisco: Chandler Publishing, 1965.

Seeley, John. *The Expansion of England – Two Courses of Lectures*. Boston: Little, Brown, 1905.

Silver, Morris. *Affluence, Altruism, and Atrophy*. New York: New York University Press, 1980.

Simon, Herbert A. *Models of Man – Social and Rational*. New York: John Wiley & Sons, 1957.

Singer, J. David, et al. *Explaining War*. Beverly Hills: Sage Publications, 1979.

Smart, Ian. "The Great Engines: The Rise and Decline of a Nuclear Age." *International Affairs* 51 (1975):544 – 53.

Smith, Adam. *The Wealth of Nations*. New York: Modern Library, 1937.

Spengler, Joseph J. "Theories of Socio-Economic Growth." In *Problems in the Study of Economic Growth,* pp. 46–114. New York: National Bureau for Economic Research, 1949.

Sprout, Harold, and Sprout, Margaret. *Foundations of International Politics.* Princeton: D. Van Nostrand, 1962.

"The Dilemma of Rising Demands and Insufficient Resources." *World Politics* 20 (1968):660–93.

Toward a Politics of the Planet Earth. New York: Van Nostrand Reinhold, 1971.

"National Priorities: Demands, Resources, Dilemmas." *World Politics* 24 (1972):293–317.

Steinbruner, John D. *The Cybernetic Theory of Decision – New Dimensions of Political Analysis.* Princeton: Princeton University Press, 1974.

Strachey, John. *The End of Empire.* New York: Frederick A. Praeger, 1964.

Strayer, Joseph R. *On the Medieval Origins of the Modern State.* Princeton: Princeton University Press, 1970.

Syme, Ronald. *The Roman Revolution.* Oxford: Clarendon Press, 1939.

Taagepera, Rein. "Growth Courses of Empires." *General Systems* 13 (1968):171–5.

Taylor, Michael. *Anarchy and Cooperation.* New York: John Wiley & Sons, 1976.

Teggart, Frederick J. *Rome and China; A Study of Correlations in Historical Events.* Berkeley: University of California Press, 1939.

Theory and Processes of History. Berkeley: University of California Press, 1941.

Thucydides. *The Peloponnesian War.* New York: Modern Library, 1951.

Tilly, Charles, ed. *The Formation of National States in Western Europe.* Princeton: Princeton University Press, 1975.

Tolstoy, L. N. *War and Peace.* 2 vols. Baltimore: Penguin Books, 1961.

Toynbee, Arnold J. *Survey of International Affairs 1930.* London: Oxford University Press, 1931.

A Study of History. Vols. 3 and 12. London: Oxford University Press, 1961.

Tucker, Irwin St. John. *A History of Imperialism.* New York: Rand School of Social Science, 1920.

Tucker, Robert W. *The Inequality of Nations.* New York: Basic Books, 1977.

Tullock, Gordon. *The Politics of Bureaucracy.* Washington, D. C.: Public Affairs Press, 1965.

Veblen, Thorstein. *Imperial Germany and the Industrial Revolution.* New York: Viking Press, 1939.

Vernon, Raymond. *Sovereignty at Bay – The Multinational Spread of U.S. Enterprises.* New York: Basic Books, 1971.

Viner, Jacob. *The Long View and the Short: Studies in Economic Theory and Policy.* New York: Free Press, 1958.

von Ranke, Leopold. "The Great Powers." In *Leopold Ranke – The Formative Years,* edited by Theodore H. von Laue, pp. 181–218. Princeton: Princeton University Press, 1950.

Walbank, F. W. *The Awful Revolution: The Decline of the Roman Empire in the West.* Liverpool: Liverpool University Press, 1969.

Waldman, Sidney R. *Foundations of Political Action – An Exchange Theory of Politics.* Boston: Little, Brown, 1972.

Wallace, Michael David. *War and Rank Among Nations.* Lexington, Mass.: D. C. Heath, 1973.

Wallerstein, Immanuel. *The Modern World System – Capitalist Agriculture and the Origins of the European World-Economy in the Sixteenth Century.* New York: Academic Press, 1974.

Waltz, Kenneth N. *Man, the State and War.* New York: Columbia University Press, 1959.

   Theory of International Politics. Reading, Mass.: Addison-Wesley, 1979.

   "The Spread of Nuclear Weapons" Unpublished. March, 1981.

Weber, Max. *Economy and Society, An Outline of Interpretive Sociology.* 3 vols. New York: Bedminster Press, 1968.

Wesson, Robert G. *The Imperial Order.* Berkeley: University of California Press, 1967.

   State Systems – International Pluralism, Politics, and Culture. New York: Free Press, 1978.

White, Lynn, Jr. *Medieval Technology and Social Change.* London: Oxford University Press, 1964.

Wight, Martin. "Why Is There No International Theory?" In *Diplomatic Investigations: Essays in the Theory of International Politics,* edited by Herbert Butterfield and Martin Wight, pp. 17–34. London: George Allen and Unwin, 1966.

   Systems of States, edited by Hedley Bull. Leicester: Leicester University Press, 1977.

   Power Politics, edited by Hedley Bull and Carsten Holbraad. London: Penguin Books, 1979.

Wiles, P. J. D. *Economic Institutions Compared.* New York: John Wiley & Sons, 1977.

Wilson, Charles. *England's Apprenticeship, 1603–1763*. London: Longmans, 1965.

Economic History and the Historian – Collected Essays. London: Weidenfeld and Nicolson, 1969.

Wittfogel, Karl. *Oriental Despotism: A Comparative Study of Total Power*. New Haven: Yale University Press, 1957.

Wohlstetter, Albert. "Theory and Opposed-Systems Design." In *New Approaches to International Relations*, edited by Morton A. Kaplan, pp. 19–53. New York: St. Martin's Press, 1968.

Wolfers, Arnold, and Martin, Laurence W., eds. *The Anglo-American Tradition in Foreign Affairs: Readings from Thomas More to Woodrow Wilson*. New Haven: Yale University Press, 1956.

Wolin, Sheldon S. *Politics and Vision – Continuity and Innovation in Western Political Thought*. Boston: Little, Brown, 1960.

Wright, Quincy. *A Study of War*. 2 vols. Chicago: University of Chicago Press, 1942.

Young, Oran. *The Politics of Force – Bargaining During International Crises*. Princeton: Princeton University Press, 1968.

"The Perils of Odysseus: On Constructing Theories of International Relations." *World Politics* 24 (Supplement) (1972):179–203.

"Anarchy and Social Choice: Reflections on the International Polity." *World Politics* 30 (1978):241–63.

Index